W9-AWR-158

Market Structure and Foreign Trade

Market Structure and Foreign Trade
Increasing Returns, Imperfect Competition, and the International Economy

Elhanan Helpman and
Paul R. Krugman

The MIT Press
Cambridge, Massachusetts
London, England

© 1985 by The Massachusetts Institute of Technology

All rights reserved. No part of this book may be reproduced in any form by any electronic or mechanical means (including photocopying, recording, or information storage and retrieval) without permission in writing from the publisher.

This book was set in Apollo
by Asco Trade Typesetting Limited, Hong Kong,
and printed and bound in the United States of America.

Library of Congress Cataloging in Publication Data

Helpman, Elhanan.
  Market structure and foreign trade.

  Bibliography. p.
  Includes index.
  1. International economic relations.   2. Industrial organization (Economic theory)
3. Economies of scale.   4. Competition, Imperfect   I. Krugman, Paul R.   II. Title.
HF1412.H45   1985   382   84-21823
ISBN 978-0-262-08150-4 (hc. : alk. paper) — 978-0-262-58087-8 (pb. : alk. paper)

20 19 18 17 16 15 14 13 12 11

Contents

Preface   xi

Introduction   1

I Preliminaries   9

  1 The Factor Proportions Theory   11

    1.1 Integrated Equilibrium   12

    1.2 Factor Price Equalization   13

    1.3 Trade Pattern   16

    1.4 Nontraded Goods   19

    1.5 The Volume of Trade   22

    1.6 Unequal Factor Rewards   24

    1.7 Gains from Trade   28

    References   29

  2 Technology and Market Structure   31

    2.1 Economies of Scale at the Level of the Firm   32

    2.2 Economies of Scale and Market Structure   34

    2.3 External Economies   36

    2.4 Dynamic Scale Economies   38

    2.5 Specific Inputs and Integrated Firms   39

    2.6 Conclusions   40

    References   40

II   Homogeneous Products   43

3   External Effects   45

   3.1   Production Functions   45

   3.2   Resource Allocation within a Representative Country   47

   3.3   Autarky Equilibrium   50

   3.4   Trading Equilibrium   50

   3.5   Gains from Trade   51

   3.6   Trade Structure   55

   3.7   Factor Price Equalization   59

   3.8   Nonuniqueness   63

   3.9   More on Gains from Trade   64

   References   66

4   Contestable Markets   67

   4.1   The Concept of Market Contestability   67

   4.2   Integrated Equilibrium   71

   4.3   Trading Equilibrium   72

   4.4   Robustness of Factor Price Equalization   75

   4.5   Unequal Factor Rewards   77

   4.6   Gains from Trade   79

   Appendix 4A: Existence of Equilibrium   80

   Appendix 4B: Losses from Trade   81

   Reference   83

5   Oligopoly   85

   5.1   Seller Concentration: Partial Equilibrium   86

   5.2   Seller Concentration: General Equilibrium Trade
          Patterns   88

   5.3   Seller Concentration: Welfare   96

   5.4   Free Entry   100

   5.5   Market Segmentation   104

   References   111

III   Differentiated Products   113

  6   Demand for Differentiated Products   115
      6.1   The General Formulation   115
      6.2   Love of Variety Approach   117
      6.3   Ideal Variety Approach   120
      References   129

  7   Trade Structure   131
      7.1   Behavior of Firms   132
      7.2   Integrated Equilibrium   134
      7.3   Trade Patterns: Free Entry   140
      7.4   Unequal Factor Rewards   143
      7.5   Many Goods and Factors   144
      7.6   Restricted Entry   146
      7.7   Predictors of the Intersectoral Pattern of Trade   151
      References   157

  8   Trade Volume and Composition   159
      8.1   Trade Volumes in the Simple Model   159
      8.2   Trade Volume: Generalizations   165
      8.3   Trade Composition in the Simple Model   168
      8.4   Trade Composition: Generalizations and Empirical
            Hypothesis   169
      Appendix 8A: Geometric properties of Volume and Share
      Isocurves   174
      References   178

  9   Welfare   179
      9.1   Basic Considerations   179
      9.2   S-D-S Preferences   181
      9.3   Lancaster Preferences   183
      9.4   Equilibrium Scale and Diversity   187
      9.5   Trade and Income Distribution   190
      References   195

10   Transport Costs and Nontraded Goods   197

     10.1   The Model with Nontraded Goods   198

     10.2   Nontraded Goods Produced with Increasing Returns   201

     10.3   Factor Mobility   204

     10.4   Transport Costs and Market Size Effects   205

     References   209

11   Intermediate Inputs   211

     11.1   Integrated Equilibrium   211

     11.2   Trading Equilibrium: Tradable Differentiated
            Products   214

     11.3   Trading Equilibrium: Nontraded Intermediates   217

     11.4   A Generalization: Forward and Backward Linkages   220

     Appendix 11A: A Model of Differentiation in Intermediate
     Goods   223

     References   224

IV   **Multinational Corporations**   225

12   Single-Product Firms   227

     12.1   The Basic Model   228

     12.2   Equilibrium in an Integrated Economy   230

     12.3   The Pattern of Trade   231

     12.4   The Volume of Trade   238

     12.5   Intraindustry and Intrafirm Trade   241

     References   244

13   Vertical Integration   247

     13.1   The Structure of Production   247

     13.2   The Integrated Economy   249

     13.3   Trade Patterns   250

     13.4   Trade Volumes and Trade Shares   255

     References   259

14 Summary and Conclusions 261

14.1 The Pattern, Volume, and Composition of Trade 261

14.2 Trade and Welfare 263

14.3 Future Directions 265

Index 267

Preface

In the last few years trade theorists have finally begun to come to grips with the role of increasing returns and imperfect competition in the world economy. As participants in this effort, however, we have come to feel that new theoretical work in this area has left important gaps and that it has not had the effect it should have. We wrote this book in order to fill in some of the gaps and to present an integrated view of the theory. We hope that by presenting an integrated treatment of a variety of issues involving increasing returns, imperfect competition, and international trade, we can help make this branch part of the core of trade theory rather than merely a promising new area.

We offer here a monograph rather than a textbook. Although it reviews and restates known results, it also contains a good deal of new work. The chapters on contestable markets, oligopolies, welfare, and multinational corporations, for example, are entirely new. New insights and results are also available in chapters that cover older ground, such as the treatment of external economies, intermediate inputs, and trade composition. The book is suitable, however, as a supplementary graduate text and for advanced undergraduate courses. Some of the material is somewhat technical, but most of the main points are made with simple models.

The book was written at MIT during the academic year 1983–84. While we were writing it, Helpman was a visiting professor in the Department of Economics at MIT, on leave from Tel-Aviv University. We received helpful comments on drafts of the book from Richard Brecher, Avinash Dixit, Wilfred Ethier, Torsten Persson, Lars Svensson, and Martin Weitzmann. Gene Grossman and Assaf Razin provided valuable comments on chapter 4. In addition the work reflects suggestions made by participants in seminars at Columbia, Princeton, Harvard, MIT, Dartmouth, University of Western Ontario, and Michigan State. We remain of course fully responsible for any errors.

We would like to thank all those who provided comments, as well as the gallant typists in the Sloan School of Management, the MIT Department of Economics, and the National Bureau of Economic Research who worked on portions of the book. Finally, we would like to thank our wives, who were tolerant and supportive through many months of nonstop shop talk.

Market Structure and
Foreign Trade

Introduction

Why do countries trade with each other? What are the effects of international trade? It may seem surprising that these questions are still the subject of debate, close to one hundred and seventy years after the publication of Ricardo's *Principles*. In the last few years, however, a long-standing undercurrent of discontent with standard trade theory has finally surfaced in the form of new models offering alternative approaches to international trade. These new approaches break with traditional analysis by stressing the importance of increasing returns to scale and imperfect competition in understanding how the international economy works. The impact of these new approaches on research has been substantial. It was not very long ago that discussions of the relationship between trade and industrial organization had to start by justifying the juxtaposition of such unrelated fields. Today the border country between the theory of international trade and the theory of industrial structure is one of the most active areas in international economics.

A somewhat disturbing feature of these recent developments, however, has been the proliferation of special models, each with its own assumptions, seemingly inconsistent not only with traditional trade theory but with each other. This proliferation is for the most part a healthy thing, an indication that old assumptions are being challenged and that innovation is taking place. At some point, however, it becomes necessary that we attempt a synthesis that defines the common elements in the variety of new models and at the same time reestablishes some continuity with older traditions.

Our purpose in this book is to provide an integrated approach to the analysis of trade in a world characterized by increasing returns and imperfect competition. By an "integrated approach" we do *not* mean a survey. What we have tried to do here is something more ambitious than simply restating a number of existing models in a common notation. Instead, we develop a new approach to trade theory (which of course builds on the earlier work of many economists), allowing us to treat a number of existing models as special cases and to treat a number of additional issues as well. Most of the analysis in this book is new, in both analytical technique and substantive results. At the same time we believe that our approach reveals a similarity in "deep structure" among models that may look quite different on the surface, and it helps clarify the continuity between traditional trade theory and new approaches. We hope that our integrated approach will help move the study of increasing returns and imperfect competition from its current status as a promising new subfield of trade theory into a central position at its core.

Why We Need New Theories of Trade

The traditional general equilibrium approach to international trade is a powerful and elegant intellectual construct, capable of yielding many useful insights about a trading world economy. A proposal that this approach share its position as the central element of trade theory with alternative approaches is therefore not something to be offered lightly. The only good reason for challenging the traditional approach is that it does not seem to do an adequate job of explaining the world and alternative approaches seem to offer an opportunity to do better.

We can identify four major ways in which conventional trade theory seems to be inadequate in accounting for empirical observation: its apparent failure to explain the volume of trade, the composition of trade, the volume and role of intrafirm trade and direct foreign investment, and the welfare effects of trade liberalization. Let us consider each of these in turn.

Conventional trade theory explains trade entirely by differences among countries, especially differences in their relative endowments of factors of production. This suggests an inverse relationship between similarity of countries and the volume of trade between them. In practice, however, nearly half the world's trade consists of trade between industrial countries that are relatively similar in their relative factor endowments. Further both the share of trade among industrial countries and the share of this trade in these countries' imcomes rose for much of the postwar period, even as these countries were becoming more similar by most measures.

If differences between countries were the sole source of trade, we would expect the composition of trade to reflect this fact. In particular, countries should export goods whose factor content reflects their underlying resources. This is in fact by and large true of countries' *net* exports. But to casual observation, and on more careful examination, actual trade patterns seem to include substantial two-way trade in goods of similar factor intensity. This "intraindustry" trade seems both pointless and hard to explain from the point of view of a conventional trade analysis.

When we turn to intrafirm trade and direct foreign investment, the problem with conventional trade theory is that it is simply an inappropriate framework. In the perfectly competitive, constant-returns world of traditional theory there are no visible firms and thus no way to discuss issues hinging on the scope of activities carried out within firms. Again, in reality much international trade consists of intrafirm transactions rather than arm's-length dealings between unrelated parties, and multinational firms are a prominent part of the international landscape. We would like to have a trade theory that can both explain why this is so and tell us what difference it makes.

Finally, studies of trade liberalization seem to suggest that conventional trade theory misses important aspects of the welfare effects of trade. Standard models associate trade with a reallocation of resources that increases national income in aggregate but leaves at least some factors with reduced real income. What seems to have happened in such important episodes of trade liberalization as the formation of the EEC and the U.S.-Canadian auto pact is quite different, however. Little resource reallocation took place; instead, trade seems to have permitted an increased productivity of existing resources, which left everyone better off.

These four empirical weaknesses of conventional trade theory are not its only problems. We emphasize them here, however, because they become understandable once economies of scale and imperfect competition are introduced into our analysis.

Increasing Returns and Imperfect Competition

In reality many industries do not seem to be characterized either by constant returns or perfect competition. By itself, however, this observation would not make a compelling case for introducing these considerations into trade theory, since all economic theories leave out many aspects of reality. The reason for emphasizing the role of increasing returns rather than something else, such as the role of consumer psychology, is that economies of scale seem to allow a straightforward explanation of our empirical puzzles.

Consider first the problem of trade between similar countries. If there are country-specific economies of scale, such trade poses no puzzle. Even if differences in factor rewards or technology do not create an incentive for specialization and trade, the advantages of large-scale production will still lead countries to specialize and trade with one another. We will show that specialization and trade will persist even when countries have identical relative factor endowments for a wide variety of models.

Increasing returns also provide a simple explanation of intraindustry trade.

It seems apparent that specialization which takes place to realize economies of scale rather than because of differences in factor rewards can easily involve two-way trade in goods with similar factor content.

In part III of this book we will develop an approach to trade in which intraindustry trade is well defined and show that the importance of this trade is greater, the more similar countries are in their resources.

The relationship between increasing returns, intrafirm trade, and direct foreign investment is more indirect, relying on less well formalized insights, but it still seems clear. Whenever there are inputs such as headquarters services and intermediate goods that are both produced under increasing returns and specific to particular users, there will be strong incentives to avoid the problems of bilateral monopoly by integrating upstream and downstream activities in a single firm. If at the same time there are incentives, such as differences in factor rewards, for locating upstream and downstream activities in different countries, the result will be multinational firms engaging in intrafirm trade.

Finally, the experience of trade liberalizations that produce all-round gains without significant resource reallocation is not all paradoxical in a world characterized by increasing returns, where intraindustry specialization and trade may produce gains in efficiency through an increased scale of production.

Increasing returns then, seem to be useful for explaining important features of the international economy. Yet they have only recently been integrated into the basic theory of international trade because except under very special circumstances increasing returns are inconsistent with perfect competition. Since there is no generally accepted theory of imperfect competition, this has seemed to prevent the study of trade in the presence of increasing returns from being more than a collection of special cases.

Even if this were true, it would not be a good reason to ignore the role of economies of scale and imperfect competition in trade. It is better to have a collection of examples that seem to capture what is actually going on than to restrict oneself to a fully integrated theory that does not. In any case, although recent theoretical work on international trade has been marked by a proliferation of special assumptions, the insights gained from this work often seem more general than the particular models that suggest them.

In this book we will try to develop an approach to the modeling of trade in a world of increasing returns and imperfect competition that confirms the impression of a fairly general set of insights behind the special assumptions of particular models. The result is still not a general theory—this is not possible until economists agree on a general theory of imperfect competition. But we believe that we have developed an approach that does provide an integrating framework for a variety of special models.

Method of the Book

This book is built around the two classic questions of trade theory: First, what determines the pattern of international trade? Second, is international trade beneficial? These are not the only questions one might ask, or even the most relevant for policy. They have been valuable historically as a way of structuring discussion, however, and we use them in the same way here. To answer each question, we have a general method that we apply to a variety of particular models.

Our method for the analysis of the trade pattern is to begin by constructing a reference point, the "integrated economy." This is a description of what the world economy would look like if factors of production were perfectly mobile; the description depends on the underlying assumptions about technology, the structure of production, the behavior of firms, and so on.

We then "carve up" this integrated economy into separate countries, and ask the following question: Under what conditions will the integrated economy be reproduced through trade? In answering this question, we find what we also learn a great deal about the pattern of international trade because we can determine what transactions are needed to offset the fact that the world is divided into countries.

For example, to reproduce the integrated equilibrium in a world of constant returns, countries must indirectly trade the services of productive factors by trading goods produced with different factor intensities—which is the essence of the factor proportions theory of trade. If we add to this world some goods produced with country-specific economies of scale, to reproduce the integrated economy, we must concentrate production of each such good in a single country, giving an additional source of specialization and trade. If there are intermediate inputs that are produced with economies of scale and are not tradable, then to reproduce the integrated economy the trading economy must concentrate production of each such input and all the sectors using that input into an "industrial complex" located in a single country. If the integrated economy contains multiactivity firms, but the distribution of resources in the trading world leads to a geographical separation of these activities, to reproduce the integrated economy, we must have multinational firms. In each case asking what is needed to reproduce the integrated economy is a way of revealing the essential role of an international economic linkage.

The method just described applies to any number of countries, factors, and goods. The essential points can be made, however, with two-country, two-factor examples, which we use liberally throughout the book. These examples have a distinctive geometry; we have found the "parallelograms in a box" diagrammatic technique extremely useful for building our intuition and hope that others will find the same.

Unfortunately trade does not always lead to reproduction of an integrated economy, and we have no general analysis when it does not. What we can do is twofold: we can establish the conditions under which the integrated economy is reproduced, and we can explore what happens when it is not by special cases and examples. Some of these special analyses suggest points that have the appearance of being both more general than the examples and important in reality. For example, when markets are separated by transport costs, which of course prevents reproduction of the integrated equilibrium, we have examples suggesting both a tendency of oligopolistic firms to engage in dumping and a tendency for increasing-returns industries to concentrate in countries with large domestic markets.

Turning next to the welfare effects of trade, here we also have a general method. We know that in a world of constant returns and perfect competition gains from trade are ensured. Once increasing returns and imperfect competition are introduced, there are both extra sources of potential gain and risks that trade may actually be harmful. Our approach is to derive cost-oriented *sufficient conditions* for gains from trade. The form of these sufficient conditions typically reveals key welfare effects over and above those captured by traditional models. For example, in models with oligopolistic firms a sufficient condition for gains from trade is that an appropriately weighted average of output per oligopolistic firm rises as a result of trade; this condition reveals that increased competition in oligopolistic industries can be a source of gains. In models with differentiated products the sufficient conditions we derive reveal the role of diversity and scale of production at a global level.

For the most part, our sufficient conditions are stated in terms of *outcomes* of trade. In other words, we show that gains from trade are ensured if, for example, the *world* output from increasing-returns sectors is on average larger than the *domestic* output before trade. Ideally we would like to go beyond this to derive predictions about trade and welfare from "primitives": tastes, technology, and factor endowments. This is more difficult; we study it where possible by special cases and examples.

The Book's Structure

Part I of the book lays some groundwork for the analysis. It begins with a restatement of conventional factor proportions theory—a restatement that uses the "integrated economy" as a reference point, however. It then describes several alternative strategies for modeling market structure when returns to scale are not constant.

Part II of the book develops approaches to trade based on three different ways of handling increasing returns. The first is based on the assumption that economies of scale are external to firms; the second instead assumes average cost pricing enforced in imperfectly competitive industries by the contestability of markets; the third assumes noncooperative behavior by oligopolistic firms.

Part III of the book introduces a particular approach that has proved very valuable as a tool for thinking about many aspects of international trade. This is the "differentiated products" approach. We begin with some necessary technical tools, then develop a basic analysis of the pattern of trade. We then use the basic analysis to analyze a series of topics: the volume and composition of trade, the welfare effects of trade, the effects of transport costs, and the role of intermediate inputs.

Finally, part IV turns to the theory of multinational firms and intrafirm trade. It begins with a minimal model of a world economy with direct foreign investment, then develops a more complex analysis with vertical integration and intrafirm trade.

I   Preliminaries

This book begins with some preparation of the ground. First, in chapter 1, we provide an exposition of the most influential conventional approach to trade, the factor proportions theory. This exposition serves in part as a background, but it also serves to introduce some key concepts and techniques that we will use repeatedly throughout the book. In chapter 2 we explore in general terms how it might be possible to extend our analysis to allow for increasing returns and imperfect competition, and we describe the approaches that will be followed in the rest of the book.

1   The Factor Proportions Theory

The core of modern analysis of trade is the factor proportions theory—the Heckscher-Ohlin model and its extensions. In this book we go beyond this theory to develop an approach that allows for many more phenomena than can be encompassed by Heckscher-Ohlin-based models. Our approach builds on a factor proportions foundation, however. Indeed, one of our major purposes is to show that many of the insights gained from traditional theory continue to be useful even in a world where increasing returns and imperfect competition are important. Thus we begin this book with a brief exposition of the basic elements of the factor proportions approach.

We present the theory in a way that is perhaps somewhat unfamiliar, although not new. Much of the traditional expositional apparatus of trade theory is built around $2 \times 2 \times 2$ examples; in our analysis it will generally be important that there be more goods than factors. This means that it will be useful if from the start we develop a framework suitable for a multidimensional analysis.

Our approach builds on a long tradition of research in this area, but it is most intimately related to the recent treatment in Dixit and Norman (1980, chapter 4). The central idea is to use as a reference point a hypothetical construct, which we will call the *integrated equilibrium*. This is defined as the resource allocation the world would have if goods and factors were both perfectly mobile. We then ask whether it is possible to achieve the same resource allocation if factors of production are instead divided up among countries and there is no international factor mobility. We find in general that there is a set of allocations of factors to countries for which this is possible. If factor endowments lie within this set, factor prices will be equalized through trade.

If factor prices *are* equalized, and if countries have identical homothetic preferences, we are then able to deduce a relationship between factor endowments and trade, which was first suggested by Vanek (1968): if we look at the factor services embodied in a country's trade, we will find that a country is a net exporter of the services of factors of which it has a relatively large share of the world's supply.

We will develop this approach in what follows. We will also develop two extensions. First is an extension to a world in which not all goods are traded. Second is an extension to the case where countries' factor endowments do not lie in the factor price equalization set. We will also discuss gains from trade and the dependence of the volume of trade on factor endowments.

1.1 Integrated Equilibrium

In this section we describe the equilibrium of an integrated world economy. Although at this stage we need not make restrictive assumptions about preferences, we do make them in anticipation of future needs:

1. There are N factors of production which are inelastically supplied. The N-dimensional vector $\bar{V} = (\bar{V}_1, \bar{V}_2, \ldots, \bar{V}_N)$ describes the available quantities of these factors in the world economy. We will also use N to denotes the set of inputs.

2. There are I goods produced with quasi-concave, constant returns to scale production functions. We will also use I to denote the set of goods. Every production function has associated with it a unit cost function:

$c_i(w), \quad i \in I,$

where w is the N-dimensional vector of input prices (factor rewards).

3. Preferences are well behaved and homothetic. As a result the share of spending on every good is a function only of commodity prices, represented by

$\alpha_i(p), \quad i \in I,$

where p is an I-dimensional vector of commodity prices.

4. There is perfect competition.

5. All I goods are produced in the integrated equilibrium.

Using these assumptions, the equilibrium conditions for the integrated economy can be represented in a simple way. It is useful, first, to define for this purpose per unit output demand functions for factors of production. As is well known (e.g., see Varian 1978, chapter 2), these can be derived from the unit cost functions as follows:

$$a_{li}(w) = \frac{\partial}{\partial w_l} c_i(w), \quad l \in N, i \in I,$$

where $a_{li}(w)$ is the use of factor l per unit output of good i.

Using $\overline{X}_i$ to denote the output level of good i in the integrated equilibrium, the equilibrium conditions are

$$p_i = c_i(w), \quad \text{for all } i \in I, \tag{1.1}$$

$$\sum_{i \in I} a_{li}(w) \overline{X}_i = \overline{V}_l, \quad \text{for all } l \in N, \tag{1.2}$$

$$\alpha_i(p) = \frac{p_i \overline{X}_i}{\sum_{j \in I} p_j \overline{X}_j}, \quad \text{for all } i \in I. \tag{1.3}$$

The first condition states that all goods are priced according to marginal cost, as required in a competitive equilibrium. The second condition assures clearing of factor markets, and the third assures clearing of commodity markets.

We need for future use a notation for sectoral factor employment vectors in the integrated equilibrium. We define therefore

$$\overline{V}(i) = [a_{1i}(w), a_{2i}(w), \ldots, a_{Ni}(w)] \overline{X}_i, \quad \text{for all } i \in I,$$

as the vector of employment in sector i in the integrated equilibrium. These vectors have a simple geometric representation when there are only two factors of production. A three-sector (good) version is illustrated in figure 1.1, in which the first factor is labor (L) and the second factor is capital (K). The employment vector $\overline{V}(1)$ is represented by OQ_1, the employment vector $\overline{V}(2)$ is represented by $Q_1 Q_2$, and the employment vector $\overline{V}(3)$ is represented by $Q_2 \overline{V}$. In this figure sector 1 is the most capital intensive, sector 2 employs an intermediate capital/labor ratio, and sector 3 is the least capital intensive (or the most labor intensive).

1.2 Factor Price Equalization

Now suppose that the world economy is divided into $J \geq 2$ countries, with every country j receiving an endowment $V^j = (V^j_1, V^j_2, \ldots, V^j_N)$ of factors of production. Assuming that every country has the same homothetic preferences as summarized by the budget share functions $\alpha_i(p)$, $i \in I$, we may ask what is the nature of the set FPE (factor price equalization) of endowment distributions $V = (V^1, V^2, \ldots, V^J)$ in which every country can fully employ its resources, using the techniques of production that are used in the integrated equilibrium. This set is of interest because for every endowment distribution that belongs to it, the equilibrium price-factor-reward structure is the same as in the integrated equilibrium.

The last point is easily verified by observing that given the integrated

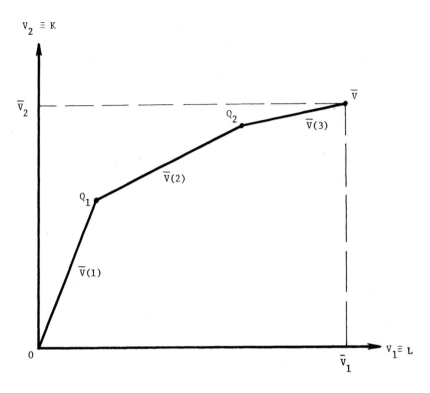

Figure 1.1

equilibrium w, every firm will employ the integrated equilibrium techniques of production and full employment will prevail in every country. Hence the world economy *can* produce in the trading equilibrium the output levels $\bar{X}_i$, $i \in I$, in the sense that there exist output levels X_i^j in country j, $j \in J$, $i \in I$, such that

$$\sum_{j \in J} X_i^j = \bar{X}_i, \quad \text{for all } i \in I.$$

Since aggregate world income in this trading equilibrium is equal to the income level in the integrated equilibrium, and since every country spends the integrated equilibrium budget shares on all goods, then there is commodity market clearing in the trading equilibrium. This proves that for $V \in \text{FPE}$ there is factor price equalization in the trading equilibrium and the trading equilibrium replicates the integrated equilibrium.

We are now in a position to characterize the set FPE for a given number of countries J. Formally

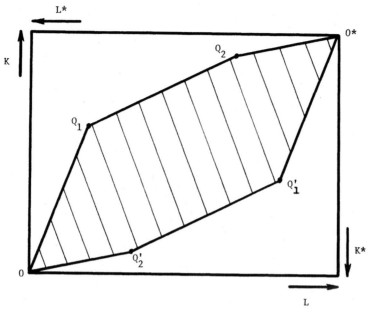

Figure 1.2

$$FPE = \left\{ (V^1, V^2, \ldots, V^J) | \exists \lambda_{ij} \geq 0, \sum_{j \in J} \lambda_{ij} = 1 \quad \text{for all } i \in I \text{ such that} \right.$$

$$\left. V^j = \sum_{i \in I} \lambda_{ij} \bar{V}(i) \quad \text{for all } j \in J \right\}. \tag{1.4}$$

By defintion, for $V \in FPE$ every country can fully employ its resources when using the integrated equilibrium techniques of production. In particular, given λ_{ij}, these resources are fully employed when the output levels are

$$X_i^j = \lambda_{ij} \bar{X}_i, \quad \text{for all } i \in I, j \in J,$$

in the trading equilibrium.

The set FPE is constructed from convex combinations of the integrated equilibrium sectoral employment vectors, and it has a simple geometrical representation (the algebra and the two-sector geometry appeared in Travis 1964, chapter 2). It is represented by the shaded area in figure 1.2 for the case of two countries, two factors, and three goods. In this figure O is the home country origin and O^* is the origin of the foreign country. The vectors OQ_1, Q_1Q_2, and Q_2O^* represent the employment vectors $\bar{V}(1)$, $\bar{V}(2)$, and $\bar{V}(3)$, respectively, relative to the origin of the home country, and the vectors $O^*Q'_1$, $Q'_1Q'_2$, and Q'_2O represent the same employment vectors relative to the origin of

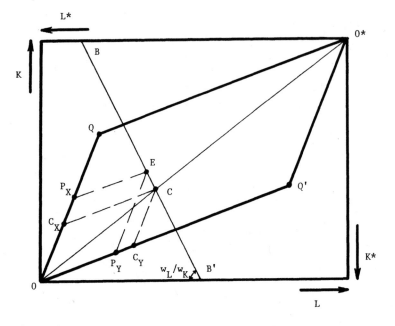

Figure 1.3

the foreign country. This FPE set is not empty because it always contains the diagonal OO^*. Since it is a convex symmetrical set around the diagonal, its boundaries define the limits of dissimilarity in factor composition which is consistent with factor price equalization. Hence for sufficiently similiar compositions there is factor price equalization in the trading equilibrium.

It is clear from this analysis that the likelihood of factor price equalization depends on the relative "size" of the set FPE. In particular, if this set is of lower dimension than N, it is very unlikely that we will observe factor price equalization. This implies that an analysis of trade patterns that require FPE makes sense only when the number of goods is at least as large as the number of factors.

1.3 Trade Pattern

We begin by examining the $2 \times 2 \times 2$ model. A typical factor price equalization set for this model is represented by the parallelogram OQO^*Q' in figure 1.3, in which OQ is the employment level in the first industry, say X, and QO^* is the employment level in the second industry, say Y, in the integrated equilibrium.

Suppose that E describes the distribution of factor endowments. Since E is above the diagonal OO^*, the home country is relatively capital rich. Drawing through E a negatively sloped line whose slope is w_L/w_K—where w_l is the reward to factor l, $l = L, K$, in the integrated equilibrium—we obtain point C as the intersection point of this line with the diagonal. Point C divides the diagonal into two segments that are proportional to the countries' gross domestic product (GDP) levels. Thus $\overline{OC}/\overline{CO}^*$ is equal to the relative GDP level of the home country.

Now we can choose units of measurement so that $\overline{OQ} = \bar{X}$, $\overline{OQ'} = \bar{Y}$, and $\overline{OO}^* = \overline{GDP}$, where $\overline{GDP}$ is the income level of the integrated world economy. In this case, by constructing parallelograms between O and E and O and C, we obtain a representation of the home country's production and consumption levels. Output of X is $\overline{OP}_X$, output of Y is $\overline{OP}_Y$, consumption of X is $\overline{OC}_X$, and consumption of Y is $\overline{OC}_Y$. It is therefore clear that the home country, which is relatively capital rich, exports the relatively capital-intensive good X (the quantity of exports is $\overline{C_X P_X}$), and it imports good Y (the quantity of imports is $\overline{P_Y C_Y}$), which is the prediction of the Heckscher-Ohlin model. As usual it is assumed in this discussion that there is no two-way trade in identical goods.

One can also use figure 1.3 to describe the net factor content of trade. Since the composition of consumption is the same in every country (due to the existence of free and costless trade in all goods and of identical homothetic preferences), then the composition of the factor content of consumption is the same in every country and it is identical to the world endowment $\bar{V}$. Therefore the vector OC describes the factor content of consumption in the home country. Hence the vector EC, which is the difference between the endowment and the implicit consumption of factor services, is the factor content of net trade flows. It is apparent that the home country is a net importer of labor services and a net exporter of capital services.

When the number of traded goods exceeds the number of factors of production the pattern of production and the pattern of trade are not uniquely determined. The factor content of net trade flows *is* uniquely determined, however (this was noted by Travis 1964, p. 143). We demonstrate this point in figure 1.4.

Factor employment levels in the integrated equilibrium are represented by OQ_1 in the first industry, $Q_1 Q_2$ in the second, and $Q_2 O^*$ in the third. The last two employment levels are also represented by $O\tilde{Q}_2$ and OQ'_2, respectively. Now, if E is the endowment allocation, then $X_1 = \overline{OP}_1$, $X_2 = 0$, and $X_3 = \overline{OP}_3$ is one equilibrium production configuration, and $X_1 = \overline{OP'}_1$, $X_2 = \overline{OP'}_2$, $X_3 = 0$ is another equilibrium production configuration (this type of indeterminacy in production is discussed in detail in Melvin 1968). It is clear from the figure that under the former configuration the home country exports

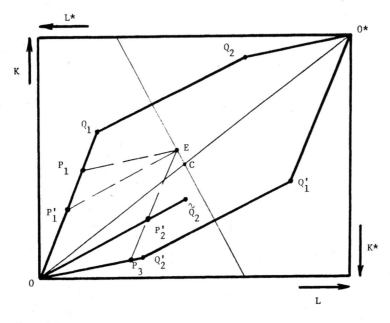

Figure 1.4

good 1 and that it imports it under the latter configuration. However, the vector of the factor content of net trade flows is given by EC under every configuration (every convex combination of these two configurations is also an equilibrium configuration). This observation justifies the approach of Vanek (1968), who devised a scheme for predicting the *factor content* of net trade flows for the case of many goods and factors, given $V \in \text{FPE}$.

Let t^j_V be the N-dimensional vector of the factor content of country j's net imports, and let s^j be the relative size of country j as measured by GDP:

$$s^j = \frac{w \cdot V^j}{w \cdot \bar{V}}.$$ (1.5)

Then

$$t^j_V = s^j \bar{V} - V^j \quad \text{for all } j \in J,$$ (1.6)

because $s^j \bar{V}$ is the factor content of consumption. Given $w \cdot t^j_V = 0$ (balanced trade), some components of t^j_V are positive, and others are negative. Hence, if we chose the numbering of factors of production so that

$$\frac{V^j_1}{\bar{V}_1} > \frac{V^j_2}{\bar{V}_2} > \cdots > \frac{V^j_m}{\bar{V}_m} > s^j > \frac{V^j_{m+1}}{\bar{V}_{m+1}} > \cdots > \frac{V^j_N}{\bar{V}_N}$$ (1.7)

(where for simplicity we disregard possible equalities), then (1.6) implies

$$t^j_{V_l} < 0, \quad \text{for } l = 1, 2, \ldots, m,$$

$$t^j_{V_l} > 0, \quad \text{for } l = m + 1, m + 2, \ldots, N;$$

that is, country j is a net exporter of the services of the first m factors of production and a net importer of the services of the last $N - m$ factors of production. However, we have renumbered the factors of production in an increasing order of relative availability (as compared to the world economy). Hence country j is a net exporter of services of those factors with which it is relatively well endowed and a net importer of services of those factors with which it is relatively poorly endowed.

This is a general statement of the factor content version of the Heckscher-Ohlin theory in the presence of factor price equalization. Its empirical validity has been studied carefully by Leamer (1984), with the results being favorable to the factor proportions theory.

Finally, observe that balanced trade is not required for the validity of Vanek's chain argument. If s^j is interpreted as the share of country j in *spending* rather than in *income*, then the chain argument still goes through. However, balanced trade—which obtains when the share of the country in spending is the same as in income—ensures that the share of spending is in between $V_1/\overline{V}$ and $V_N/\overline{V}_N$, so that some factor service is imported while some other is exported. Large trade surpluses may make a country export *all* factor services, and large trade deficits may make it import *all* factor services.

1.4 Nontraded Goods

Our discussion so far has depended on the assumption that all goods are traded. For some purposes, however, it is important to allow for the possibility that there are also goods that cannot be traded. We begin this section by characterizing the factor price equalization set in the presence of nontraded goods. Then we show that for endowment allocations that belong to this set, the factor content of net trade vectors still obeys Vanek's chain rule.

Suppose that the set of goods I can be partitioned into I_T and I_N, $I_T \cup I_N = I$, where I_T is the set of traded goods and I_N is the set of nontraded goods. Then, if a division of the world economy into J countries is to reproduce the integrated equilibrium, not only must every country be able to employ its resources fully, using the integrated equilibrium techniques of production, but it must do so by supplying its own demand for nontraded goods. Given identical homothetic preferences, however, self-sufficiency in nontraded goods requires it to devote to the nontraded sectors resources in proportion to

$$\sum_{i \in I_N} \bar{V}(i),$$

where the factor of proportionality is the share of the country in world spending.

For the purpose of this section we assume balanced trade, so that the share of a country in world spending is equal to its share in world income. Under this assumption the factor price equalization set can be characterized as follows:

$$\text{FPE} = \left\{ (V^1, V^2, \ldots, V^J) | \exists \lambda_{ij} \geq 0, \sum_{j \in J} \lambda_{ij} = 1, \text{ for all } i \in I, \text{ and} \right.$$

$$\lambda_{ij} = \frac{w \cdot V^j}{w \cdot \bar{V}}, \text{ for all } i \in I_N, \text{ such that} \tag{1.8}$$

$$\left. V^j = \sum_{i \in I} \lambda_{ij} \bar{V}(i), \text{ for all } j \in J \right\}.$$

By comparing (1.8) with (1.4), it is readily seen that the FPE defined in (1.8) is smaller than the FPE defined in (1.4), because in (1.8) there are more restrictions imposed on the λ_{ij}'s. These restrictions assure that full employment can be obtained when every country produces its own consumption of nontraded goods. The set FPE defined in (1.8) is not empty, because like the one defined in (1.4) it contains the "diagonal" (all points generated by V^j proportional to $\bar{V}$ in all countries).

It is clear from the construction of the set FPE in (1.8) that when V belongs to it, there is a trading equilibrium with factor price equalization in which the markets for nontraded goods clear separately in every country. Moreover, since the factor content of consumption in $s^j \bar{V}$ in every country (where s^j is the share of country j in spending), then (1.6) and (1.7) are applicable, which means that the factor content of net trade flows obeys Vanek's chain rule.

At this stage, however, it should be made clear that the relative size of the factor price equalization set in the presence of nontraded goods depends on the relationship between the number of *traded* goods and the number of factors of production. Thus, if this set is to have full dimensionality in factor space, the number of *traded* goods needs to be at least equal to the number of factors (e.g., Komiya 1967).

In the remainder of this section we show how to construct geometrically the factor price equalization set for the case of two factors, two countries, and three goods, one of which is nontraded.

Consider figure 1.5, in which OQ_1, Q_1Q_2, and Q_2O^* describe the sectoral employment levels in the integrated equilibrium. If all goods were traded, then the hexagon $OQ^1Q_2O^*Q_1'Q_2'$ would have described the factor price equaliza-

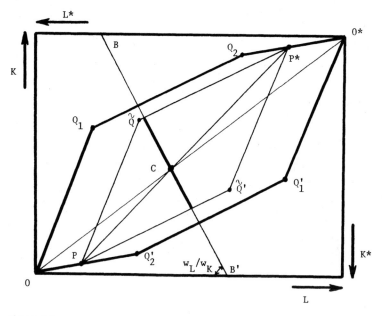

Figure 1.5

tion set. Suppose, however, that the most labor-intensive good, good 3, is not traded. Then clearly an endowment allocation close to Q_2 will not bring about factor price equalization because the foreign country would not be able to employ fully its factors of production with the integrated equilibrium techniques of production, given that it has to supply its own demand for good 3. This is seen from the fact that after the foreign country allocates to the nontraded sector the required inputs in sector 3, the remaining capital/labor ratio is lower than that used in the traded sectors. Hence fully employment is impossible. This means that the factor price equalization set is smaller than $OQ_1Q_2O^*Q_1'Q_2'$.

We now construct the factor price equalization set for the case where the labor-intensive good is not traded. First, let us construct allocation points that belong to this set and at which the relative size of countries is given by point C. Obviously in this case an equilibrium requires the employment vector in the nontraded sector, OQ_2', to be distributed between the home and foreign country in the proportion $\overline{OC}/\overline{CO}^*$. This is obtained by drawing through C a line parallel to an imaginary line that connects O^* with Q_2'. The result is PP^*, with OP being the employment vector in the nontraded sector of the home country and O^*P^* being the employment vector in the nontraded sector of the foreign country. It remains to construct feasible allocations of employment

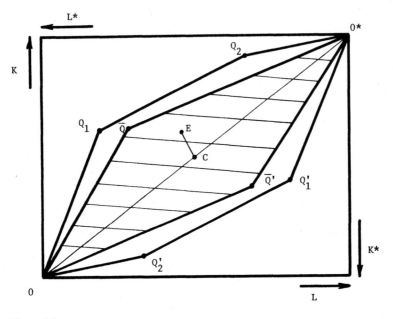

Figure 1.6

levels to the traded sectors in both countries. This is achieved by constructing the parallelogram $P\tilde{Q}P^*\tilde{Q}'$.

Now, drawing through C the equal income line BB (whose slope is w_L/w_K), points on this line *that belong* to $P\tilde{Q}P^*\tilde{Q}'$ also belong to FPE. This is represented by the heavy part of BB. Repeating this procedure for every point C on the diagonal OO^*, we obtained the factor price equalization set described by the shaded area in figure 1.6. This set is a parallelogram. The breakpoint $\bar{Q}'$ occurs when, by sliding C in figure 1.5 toward O, the southeast end of the part of BB in $P\tilde{Q}P^*\tilde{Q}'$ coincides with $\tilde{Q}'$, and the breakpoint $\bar{Q}$ occurs when the northwest end of BB in $P\tilde{Q}P^*\tilde{Q}'$ coincides with $\tilde{Q}$.

If E is the endowment point in figure 1.6, then the vector of factor content of net trade flows is given by EC, where the slope of the line EC is the relative wage.

1.5 The Volume of Trade

Our discussion of the indeterminancy in the pattern of production and trade when the number of traded goods exceeds the number of factors of production makes it clear that in this case the *volume* of trade is also indeterminate. Therefore in this section we confine attention to the "even" case. In particular, since the current analysis is designed to serve as background and reference model to the discussion of trade volumes in the presence of differentiated products (chapter 8), we restrict our discussion to the $2 \times 2 \times 2$ case.

Consider the factor endowments in the factor price equalization set. We want to compare the dependence of the volume of trade on the factor distribution points. In particular, we want to construct equal-volume-of-trade curves.

A standard definition of the volume of world trade is the sum of exports across countries. As long as we consider factor endowments in the set FPE, there is no difference between comparisons of nominal and real trade volumes. Thus in the two-country, two-sector case the volume of trade is

$$VT = p_X(X - s\bar{X}) + p_Y(Y^* - s^*\bar{Y}),$$

where good X is exported by the home country and good Y is exported by the foreign country (X is also the output level of X in the home country and Y^* is the output level of Y in the foreign country). Assuming balanced trade, the volume of trade can be represented in the following two alternative forms:

$$VT = 2p_X(X - s\bar{X}), \tag{1.9a}$$

$$VT = 2p_Y(Y^* - s^*\bar{Y}). \tag{1.9b}$$

Now in the factor price equalization set s is a linear function of home country factor endowments [see (1.5)] and X is a linear function of home country factor endowments (X is solved from $a_{LY}Y + a_{LX}X = L$ and $a_{KY}Y + a_{KX}X = K$, where a_{li} are the factor imputs per unit output in the integrated equilibrium). Hence (1.9a) implies

$$VT = v(L, K) \equiv \gamma_L L + \gamma_K K \tag{1.10}$$

for some (γ_L, γ_K), whenever (L, K) is in the factor price equalization set. This means that the equal volume of trade curves in the FPE set are straight parallel lines. In particular, since the volume of trade is constant and equal to zero on the diagonal OO^*, then all equal trade volume lines are parallel to the diagonal (this implies $-\gamma_L/\gamma_K = \bar{K}/\bar{L}$). These lines are drawn in figure 1.7. It is also easy to check that if (1.10) applies to endowment points above the diagonal, then $\gamma_L < 0$ and $\gamma_K > 0$, and if it applies to points below the diagonal, then $\gamma_L > 0$ and $\gamma_K < 0$ [(1.10) applies to points above the diagonal if X is relatively capital intensive and to points below the diagonal if X is relatively labor intensive].

It is clear from figure 1.7 that the volume of trade is larger, the larger the difference across countries in factor composition. This result is intuitively

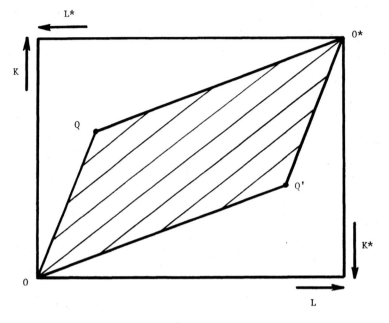

Figure 1.7

appealing for a model in which differences in factor composition are the sole basis for trade.

We should also note that figure 1.7 implies that in some sense relative country size has no effect on the volume of trade.

1.6 Unequal Factor Rewards

We now study the factor content of net trade flows in the absence of factor price equalization. For this purpose we do not require preferences to be homothetic and identical across countries; we derive predictions on *bilateral* trade flows instead of the trade flows between a country and the rest of the world.

The basic insight (due to Brecher and Choudhri 1982) that serves as a basis for the more general analysis that follows is obtained from figure 1.8 for a two-factor, four-good, and three-country case. It depicts a Lerner diagram in which the isoquants of the four goods each represents a Krona worth of output (i.e., the isoquant of good i represents the output level $1/p_i$). For every country j the ray K^j/L^j represents the capital/labor ratio of its endowment, and the downward sloping line with slope w^j_L/w^j_K represents its unit cost line.

The fact that the more capital per worker a country has, the higher is its

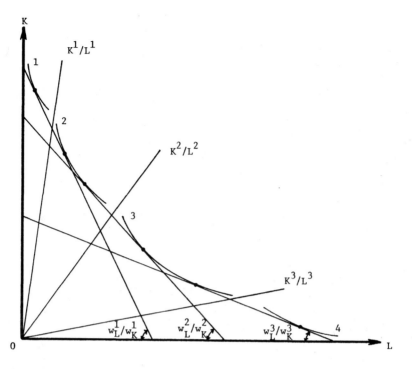

Figure 1.8

wage rental ratio, is established from properties of the maximum gross domestic product function (e.g., Dixit and Norman 1980, chapter 2) which is defined as

$$\Pi(p, V) = \max_{\{v_1, v_2, \ldots, v_N\}} \left\{ \sum_{i \in I} p_i f_i(v_i) \,|\, v_i \geq 0, \sum_{i \in I} v_i \leq V \right\}$$

where $f_i(\cdot)$ is the production function in sector i. $\Pi(p, V)$ is positively linear homogeneous and concave in V, and the competitive reward to factor l is given by

$$w_l = \frac{\partial}{\partial V_l} \Pi(p, V), \quad \text{for all } l \in N.$$

Hence in the two-factor case an equal gross domestic product curve has the shape exhibited in figure 1.9, and the slope of this curve equals the competitive wage rental ratio. Apart from possible linear segments, the wage rental ratio rises with the capital/labor ratio. A proportional exlpansion in the endowment of labor and capital produces a radial expansion of the GDP curve,

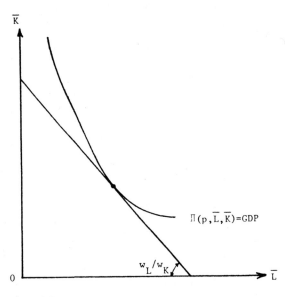

Figure 1.9

so that the wage rental ratio depends on the composition of factor endowments but not on their absolute size.

In the equilibrium described by figure 1.8, the first country, which has more capital per worker than the other two, produces goods 1 and 2; the second country, with the intermediate capital/labor ratio, produces goods 2 and 3 (it may share good 2 with country 1 and good 3 with country 3); and the third country, which has the smallest amount of capital per worker, produces goods 4 and 3. It is, however, clear from this figure that the more capital rich a country is, the *more* capital and *less* labor it uses per Krona worth of output in *all* lines of production. It is also easy to see that the existence of factor-intensity reversals would not change this result. Hence independently of the bilateral pattern of trade between a pair of countries, the more capital-rich country's exports embody more capital per worker than its imports, if we calculate factor content with the *exporter's* techniques of production.

In order to generalize this result, let T^{jk} be the vector of commodity imports by country j from country k. Then we define the factor content of this import vector by

$$T_V^{jk} = \sum_{i \in I} a_i(w^k) T_i^{jk}, \quad \text{for all } j, k \in J \tag{1.11}$$

where

$$a_i(w^k) \equiv [a_{1i}(w^k), a_{2i}(w^k), \dots, a_{Ni}(w^k)]$$

is the vector of factor inputs per unit output. In this definition the techniques of production of the exporter are used to calculate factor content.

Competiton implies

$$p_i \leq c_i(w^k) \equiv w^k \cdot a_i(w^k), \tag{1.12}$$

with equality holding when good i is produced by country k. Combining (1.12) with (1.11) yields

$$w^k \cdot T_V^{jk} = p \cdot T^{jk}, \quad \text{for all } j, k \in J. \tag{1.13}$$

Now, since

$$c_i(w^j) \equiv w^j \cdot a_i(w^j) \leq w^j \cdot a_i(w^k), \quad \text{for all } k, j \in J,$$

then using this result and (1.11) and (1.12), we obtain

$$p \cdot T^{jk} \leq \sum_{i \in I} c_i(w^j) T_i^{jk} \leq \sum_{i \in I} w^j \cdot a_i(w^k) T_i^{jk} = w^j \cdot T_V^{jk},$$

or

$$p \cdot T^{jk} \leq w^j \cdot T_V^{jk}, \quad \text{for all } j, k \in J. \tag{1.14}$$

The combination of (1.13) and (1.14) implies the following restrictions on the factor content of bilateral trade flows (due to Helpman 1984):

$$(w^j - w^k) \cdot T_V^{jk} \geq 0, \quad \text{for all } j, k \in J. \tag{1.15}$$

Hence country j imports from country k goods whose factor content is large on average in factor services that are cheaper in k, and by the same token it exports to k goods whose factor content is large, on average, in factor services that are cheaper in j. In the two-factor case this reduces to the Brecher-Choudhri result.

It should be observed that in the presence of many factors the cross-country differences in relative factor rewards is not uniquely determined by differences in the composition of factor endowments, as it is in the two-factor case. The link between factor rewards and factor composition is given in this case by

$$(w^j - w^k) \cdot (\lambda^j V^j - \lambda^k V^k) \leq 0, \quad \text{for all } j, k \in J, \text{ for all } \lambda^j, \lambda^k \geq 0 \tag{1.16}$$

(see Helpman 1984 for a proof). Indeed, this implies in the two-factor case that the country with a larger capital/labor ratio cannot have a lower wage/rental ratio.

Equation (1.15) provides a restriction on the factor content of bilateral trade flows for all preference structures. It holds trivially in the presence of factor price equalization, and it is therefore useful only when factor prices are *not* equalized. Since it depends on trading equilibrium data, it represents a testable hypothesis.

1.7 Gains from Trade

Our interest in this section, as well as in most other parts of this book, is in aggregative welfare effects rather in distributional issues. For this reason we consider gains from trade for economies with a representative individual. For such economies gains from trade are ensured if in the trading equilibrium the economy can afford to purchase its autarky consumption vector. Since in autarky consumption equals production, this condition reads

$$p \cdot X^A \le p \cdot X, \tag{1.17}$$

where X^A is the economy's autarky output vector, X is its free trade output vector, and p is the free trade price vector.

The proof that (1.17) is sufficient for gains from trade is as follows. Let $e(p, u)$ be the mimimum expenditure function (see Varian 1978, chapter 3).

Then, if X^A provides the utility level u^A, we have

$$e(p, u^A) \le p \cdot X^A,$$

which implies, by (1.17),

$$e(p, u^A) \le p \cdot X.$$

If, however, u is the utility level in balanced free trade, then

$$p \cdot X = e(p, u),$$

and we obtain

$$e(p \cdot u^A) \le e(p, u),$$

which implies $u^A \le u$, thus proving gains from trade.

We will use condition (1.17) on several occasions later in the book. At this stage it remains to be shown that *it is satisfied* in a balanced free trade equilibrium. We will prove this point by means of a method that will be used repeatedly throughout the book.

From (1.12)

$$p \cdot X^A \le \sum_{i \in I} c_i(w) X_i^A = \sum_{i \in J} w \cdot a_i(w) X_i^A.$$

However,

$$w \cdot a_i(w) \leq w \cdot a_i(w'), \quad \text{for all } w' > 0,$$

and in particular, for $w' = w^A$, the autarky factor reward vector. Hence

$$p \cdot X^A \leq w \cdot \sum_{i \in I} a_i(w^A) X_i^A = w \cdot V,$$

where the last equality is obtained from factor market-clearing conditions [see (1.2)]. But $w \cdot V = p \cdot X$ in an economy where there are no pure profits. Hence

$$p \cdot X^A \leq p \cdot X,$$

which is (1.17).

Our proof is rather roundabout, and it serves mainly to introduce the reader to the method. Condition (1.17) is always satisfied in competitive economies with convex technologies because the competitive process leads to an allocation of resources whose value of output is maximal.

References

Brecher, Richard E., and Choudhri, Ehsan V. "The Factor Content of International Trade without Factor Price Equalization." *Journal of International Economics* 12 (1982): 277–283.

Dixit, Avinash, and Norman, Victor. *Theory of International Trade.* Cambridge, England: Cambridge University Press, 1980.

Helpman, Elhanan. "The Factor Content of Foreign Trade." *Economic Journal* 94 (1984): 84–94.

Komiya, Ryutaro. "Non-Traded Goods and the Pure Theory of International Trade." *International Economic Review* 8 (1967): 132–152.

Leamer, Edward E. *Sources of International Comparative Advantage: Theories and Evidence.* Cambridge, Mass.: The MIT Press, 1984.

Melvin, James R. "Production and Trade with Two Factors and Three Goods." *American Economic Review* 58 (1968): 1249–1268.

Travis, William P. *The Theory of Trade and Protection.* Cambridge, Mass.: Harvard University Press, 1964.

Vanek, Jaroslav. "The Factor Proportions Theory: The N-Factor Case." *Kyklos* 24 (1968): 749–756.

Varian, Hal R. *Microeconomic Analysis.* New York: Norton, 1978.

2 Technology and Market Structure

Like most traditional trade theory, the factor proportions theory of international trade described in chapter 1 rests on the simplifying assumption of constant returns to scale. It has been known for a long time, however, that relaxing the assumption of a constant-returns technology can have a significant impact on our view of trade. Even while helping create the factor proportions theory, Ohlin (1933) pointed out that economies of scale in production provide an incentive for international specialization and trade that can supplement the incentives created by cross-country differences in factor endowments and give rise to trade even in the absence of such differences. Yet until recently the assumption of constant returns remained the basis of the bulk of trade theorizing.

The reason for the long dominance of trade theories based on a constant-returns technology is that as soon as this assumption is relaxed, we must confront the issue of market structure. Except under special circumstances a world where returns to scale are not constant will not be a world of perfectly competitive markets. Since there is no generally accepted theory of imperfect competition, it has seemed impossible to say anything general about trade in a world whose technology allows for increasing returns.

In subsequent chapters of this book we will analyze international trade under several alternative assumptions about the nature of competition. We will show that some important conclusions about both the positive and normative aspects of trade are valid for a variety of market structures. This means that it is possible to have a theory of trade in the presence of increasing returns without committing ourselves to any one theory of imperfect competition. Clearly, however, market structure is not completely arbitrary. Even if technology does not fully determine the nature of competition, it sets limits on what is possible.

The purpose of this chapter is to provide an analysis of the relationship between the characteristics of technology and the nature of market structure.

This discussion will be useful as an introduction to some concepts we use later in the book and as a justification for our choices of issues and assumptions in subsequent chapters.

This chapter is in five sections. The first section presents some basic definitions and concepts. The second describes the major approaches we will take to modeling imperfectly competitive markets—contestable markets, Cournot and Bertrand oligopoly, and monopolistic competition. The third section describes an alternative approach that avoids the problem of modeling market structure, the assumption that economies of scale are external to firms.

In the fourth section we discuss the relationship between the static analysis that we use in this book and dynamic conceptions of scale economies. Finally, the last section discusses the role of specific inputs in creating an incentive to form multiproduct firms, which is crucial in explaining the existence of multinational enterprises.

2.1 Economies of Scale at the Level of the Firm

The easiest form of scale economies to give a real-world justification is increasing returns at the level of an individual firm. Other things equal, a larger firm will be better able to overcome indivisibilities, allowing either fuller use of capacity or the use of more specialized and hence more efficient equipment. At the same time some overhead costs are independent of the scale of production and thus fall per unit as production increases. And simple physics can provide advantages to large scale, for example, in process industries where the relationship between volume and surface area provides an incentive to make pipes, storage tanks, and other implements, as large as possible.

How important are these internal economies of scale? In the 1950s and early 1960s much of the quantitative evidence seemed to suggest that in the United States, at least, such economies were largely exhausted, that optimal plant sizes were generally small relative to the market. More recently workers in industrial economics have revised their assessment of the importance of such scale economies upward (see Scherer 1980). This reflects several factors. First, "industries" often produce many products, so that even when optimal plant size is only a few percent of total industry output, there may be many products produced at less than optimal scale. Second, there appear to be important economies of multiplant operation not captured by plant-based estimates of scale economies. Third, there are probably important dynamic scale economies internal to firms.

We should note, however, that though economists have become more willing to accept the importance of scale at the level of the firm, other observes—who have traditionally laid more stress on scale economies than economists—have become more skeptical. Very recent managerial literature now stresses the problems of incentive, control, and morale which arise as organizations grow large and which can outweigh purely technical factors. Nevertheless, there is no doubt that economies of scale internal to firms are important enough to make their implications worth studying. This is particularly true in international economics, since most countries have domestic markets much smaller than those of the United States.

So far we have used the term economies of scale loosely. It is helpful to have a more formal statement. Consider a single-product firm which produces output x using a vector of inputs v according to the production function

$$x = f(v). \tag{2.1}$$

We will say that $f(\cdot)$ exhibits local economies of scale if $f(\lambda v) > \lambda f(v)$ for λ greater than, but sufficiently close to, one. An index of local scale economies is the elasticity of x with respect to λ, evaluated at $\lambda = 1$:

$$\tilde{\theta}(v) = \frac{\sum_{l \in N} f_l(v) v_l}{f(v)}, \tag{2.2}$$

where $f_l(\cdot)$ is $\partial f(v)/\partial v_l$.

It will usually be more convenient, however, to work with a cost-based index of scale economies. The production function $f(\cdot)$ implies a minimum cost function $C(w, x)$, where w is the vector of input prices. An alternative index of economies of scale is the inverse of the elasticity of cost with respect to output (or, equivalently, the ratio of average to marginal cost):

$$\theta(w, x) = \frac{C(w, x)/x}{C_x(w, x)}. \tag{2.3}$$

Not surprisingly, in the vicinity of an optimum position these two measures of scale economies will be equivalent (see Hanoch 1975); that is, at the cost-minimizing input choices corresponding to a given output and set of factor prices, $\theta(e, x) = \tilde{\theta}(v)$.

It is worth repeating that $\theta(\cdot)$ is only a local index of scale economies, which in general depends on both w and x. It will sometimes be useful, however, to assume that $f(\cdot)$ is homothetic. When this is true, we can rewrite the function in the form

$$x = \tilde{f}(v)\bar{f}(x),$$

where $\tilde{f}(v)$ is linearly homogeneous in its arguments. When we can do this, we can think of $\tilde{f}(v)$ as an index of "factor input," and $\bar{f}(x)$ as a productivity effect. Correspondingly we can write the average cost function in the form

$$c(w, x) = \tilde{c}(w)\overline{c}(x),$$

where $\tilde{c}(w)$ is again linearly homogeneous and can be interpreted as an index of the *cost* of "factor input."

The assumption of homotheticity will often be a helpful simplification, because it will allow us to analyze input choices in terms of the functions $\tilde{f}(\cdot)$ or $\tilde{c}(\cdot)$ without having to worry about interactions between input choices and the scale of production.

The crucial fact about internal economies of scale is of course that if they persist, they are inherently inconsistent with competitive equilibrium. As long as $\theta(\cdot) > 1$, marginal cost pricing implies losses. So internal scale economies must be associated with a market structure that allows prices above marginal cost. Our next step then must be to discuss alternative theories of market structure.

2.2 Economies of Scale and Market Structure

The presence of economies of scale at the level of the firm implies that price-taking behavior is inconsistent with non-negative profits and thus that markets cannot be perfectly competitive. To go beyond this insight, however, it is necessary to be specific about how price-setting firms behave. There is no general theory of the behavior of imperfectly competitive firms, but we will lay out some basic issues and describe the particular approaches we will use later in the book.

The first question we need to ask is whether firms with market power act in a cooperative or a noncooperative fashion. In reality the answer is that there is at least some cooperation. Formal cartels and price-fixing arrangements, though illegal in the United States, are not uncommon elsewhere and not unknown even where they are not legal. More generally, tacit cooperation to avoid price wars through price leadership and other coordinating devices is common. The theory of cooperative behavior in oligopolistic industries is not well developed, however. Thus in this book we will restrict ourselves to an analysis of markets where the participants behave noncooperatively.

Even if we rule out collusion, the outcome of noncooperative behavior by firms depends to a considerable extent on additional details. In particular, the outcome of competition in an industry depends on two factors: the strategic variables in terms of which the noncooperative game is played and the conditions of entry into and exit from the industry.

Most theoretical work on oligopoly assumes that the strategic variables of firms are either outputs—the Cournot assumption—or prices—the Bertrand assumption. In the first case each firm chooses its profit-maximizing output level, taking other firms' outputs as given. In the second case each firm chooses its profit-maximizing *price*, taking other firms' *prices* as given. There has always been a tension between these two approaches. As a description of firm behavior, the Bertrand assumption seems to most observers to be more realistic. Yet the results that come from Cournot models often seem more plausible. We will make use of both assumptions at different points in the book.

The issue of entry and exit has also been a major theme in industrial organization. There are two important questions arising from the possibility that new firms could enter an imperfectly competitive industry. The first is whether entry will eliminate economic profits. We will consider both models in which entry eliminates profits and models in which barriers to entry allow some pure profits to persists. We will not, however, tackle the second question, which is that of entry deterrence: the measures that firms in an industry might take to discourage potential competitors.

Bearing in mind these general considerations, in this book we will actually develop theoreis of trade in the presence of three kinds of imperfectly competitive market structures:

1. *Contestable markets.* This concept has been promoted by Baumol, Panzar, and Willig (1982) as a benchmark case for the analysis of industry structure. In terms of our preceding discussion, the theory of contestable markets combines the assumptions of Bertrand behavior by firms and costless unrestricted entry and exit. Although the originators of the concept of contestable markets were largely interested in the analysis of multiproduct firms, we will only use it in the case of single-product firms, where it has a simple implication: every good subject to economies of scale at the level of the firm will be produced by a single firm, and that firm will price the good at average cost. We use the contestable markets theory as the basis for the analysis in chapter 4.

2. *Cournot oligopoly.* Chapter 5 of the book offers an alternative approach, one based on the traditional Cournot assumption of noncooperative behavior with outputs as the strategic variables. We consider both the case where firms earn some pure profits, and the case where free entry drives profits to zero.

3. *Monopolistic competition.* The monopolistic competition approach is, like the contestable markets approach, based on the assumption of Bertrand competition: each firm takes competitors' prices as given. We now suppose, however, that firms are able to differentiate their products so that they are not perfect substitutes for either the products of existing competitors or the products of potential entrants. Each firm thus acts as a monopolist facing a downward-sloping demand curve.

Within this approach we consider two alternative cases of entry. The first is one where entry is restricted, so that there may be economic profits in imperfectly competitive sectors. This case is typically referred to as Bertrand oligopoly. The second case is where there is free entry that drives profits to zero. This last variant is Chamberlin's famous "large group" case and is the one we use most.

The monopolistic competition approach to market structure can be used to shed light on a surprisingly wide variety of issues in international economics. Thus we devote the whole of part II of the book to developing this approach and applying it. Further the analysis of multinational firms in part III also assumes a monopolistically competitive market structure.

2.3 External Economies

Although most of this book will be concerned with the analysis of trade under the market structures just described, we will actually begin our analysis of trade under increasing returns with the one case where increasing returns are consistent with perfect competition. This is the case where returns to scale are constant at the level of the firm, and social increasing returns take the form of external economies. We devote only one chapter to this case. Until recently, however, external effects were the standard way to introduce scale economies into international trade. Thus the uses and limitations of the approach need some discussion.

In principle, external effects can arise from any economic activity. Thus a general external economy model would have production functions at the firm level of the form:

$$x = f(v, \xi), \tag{2.4}$$

where ξ is a vector of all possible "external" influences. The traditional formulation has assumed that the only relevant element of ξ is the output of the domestic industry—for example, Japanese productivity in computers depends on the size of the Japanese computer industry. More generally, however, the vector of external effects surely need not be restricted either to industry-specific or country-specific variables. Japanese computer productivity could easily depend both on the size of the U.S. computer industry—an *international* external effect—and on the size of Japan's semiconductor industry—an *interindustry* effect.

Still, the usual assumption is that the relevant external effect is of the output of the *national* industry on the productivity of individual firms within that industry. This allows us to have constant returns from the point of view of any individual firm—$f(\lambda v, X) = \lambda f(v, X)$, where X is the industry's output—while having increasing returns form the point of view of the industry as a whole. The usual formulation is in fact to assume that scale effects enter multiplicatively:

$$X = g(X)\tilde{f}(v), \qquad (2.5)$$

where $\tilde{f}(\cdot)$ exhibits constant returns. In either the special form (2.5) or a more general form, the external economies assumption lets us write an industry production function $X = F(v)$, which exhibits increasing returns, with an assumption of *average* cost pricing.

But how does one justify the way industry output enters into the firm's production function? One justification, invoked by authors from Marshall (1920) to Ethier (1979), is the argument that a larger industry is able to support production of a wider variety of intermediate inputs at lower cost. If this is the reason for industry economies of scale, however, the problem of handling the effects of scale economies on market structure has not really been solved. Rather, it has been concealed through an incomplete specification of the model. As we will show in chapter 11, certain special assumptions about the market structure of the intermediate goods industry can cause the economy to behave "as if" there are true technological external economies, but this is by no means a general result.

A second potential justification for the external economy type of model is to argue that it is really an internal economy story in which something is constraining firms to price at average cost. As we have already mentioned, the threat of entry by competitors can, under some hypotheses about behavior, lead to average cost pricing by monopolists. As we will show in chapter 4, however, average cost pricing imposed by the threat of entry is not always the same in its implications for international trade as average cost pricing resulting from perfect competition and constant private returns to scale.

Finally, it is possible to argue that there are external economies resulting from the inability of firms to appropriate knowledge completely. Information gained by one firm, whether through explicit R & D (research and development) or through experience, will often be acquired by the firms through word of mouth or deliberate "reverse engineering." This is a true externality; however, it is hard to envisage it leading to a relationship such as (2.4). In the first place innovative industries will ordinarily not be perfectly competitive. Further an emphasis on the generation of knowledge points one in the direction of a dynamic rather than a purely static model.

Given these objections, it seems that one should regard the static external economies model as at best a rough proxy for more complex models. This does not mean that models that assume pure external economies cannot yield useful insights. It does mean that they should be used cautiously and that the results should always be checked for plausibility, given the underlying explanations of increasing returns.

One question for which this appeal to the implicit underlying model is especially important is the question of the unit to which external economies apply. Traditionally this has been assumed to be the nation. Still, as Ethier (1979) has pointed out, if "external" economies arise from economies of scale in the production of intermediate goods, and if these intermediates are (cheaply) tradable, we should think of economies of scale as applying at the international rather than the national level. The key point here is that it is the *tradability* of the intermediate goods that is crucial. Where intermediate inputs are not tradable, the scale economies are national, not international. This point comes out clearly in the explicit model of trade with intermediate goods developed in chapter 11, but the point can easily be missed if the underlying model of production and market structure is concealed within an external economies formulation.

A similar source of potential confusion arises if external economies are assumed to result from incomplete appropriability of knowledge. In this case the question of which unit is relevant for externalities depends crucially on the details of how innovations diffuse. If information spreads by word of month, the relevant unit will be a nation or an even smaller unit—say, the Boston metropolitan area. If, on the other hand, firms can reap the benefits of other firms' innovations by taking their products apart and seeing how they work, external economies should be thought of as international in their effect.

Despite these criticisms the external economies approach to incorporating increasing returns remains useful. It should, however, be demoted from its traditional position as the basic approach to trade with economies of scale.

2.4 Dynamic Scale Economies

In practice, it is likely that one of the most important sources of economies of scale (and of imperfect competition) lies in the dynamic process by which firms and industries improve their technologies. Recent industrial organization literature has emphasized the role of the learning curve in generating industry concentration, whereas the most plausible accounts of external economies involve diffusion of knowledge, and inherently dynamic issue.

We do not attempt in this book to do any explicit modeling of dynamic scale economies. To a degree we believe that our static models can proxy for these dynamic effects. However, the interpretation of this proxy role must be made carefully. There are major potential pitfalls in mixing static and dynamic analysis.

The most important danger is in misinterpreting the nature of the mapping from dynamics into statics. To the extent that a static model is used as a proxy for a dynamic world, it should be viewed as a representation of the whole time path of that world, not a snapshot at a particular point in time.

It particular, the comparison of equilibria involved in comparative statics exercises—such as the comparison of autarky with free trade—should be understood as a comparison between two alternative histories, not as a change that takes place over time. We will often follow the common shortcut of talking about "before trade" versus "after trade," but what we really mean is "if trade had *not* been allowed" versus "if trade *had* been allowed."

This is not a pedantic point, because even careful theorists sometimes get it wrong. For example, Negishi (1972) argued that since economies of scale resulting from learning are irreversible, if scale economies take this form one cannot suffer a loss of scale through the resource allocation effects of trade. This misses the point. The question is not where you are after trade compared with where you were before, but where you are after trade compared with where you *would have been* without trade—and it is certainly possible to have smaller cumulative output in an industry in a trading equilibrium than you would have had if no trade had been allowed.

Even if one takes care to avoid this sort of misconception, using static models to think about dynamics can be risky. This is particularly true in imperfectly competitive markets, where games over time can have many possibilities not seen in one-period games. We do not think that this makes static analysis valueless, but a major goal of further work will have to be to develop a truly dynamic trade theory.

2.5 Specific Inputs and Integrated Firms

One of the most striking omissions from the theory presented in chapter 1 was any description of the size or character of firms. In a constant returns world of course nothing can be said about these questions because firms are irrelevant to the equilibrium. In real-world discussions of trade, however, firms are highly visible features of the landscape. The size and character of firms are widely believed to matter, especially when the boundaries of firms extend across national boundaries so that firms become multinational.

The theory of the firm is not as well developed as we might like it to be. One strong insight does stand out from the work of such authors as Williamson (1975). This is the role of specific inputs in giving rise to integrated firms.

Suppose that technology dictates that only a small number of firms produce an input that is highly specific to an activity which itself is carried out by only a few firms. Then there will be a strong incentive to create integrated firms producing their own specific inputs. Otherwise, firms will be confronted with what Williamson has called the "horrors of bilateral monopoly" where determination of the price and output of the specific inputs becomes the subject of a bargaining game. This game is likely to be costly either through failure to reach agreement or through failure to reach an efficient agreement.

The important implication for our purposes is the following. Suppose there is an "upstream" activity such as operation of a headquarters, which is highly specific to some "downstream" activity, such as production of a differentiated product. Suppose also that both activities are subject to economies of scale. Then there is a presumption that both activities will be carried out by an integrated firm. In chapters 12 and 13 we will use this insight as the basis for an analysis of the role of multinational firms.

2.6 Conclusions

The main purpose of this chapter has been to stress that assumptions about technology and market structure are not independent and to motivate the particular approaches we take in the rest of the book. Ideally we would like to be able to provide a complete mapping from technology to market structure. We cannot do this, presumably because not enough is yet known about such issues as the roles of transaction costs and the costs of coordination and control. But we can limit the range of possibilities in a significant and useful way. Internal scale economies must involve imperfectly competitive markets; monopoly profits may be earned by firms unless they are eliminated by entry. And the existence of specific inputs produced with increasing returns creates a presumption for the existence of integrated firms.

References

Baumol, William J., Panzar, John C., and Willig, Robert D. *Contestable Markets and the Theory of Industry Structure*. New York: Harcourt Brace Jovanovich, 1982.

Either, Wilfred J. "Internationally Decreasing Costs and World Trade." *Journal of International Economics* 9 (1979): 1–24.

Hanoch, Giora. "The Elasticity of Scale and the Shape of Average Costs." *American Economic Review* 65 (1975): 492–497.

Marshall, Alfred. *Principles of Economics*. London: Macmillan, 1920.

Negishi, Takashi. *General Equilibrium Theory and International Trade*. Amsterdam: North Holland, 1972.

Ohlin, Bertil. *International and Interregional Trade*. Cambridge, Mass.: Harvard University Press, 1933.

Scherer, Fredrich. *Industrial Market Structure and Economic Performance*. Chicago: Rand McNally, 1980.

Williamson, Oliver. *Markets and Hierarchies*. New York: Norton, 1975.

II   Homogeneous Products

In this part we present three alternative approaches to modeling trade in a world with increasing returns. Chapter 3 presents the traditional approach, that of assuming that increasing returns arise solely from external economies, so that perfect competition can be preserved. Chapter 4 presents an alternative which sometimes—but not always—yields similar results, that of assuming that the threat of entry in effect constrains imperfect competitors to price at average cost. These two chapters make assumptions that minimize the importance of imperfect competition and focus on increasing returns. Chapter 5 reverses priorities and considers rather the implications of oligopolistic competition.

There are important differences between these different approaches. The main message of this part is that there are also important similarities in both the predictions of these approaches and the methods of analyses we use.

3   External Effects

The traditional way to model trade in the presence of increasing returns has been to assume that these scale economies are external to the firm. This assumption has been historically favored because it allows one to avoid the problem of market structure: with external economies one can preserve the assumption of perfect competition.

Much of the point of this book is that there are other modeling devices; perfect competition is not the only market structure in which to address the analysis of trade under increasing returns. Nevertheless, it is useful to begin with a reconsideration of the external effects approach. For one thing it is possible both to streamline and to generalize this approach; since external effects are a real issue, such an improved statement of the model is useful. At the same time the external effects model will be useful as a benchmark for evaluation of other approaches.

In this chapter then we develop a model of production that allows for quite general external affects. Special cases of these effects, which have been used extensively in the literature, are explained and discussed. We formulate conditions for gains from trade for economies with this production structure and relate them to existing results. Then we describe a variety of circumstances where we can predict trade patterns on the basis of cross-country differences in the composition of factor endowments and describe the difficulties that arise in other cases. Examples are used to illustrate some of these points.

3.1 Production Functions

The production function of a representative firm in sector i of country j, is assumed to depend on a worldwide vector of extenal effects ξ and on the vector of inputs v_i employed by the firm. Letting x_i be the firm's output level, we have

$$x_i = f_i^j(v_i, \xi), \ i \in I, j \in J, \tag{3.1}$$

where $f_i^j(\cdot)$ is strictly quasiconcave and positively linear homogeneous in v_i, with non-negative marginal products of v_i.

The vector of external effects ξ describes all the elements in the world economy that can potentially affect productivity of a firm in any sector and any country. Thus, if the worldwide size of the electronics industry affects productivity of electronics production in Japan, then this size variable is an element of ξ. And if the size of the Israeli sector that produces oranges affects productivity of oranges in Israel, then the size of this sector is also an element of ξ. Similarly, if the employment level of a particular factor of production in the chemical industry affects productivity of chemical product firms, then this employment level is an element of ξ, and if the volume of trade of a particular good affects productivity, this trade volume is also an element of ξ. Hence ξ is a very long vector and the sorting out of all the effects that its elements represent to particular country-industry combinations is assigned to the functional forms of the production functions $f_i^j(\cdot)$. We allow for output-generated external effects, input-generated external effects, and any other external effects that can be represented in this form. This formulation allows for sector-specific effects, country-specific effects, worldwide effects, and spillover effects, both across sectors and across countries. The external effects can be positive or negative.

A crucial question is how trade affects the definition of ξ. In some cases we may want to assume that in the absence of trade only *domestic* variables should appear in ξ, so that if country j does not engage in foreign trade, it faces a vector of external effects ξ^{Aj} which is country specific. Note, however, that though this is plausible in many cases, it is possible that worldwide variables affect a country that does not trade. For example, even a country committed to autarky may learn from the production experience of other countries.

Two examples may help clarify our formulation. Suppose that the productivity of the diamond industry in Israel depends only on the output of diamonds in Israel and nothing else, whereas the productivity of the Swedish electronics industry depends on the total output level of electronics in the world economy. Then we need to include among the elements of ξ the output of diamonds in Israel and the output of electronics of every country in the world economy.

Letting $i = 1$ stand for diamonds, $i = 2$ stand for electronics, $j = 1$ stand for Israel, and $j = 2$ stand for Sweden, we have

$$\xi = (X_1^1, \ldots, X_2^1, X_2^2, \ldots, X_2^J, \ldots),$$

with the dots following X_1^1 and X_2^J representing all other elements. However, given the just described external effects, the production functions $f_1^1(\cdot)$ and $f_2^2(\cdot)$ have special properties:

$$\frac{\partial f_1^1(\cdot)}{\partial \xi_k} > 0 \qquad \text{for } \xi_k = X_1^1, \text{ and it equals zero for } \xi_k \neq X_1^1,$$

where ξ_k is an element of vector ξ. Similarly

$$\frac{\partial f_2^2(\cdot)}{\partial \xi_k} > 0 \qquad \text{for } \xi_k = X_2^j, \, j \in J, \text{ and it equals zero for } \xi_k \neq X_2^j.$$

In particular, these functions can be represented in the following way:

$$f_1^1(v_1, \xi) \equiv g_1^1(v_1, X_1^1)$$

and

$$f_2^2(v_2, \xi) \equiv g_2^2\left(v_2, \sum_{j=1}^{J} X_2^j\right).$$

The Israeli production function of diamonds exhibits national sector-specific external effects, and the Swedish production function of electronics exhibits international sector-specific external effects. If these external effects are positive, then despite the fact that individual firms believe they operate under constant returns to scale, the Israeli diamond industry and the Swedish electronics industry in fact operate under increasing returns to scale.[1]

3.2 Resource Allocation within a Representative Country

Consider a typical firm from industry i of a particular country j. Since in this section we deal with a single country, we drop the country index j from the notation. Every firm has access to the same technology $f_i(\cdot)$. Hence competing firms engage in marginal cost pricing, where marginal costs are taken to be those that are perceived by the firms. Since the external effects are considered by a firm to be independent of its actions, and since $f_i(\cdot)$ is positively linear homogeneous in v_i, the firm perceives the following own output independent marginal (equals average) cost function:

1. In specific applications one has to make sure that the external effects are not too strong so as to enable production with no inputs. For example, in the case of the production function $g_i^j(v_i, X_i^j)$ the elasticity of $g(\cdot)$ with respect to X_i^j must be smaller than one.

$$c_i(w, \xi) \equiv \min_{v_i} \left(w \cdot v_i \,\middle|\, f_i(v_i, \xi) \geq 1 \right). \tag{3.2}$$

Here marginal costs depend on factor prices w and on the external effects ξ. The marginal cost function $c_i(\cdot)$ has the usual properties of cost functions with respect to w (see Varian 1978, chapter 2), whereas its properties with respect to ξ depend on the nature of the external effects (e.g., if $f_i(\cdot)$ is increasing in an element of ξ, then $c_i(\cdot)$ is declining in this element). In particular, $c_i(\cdot)$ is concave in w, and

$$\frac{\partial c_i(w, \xi)}{\partial w_l} = a_{li}(w, \xi),$$

where $a_{li}(\cdot)$ is the per unit output use of factor l.

Since firms engage in marginal cost pricing, we have

$$P_i = c_i(w, \xi), \quad i \in I, \tag{3.3}$$

where P_i is the price of product i, and the factor market-clearing conditions are

$$\sum_{i \in I} a_{li}(w, \xi) X_i = V_l, \quad l \in N. \tag{3.4}$$

These are the usual equilibrium conditions for a competitive economy with constant returns to scale technologies. The only difference is that in the current formulation the constant returns to scale are perceived by firms but do not necessarily apply to the economy as a whole and that cost and factor demand functions depend on the external effects ξ. Clearly (3.3) and (3.4) imply that the value of output in the economy can be represented by a restricted profit function (see Varian 1978, chapter 1, or Dixit and Norman 1980, chapter 2):

$$\Pi(p, V, \xi) \equiv \max_{v_i} \left(\sum_{i \in I} p_i f_i(v_i, \xi) \,\middle|\, \sum_{i \in I} v_i \leq V \right), \tag{3.5}$$

where p is the vector of commodity prices and V is the vector of available factors of production.

This function represents the economy's gross domestic product, which depends, among other things, on the external effects. Since some of the external effects are endogenous to the economy, in an equilibrium their values in the vector ξ have to be consistent with their values that are implicit in the gross domestic product function $\Pi(\cdot)$. Thus, for example, if we take the country under consideration to be Israel and we have the external effect in the diamond industry as described in the previous section, then in an equilibrium the first elements of ξ will be the actual output of diamonds in Israel implicit in $\Pi(\cdot)$.

The function $\Pi(\cdot)$ has the usual properties of restricted profit functions. It is convex in p and concave in V. Its partial derivative with respect to a factor of production equals the marginal value product of the factor of production as perceived by firms and its partial derivative with respect to the price of a good (whenever it exists) equals the output level of the good. Hence we have (see Helpman 1983)

$$w = \Pi_V(p, V, \xi), \tag{3.6}$$

$$X = \Pi_p(p, V, \xi), \tag{3.7}$$

where $\Pi_V(\cdot)$ is the gradient of $\Pi(\cdot)$ with respect to V and $\Pi_p(\cdot)$ is its gradient with respect to p.[2] Conditions (3.3)–(3.4) and (3.6)–(3.7) provide two alternative ways in which the allocation of resources within the economy can be summarized.

At this point it is convenient to pause to consider the issue of whether goods are priced according to marginal or average costs. From the point of view of firms, the answer is both. From an economy wide point of view, however, we have average but not necessarily marginal cost pricing. This can be seen most clearly in the case of the country- and industry-specific output-generated external effects that have occupied most of the literature (see Helpman 1984a). Take the special separable form that has been often used:

$$f(v_i, X_i) \equiv \bar{c}(X_i)\tilde{f}(v_i),$$

where $\tilde{f}(\cdot)$ is increasing, strictly quasi concave, and positively linear homogeneous. The function $\bar{c}(X)$ has an elasticity that is smaller than one. If $\bar{c}(\cdot)$ is an increasing function of X_i, there are economies of scale, and if it is a decreasing function, there are diseconomies of scale.

This specification of the production function has a convenient interpretation. The function $\tilde{f}(\cdot)$, which has the standard properties of a production function, can be considered as an index of factor input. This input is used with a productivity measure that depends on the scale effect, represented by $\bar{c}(\cdot)$, to yield total output. It is clear from this specification that if $\tilde{c}(w)$ represents unit costs of the factor input index (the unit cost function associated with $\tilde{f}(v_i)$), then competitive pricing according to (3.3) implies

$$p_i\bar{c}(X_i) = \tilde{c}(w),$$

where $p_i\bar{c}(X_i)$ is the reward per unit of the factor input index. It is now

---

2. When $\Pi(\cdot)$ is not differentiable with respect to p, the gradient $\Pi_p(\cdot)$ should be interpreted as the set of the slopes of all the hyperplanes that support $\Pi(\cdot)$ at p (holding constant V and ξ), and (3.7) should be replaced by: $X \in \Pi_p(p, V, \xi)$.

straightforward to see that $\tilde{c}(w) X_i / \overline{c}(X_i)$ is the *industry's* cost function so that $\tilde{c}(w) / \overline{c}(X_i)$ represents its average costs. Hence the *industry* prices its output according to average cost.

3.3 Autarky Equilibrium

In autarky every country supplies its own demand. We need not specify at this stage the structure of preferences; all we require is that in the autarky equilibrium of country j its output vector X^{Aj} equals the quantities demanded. Using (3.3)–(3.4), we have in autarky the following production equilibrium conditions:

$$p_i^{Aj} = c_i^j(w^{Aj}, \xi^{Aj}), \quad i \in I, j \in J, \tag{3.6'}$$

$$\sum_{i \in I} a_{li}^j(w^{Aj}, \xi_i^{Aj}) = V_l^j, \quad l \in N, j \in J, \tag{3.7'}$$

and we require ξ^{Aj} to contain elements that are consistent with autarky. Thus, for example, all the external effects that are transmitted across countries only via international trade have a value of zero in ξ^{Aij}, while elements that reflect domestic external effects obtain their autarky value.

It is clear from (3.7') that the autarky employment levels $V^{Aj}(i)$ can be represented as follows:

$$V^{Aj}(i) = a_i^j(w^{Aj}, \xi^{Aj}) \cdot X^j, \quad i \in I, j \in J. \tag{3.8}$$

These employment levels will prove useful in our discussion of gains from trade.

3.4 Trading Equilibrium

In a trading equilibrium commodity prices are the same in every country, because we assume free trade and no transport costs. In addition aggregate world demand for every good equals aggregate world supply. Factor rewards and output levels are determined according to (3.3)–(3.4) or (3.6)–(3.7). Using (3.3)–(3.4), we have the production equilibrium conditions:

$$P_i \leq c_i^j(w^j, \xi), \quad i \in I, j \in J, \text{ with equality if } i \text{ is produced in } j, \tag{3.6''}$$

$$\sum_{i \in I} a_{li}^j(w^j, \xi) X_i^j = V_l^i, \quad l \in N, j \in J, \tag{3.7''}$$

where p is the equilibrium vector of commodity prices and ξ is the vector of external effects that prevails in the trading equilibrium.

3.5 Gains from Trade

Graham's argument (see Graham 1923) that a country may lose from free trade was based on the observation that when trade leads to a reallocation of resources from the increasing returns to scale industry to the decreasing returns to scale industry, gross domestic product—evaluated at constant prices—declines. Later work on this subject was directed toward the identification of conditions under which there will be no real GDP decline as a result of trade. Kemp and Negishi (1970) have shown that a country always gains from trade if trade brings about an expansion of its increasing returns to scale industries and a contraction of its decreasing returns to scale industries. This condition of course excludes Graham's case, and it is based on the logic of the original argument that trade may be harmful.

It is clear from this discussion that economies of scale, or more generally external effects, can prevent a country from gaining from trade only if they bring about a fall in the economy's overall productivity following the opening of trade. Hence it should be possible to devise measures of average productivity such that when these measures increase, there are gains from trade. If this is the case, the economy gains from both the productivity increase and the opportunity to trade at prices that differ from autarky prices, the second component being the usual source of gains from trade in convex economies. This idea lies behind the following sufficient condition for gains from trade (we omit the country superscript j in what follows because the discussion is confined to a single country):

$$\sum_{i \in I} p_i f_i[V^A(i), \xi] \geq \sum_{i \in I} p_i f_i[V^A(i), \xi^A]. \tag{3.9}$$

Before proving that (3.9) is a sufficient condition for gains from trade, we discuss its meaning. It states that the value of output obtained from autarky employment levels, and evaluated with post-trade prices, is larger in the presence of post-trade external effects than autarky external effects. Put differently, it states that average productivity (measured in a particular way) is higher in the trading equilibrium, or that the contribution of trade per se, via its restructuring of the external effects, is non-negative. It is easy to see that the Kemp and Negishi (1970) conditions are a special case of (3.9).

Proof:
We will show that given (3.9), the economy can afford in the trading equilibrium its autarky consumption vector X^A. This is seen as follows:
From (3.9),

$$p \cdot X^A \leq \sum_{i \in I} p_i f_i [V^A(i), \xi].$$

However, $V^A(i)$ is a feasible allocation in the trading equilibrium. Therefore, using (3.5), we obtain

$$\sum_{i \in I} p_i f_i [V^A(i), \xi] \leq \Pi(p, V, \xi).$$

Combining both conditions yields

$$p \cdot X^A \leq \Pi(p, V, \xi),$$

which states that the economy can afford the autarky consumption vector in the trading equilibrium.

For reasons that will become apparent later in this chapter, we will often find it more useful to derive sufficient conditions for gains from trade based on a cost rather than an output measure of productivity change. In this case such a sufficient condition takes the following form:

$$\sum_{i \in I} c_i(w, \xi^A) X_i^A \geq \sum_{i \in I} c_i(w, \xi) X_i^A. \tag{3.10}$$

Thus a country gains from trade if it can produce the autarky output levels more cheaply with the trading equilibrium external effects, using trading equilibrium factor rewards to evaluate costs. This is dual to condition (3.9), but they are not identical. Clearly the Kemp-Negishi requirements also satisfy (3.10).

Proof:

This proof too consists of showing that when (3.10) is satisfied, the economy can afford in the trading equilibrium the autarky consumption vector X^A. From (3.6″) we obtain

$$p \cdot X^A \leq \sum_{i \in I} c_i(w, \xi^A) X_i^A.$$

Combining it with (3.10) yields

$$p \cdot X^A \leq \sum_{i \in I} c_i(w, \xi^A) X_i^A.$$

However,

$$c_i(w, \xi^A) = w \cdot a_i(w, \xi^A) \leq w \cdot a_i(w^A, \xi^A),$$

which yields upon substitutions into the previous inequality

$$p \cdot X^A \leq \sum_{i \in I} w \cdot a_i(w^A, \xi^A) X_i^A$$

$$= w \cdot \sum_{i \in I} a_i(w^A, \xi^A) X_i^A = w \cdot V.$$

The last equality stems from (3.7′). Hence

$$p \cdot X^A \leq w \cdot V = \Pi(p, V, \xi),$$

and the economy can afford the autarky consumption vector in the trading equilibrium.

Our sufficient conditions for gains from trade make clear the point that economies of scale that are achieved from foreign sources via international trade are more conducive to gains from trade than national economies of scale. Moreover the smaller a country is as compared to the rest of the world, the more it stands to gain from trade due to international economies of scale and the more it stands to lose via international diseconomies of scale.

We close this section with an example showing that condition (3.9) is indeed only a sufficient condition for gains from trade; in other words, it shows that a country may gain from trade even when it does not satisfy (3.9). The same example is used to demonstrate Graham's argument that a country may lose from trade. In order to be in line with Graham's nummerical example, our example has economies of scale that are sector and country specific.

Example 3.1

Consider two countries that produce and consume two commodities. Labor is the only factor of production. The first commodity is produced with sector- and country-specific output-generated positive external effects, and the second commodity is produced with constant returns to scale. The production functions are the same in both countries, and they are given by

$$g_1(L_1, \xi) = X_1^{1/2} L_1,$$ (3.11a)

$$g_2(L_2) = L_2,$$ (3.11b)

where L_i is labor employment in sector i and X_1 is the output level of the first industry in the country in which L_1 is applied. Assume also that both countries spend a share α, $0 < \alpha < \frac{1}{2}$, of their income on the first commodity (Cobb-Douglas preferences).

It is easy to verify that the following is the unique autarky equilibrium for a country with a labor size L in which both goods are produced [observe that the perceived marginal product of labor in the first industry is $(X_1^A)^{1/2}$ and that it equals w^A/p_1^A]:

$$w^A = 1,$$

$$p_1^A = (\alpha L)^{-1}, \quad p_2^A = 1,$$

$$L_1^A = \alpha L, \qquad L_2^A = (1 - \alpha)L,$$

$$X_1^A = (\alpha L)^2, \qquad X_2^A = (1 - \alpha)L.$$

The larger a country is as measured by its labor force, the higher its real wage and the better off its residents are.

Now consider trading equilibria for a world that consists of two equal size countries. One equilibrium, in which no active trade takes place, is given by the autarky allocations and prices. But there also exists a pair of equilibria with active trade which are mirror images of each other in terms of the cross-country differences in resource allocation (see Ethier 1982). Using asterisks to denote foreign country variables and no superscripts to denote home country variables, it is easy to verify that the following is a trading equilibrium (remember that $\alpha < \frac{1}{2}$):

$$p_1 = (2\alpha L)^{-1},$$

$$p_2 = 1;$$

$$w = 1, \qquad\qquad w^* = 1,$$

$$L_1 = 2\alpha L, \qquad\quad L_1^* = 0,$$

$$L_2 = (1 - 2\alpha)L, \quad L_2^* = L,$$

$$X_1 = (2\alpha L)^2, \qquad X_1^* = 0,$$

$$X_2 = (1 - 2\alpha)L, \quad X_2^* = L.$$

In this equilibrium the foreign country specializes in the production of good 2 while the home country produces both goods. The mirror image of this equilibrium is one where the roles of the home and foreign country are reversed.

By comparing real wages in terms of both goods in autarky and in trading equilibrium, one sees that in the trading equilibrium real wages are higher in terms of both goods in the home and in the foreign country. Hence, if trade leads the economies from the described autarky equilibrium to the described trading equilibrium, both countries gain from trade. A direct calculation shows, however, that conditions (3.9) and (3.10) are not satisfied by the foreign country. The reason for this is that trade leads the foreign country to shift resources from the industry with increasing return to scale to the industry with constant returns to scale. The result is a decline in the economy's average productivity. Despite this loss of productivity, the foreign country gains from trade because the concentration of the world's output of the good that is produced with increasing returns to scale in a single country leads to a reduction in its price that outweighs the productivity loss. Observe that in this example the gains from trade are in a sense the same for both countries despite their different experience in terms of resource reallocation.

Unfortunately gains from trade cannot be guaranteed. This is demonstrated by the following trading equilibrium for the case in which the countries are of unequal size:

$$L < L^* \quad \text{and} \quad \frac{L}{L + L^*} < \alpha,$$

$$p_1 = \frac{\alpha}{1 - \alpha} \cdot \frac{L^*}{L^2},$$

$$p_2 = 1;$$

$$w = \frac{\alpha}{1 - \alpha} \cdot \frac{L^*}{L} > 1, \quad w^* = 1,$$

$$L_1 = L, \qquad\qquad L_1^* = 0,$$

$$L_2 = 0, \qquad\qquad L_2^* = L^*,$$

$$X_1 = L^2, \qquad\qquad X_1^* = 0,$$

$$X_2 = 0, \qquad\qquad X_2^* = L^*.$$

Here the home country specializes in good 1 while the foreign country specializes in good 2. The home country real wage is higher in the trading equilibrium in terms of both goods. Hence the home country is better off in the trading equilibrium. However, in the foreign country we have

$$\frac{w^*}{p_2} = \frac{w^{A^*}}{p_2^{A^*}} \quad \text{and} \quad \frac{w^*}{p_1} = \frac{1 - \alpha}{\alpha} \cdot \frac{L^2}{L^*}, \quad \frac{w^{A^*}}{p_1^{A^*}} = \alpha L^*.$$

Hence for a small enough relative size of the home country, the foreign country loses from trade. In this case the decline in average productivity of the foreign country that comes with trade dominates the total welfare effect, demonstrating the original Graham point.

3.6 Trade Structure

Traditional explanations of patterns of international trade have been based on cross-country differences in various characteristics. Thus, for example, the Ricardian theory relies on differences in the sectoral ranking of relative productivity levels, and the Heckscher-Ohlin theory relies on differences in the composition of factor endowments. Both theories build on constant returns to scale technologies. Despite this tradition it has also been recognized that increasing returns have an effect of their own on trade structure. This is explicitly discussed in Ohlin (1933, p. 54) and analyzed in some detail in Matthews (1949–1950). The fact that in the presence of economies of scale there may exist active trade between countries that do not differ from each other can be seen in example 3.1 which describes trading equilibria for identical economies. The question is whether we can say more than this. Can useful predictions be made about the pattern of trade under increasing returns?

We start by providing sufficient conditions for the predictability of trade patterns along the lines of the traditional theories of comparative costs and factor proportions. The need for such conditions may be suggested by a simple example. Suppose that labor is the only factor of production and that the production functions defined in (3.1) may be written as

$$f_i^j(L_i, \xi) \equiv \frac{\bar{c}_i(\xi) L_i}{a_i^j}, \quad i \in I, j \in J, \tag{3.1'}$$

where a_i^j are constants. Then it is straightforward to see that comparative advantage of countries is determined by the coefficients a_i^j, and in particular by their relative ranking. The key to this result is the assumption that the function $\bar{c}_i(\xi)$, which summarizes the productivity contribution of the external effects, is the same in every country. Thus, although the external effects contribute different productivity levels in different industries, they contribute the same productivity level to a given industry in every country.

Take a two-sector, two-country example. In the trading equilibrium ξ is the same in both countries, and the relative costs that are perceived by home-country firms are

$$\frac{a_1}{a_2} \cdot \frac{\bar{c}_2(\xi)}{\bar{c}_1(\xi)}.$$

The relative costs that are perceived by foreign firms are

$$\frac{a_1^*}{a_2^*} \cdot \frac{\bar{c}_2(\xi)}{\bar{c}_1(\xi)}.$$

Hence the country that has a lower a_1^j/a_2^j ratio has a comparative advantage in the production of the first commodity and is expected to export it. However, contrary to the traditional Ricardian model, here it is not necessarily true that the country with the lower a_1^j/a_2^j ratio, which is the exporter of good 1, has a lower relative cost of good 1 *in autarky*. The reason is that in autarky the external effects are not the same, and so it is possible to have

$$\frac{a_1}{a_2} < \frac{a_1^*}{a_2^*}$$

and

$$\frac{a_1}{a_2} \cdot \frac{\bar{c}_2(\xi^A)}{\bar{c}_1(\xi^A)} > \frac{a_1^*}{a_2^*} \cdot \frac{\bar{c}_2(\xi^{A*})}{\bar{c}_1(\xi^{A*})}.$$

It is therefore clear that our ability to predict trade patterns under the specification (3.1′) relies on the fact that it brings about equalization of external effects across countries in a trading equilibrium.

The logic that was used to derive condition (3.1′) can also be used to derive a condition on production functions that enables the prediction of trade patterns on the basis of cross-country differences in the composition of factor endowments. For this purpose we need to assume that the extended production functions are the same in every country, or

$$f_i^j(v_i, \xi) \equiv f_i(v_i, \xi), \quad i \in I, j \in J. \tag{3.1″}$$

Clearly, since trade leads to the equalization of the external effects ξ across countries, firms in a given industry face the same production functions, including the same productivity levels of the external effects. Hence we can use the arguments from chapter 1 about the factor proportions theory in order to predict trade patterns. Those arguments rely on cross-country comparisons in the *trading* equilibrium. Predictions of trade patterns that rely on *autarky* information—like the use of autarky relative factor rewards in order to define relative factor abandance—are invalid, because in autarky production functions are effectively not the same due to the fact that the autarky external effects ξ^{Aj} differ across countries. However, predictions that are based on post-trade information—like the Vanek (1968) factor-content prediction in the presence of factor price equalization and identical homothetic preferences or the Helpman (1984b) factor-content prediction in the absence of factor price equalization—remain valid. This logic is indeed at the heart of the study of the special form of international economies of scale in Ethier (1979).

We have identified a strong condition under which it is possible to apply standard trade theories for the purpose of trade pattern predictions in the presence of external effects. It is also clear from our discussion that this condition is "almost" necessary in order to be able to predict trade patterns on the basis of the standard supply-oriented trade theories. Take for example (3.1′). If $\bar{c}_i^j(\xi)$ is not the same in every country, then comparative costs depend in a complex way on the equilibrium values of various endogenous variables, and there is no way in which one can use comparative cost in order to predict the pattern of trade [unless more detailed information about the functions $\bar{c}_i^j(\xi)$ is available]. A similar argument applies to (3.1″).

The nature of the problems posed by a failure of the condition of equality of external effects can be illustrated by another Ricardian example.

Example 3.2

Suppose that there are two countries, with only one factor of production, and that production functions take the form

$$g_i(L_i, X_i) = (X_i)^{\varepsilon_i} L_i / a_i, \quad i \in I,$$

and

$$g_i^*(L_i, X_i^*) = (X_i^*)^{\varepsilon_i} L_i / a_i^*, \quad i \in I,$$

so that there are purely national, industry-specific external effects. There is in this example a natural comparative advantage ordering of goods, according to

$$\frac{a_1}{a_1^*} < \frac{a_2}{a_2^*} < \cdots < \frac{a_I}{a_I^*}.$$

We might expect the home country to produce goods to the left of some cut, the foreign country to produce goods to the right. But given the form of the production functions, a country producing a good has an infinite productivity advantage over a country not producing it. This means that *any* pattern of specialization, and its associated level of relative wages, is an equilibrium. We have no guarantee that the comparative advantage ranking is honored. This stems from the fact that every firm sees itself as facing a horizontal average cost curve with the curve being infinitely high for firms in a country that does not produce the good.

Unfortunately the assumption that (3.1′) holds, or that (3.1″) holds is very strong indeed. For it implies that the productivity gain (or loss) from an external effect whose source is, say in England, is the same in England as in every other country. Thus, if British automobile firms experience external productivity gains whose source is in the British automobile industry, then the same productivity gains also accrue to American, Japanese, Italian, French, and all other car makers. Moreover this is the only type of external effect in existence. Hence all the externalities that stem, for example, from conglomeration or infrastructure, which are typically localized within a country, are excluded.

It turns out then that the assumption of purely external effects, though it avoids the problem of modeling imperfect competition, does not preserve the simplicity of a world where returns to scale are constant. As we saw in chapter 1, however, the precise pattern of trade in goods is hard to predict even in a constant returns world when there are many goods and factors. Our analysis there focused instead on the possibility of factor price equalization and, given this equalization, on the net trade in factor services embodied in goods. This turned out to be possible to predict. A natural question is whether the same change of question will lead to useful results under increasing returns.

3.7 Factor Price Equalization

In investigating the possibility of factor price equalization, we restrict ourselves to a particular type of external effect: industry-specific, country-specific effects of output. Further we assume that technology is the same in all countries. Thus production functions take the form

$$X_1 = g_i(v_i, X_i), \quad i \in I_E, \tag{3.12}$$

where I_E is the subset of industries where external effects are present. All other industries, indexed by I_C, produce with constant returns to scale. Although production functions are the same in all countries, for $i \in I_E$ the production functions obviously do *not* satisfy (3.1″).

As in chapter 1 our first step is to construct the equilibrium of an integrated world economy. In doing so, we will assume that all countries have identical homothetic preferences, so that expenditure shares are $\alpha_i(p)$, $i \in I$. The conditions describing equilibrium in the integrated economy are then analogues of (3.6′)–(3.7′) together with commodity market-clearing conditions. These can be represented as [compare to (1.1)–(1.3) in chapter 1]

$$p_i = c_i(w, \bar{X}_i), \quad i \in I, \tag{3.13}$$

$$\sum_{i \in I} a_i(w, \bar{X}_i)\bar{X}_i = \bar{V}, \tag{3.14}$$

$$\alpha_i(p) = \frac{p_i \bar{X}_i}{\sum_{j \in I} p_j \bar{X}_j}, \quad i \in I, \tag{3.15}$$

where $c_i(\cdot)$ and $a_{li}(\cdot)$ are independent of $\bar{X}_i$ for $i \in I_C$. They imply industry employment levels:

$$\bar{V}(i) = a_i(w, \bar{X}_i)\bar{X}_i, \quad i \in I. \tag{3.16}$$

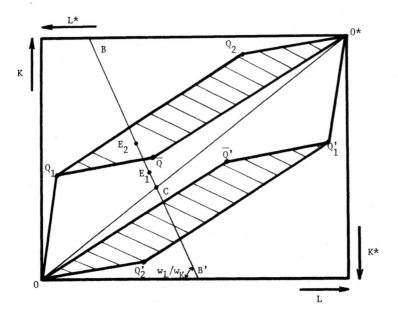

Figure 3.1

Now we ask: When we carve the world up into countries, which divisions of its resources allow us to reproduce the integrated equilibrium? The answer is similar to that given in chapter 1, except that now we add an additional condition: if we are to reproduce the integrated economy, each industry that is subject to external economies has to be located in a single country. Hence the factor price equalization set is defined by endowment allocations that are spanned by the sectoral employment levels (3.16), but with the additional requirement that for $i \in I_E$ the vector $\bar{V}(i)$ is allocated to a single country:

$$\text{FPE} = \left\{ (V^1, V^2, \ldots, V^J) \,\middle|\, \exists \lambda_{ij} \geq 0, \sum_{j \in J} \lambda_{ij} = 1, \text{ for all } i \in I, \right.$$
$$\left. \lambda_{ij} \in \{0, 1\}, \text{ for } i \in I_E, \text{ and } V^j = \sum_{i \in I} \lambda_{ij} \bar{V}(i), \text{ for all } j \in J \right\}. \tag{3.17}$$

This is a nonempty set, but it may happen to be very small and for this reason uninteresting. If, however, there are sufficiently many constant-returns industries, the factor price equalization set will be large; it will have full dimensionality in factor space. The required number of constant-returns sectors for full dimensionality of FPE is equal to the number of factors of production. This is demonstrated in figure 3.1.

The shaded areas in figure 3.1 describe the factor price equalization set for the case of two countries, two factors of production (labor L and capital K), and three goods, with only one good being subject to external economies. The origin of the home country is O and the origin of the foreign country is O^*. The vectors OQ_1, Q_1Q_2, and Q_2O^* correspond to $\overline{V}(1)$, $\overline{V}(2)$, and $\overline{V}(3)$, respectively. If all goods were produced with constant returns to scale, then $OQ_1Q_2O^*Q_1'Q_2'$ would have been the factor price equalization set. However, given that there are external economies in the production of good 1, $\overline{V}(1)$ should be allocated to only one country. If good 1 is allocated to the home country, then endowments in $Q_1Q_2O^*\overline{Q}$ allow factor price equalization; if good 1 is allocated to the foreign country, endowments in $Q_1'Q_2'O\overline{Q}'$ allow factor price equalization. Hence for endowment points in one of the shaded areas there is an equilibrium with factor price equalization.

Several remarks are in order. First, the geometry of the FPE set in figure 3.1 shows that similarity in factor composition need not increase the likelihood of factor price equalization. For example, E_1 represents a more similar factor composition than E_2, but E_1 does not belong to FPE while E_2 does. In particular, *the diagonal OO^* need not belong to the factor price equalization set.* Thus in the presence of external economies particular *dissimilarities* in factor composition may be required for factor price equalization. However, as figure 3.2 shows, similarity in factor composition *might* be consistent with factor price equalization. This point will reappear in other market structures.

Second, there may be several possible patterns of specialization and trade consistent with factor price equalization. Consider point E in figure 3.2. For that distribution of world resources there are two possible patterns of production and trade. If production of good one is concentrated in the home country, that country allocates resources Q_1P_2 to industry 2 and Q_1P_3 to industry 3. If the foreign country produces good 1, which is also consistent with factor price equalization, the home economy allocates resources OP_2' to sector 2 and OP_3' to sector 3. Notice, however, the pattern of specialization that results is of no welfare significance.

Third, increasing returns imply specialization and trade even when countries are identical. Consider figure 3.2 again. Point E happens to be a point where the countries have identical factor endowments; yet we have just seen that only one country will produce good 1, implying necessarily nonzero trade.

Fourth, although the sector with economies of scale is the most capital intensive in this equilibrium, the relatively capital-rich country *need* not have it. This is demonstrated by point E' in figure 3.2. Although at E' the home country is relatively capital rich, factor price equalization requires good 1 to

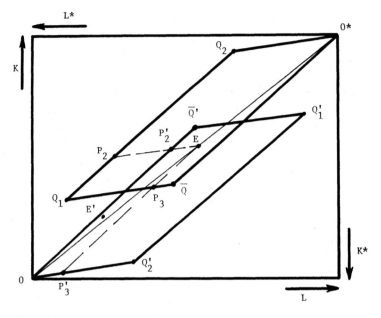

Figure 3.2

be produced in the foreign country. In this case the relatively labor-rich country necessarily exports the most capital-intensive good. The reasons for this is that country size matters too, and at E' the home country is too small to accommodate the first sector without bringing about unequal factor rewards. The last point will prove useful for understanding the problems of multiplicity of equilibria that we will discuss shortly.

Now, although there may be several possible patterns of trade in goods in the FPE set, the factor content of net trade flows is uniquely determined. This is demonstrated in figure 3.1. If, say, E_2 is the endowment point, then C describes the factor content of consumption as we explained in chapter 1. Therefore the vector E_2C describes the factor content of net trade flows. The home country, which is relatively capital rich, is a net exporter of capital content and a net importer of labor content.

In the many factors, many goods case, we have

$$t^j_V = s^j \bar{V} - V^j,$$

where t^j_V is the vector of factor content of net imports, and we can apply Vanek's chain argument. Every country exports the content of services of the factors with which it is relatively well endowed, and it imports the content of services of those factors with which it is relatively poorly endowed.

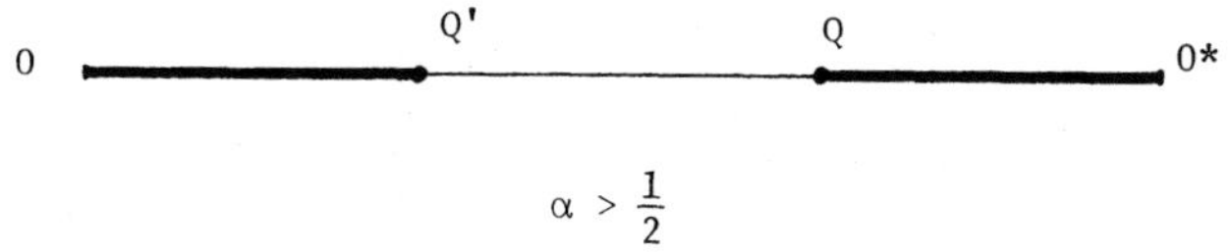

```
0  ●━━━━━━━━━━━━━━━━━━━━━━━━━━━●━━━━━━━━━━━━━●  0*
              Q'                  Q
```

$$\alpha > \frac{1}{2}$$

Figure 3.3

3.8 Nonuniqueness

We have seen that there exists an important case of external economies in which though the pattern of trade in *goods* may be indeterminate, implicit trade in factor services can be predicted from national factor endowments. The case for this prediction is not as strong in the current context, however, as it is in the case of constant returns to scale. In the constant returns to scale case the equilibrium of world production and factor prices is unique. In the presence of external economies it is not. The point is that when there are constant returns to scale and an endowment allocation belongs to the factor price equalization set, we must have factor price equalization; this is not so in the presence of external economies.

The fact that there can be many equilibria when some sectors are subject to external economies was established in section 3.6 by means of example 3.2. We showed there in a Ricardian-type example that there can be many equilibria. What we want to demonstrate now is that when production functions are the same in every country and of the type discussed in the previous section, then even when an endowment point belongs to the factor price equalization set, there may be other equilibria without factor price equalization. We use example 3.1 from section 3.5 for this purpose.

Let $\bar{L}$ be the labor force in the world economy. Then in that example the sectoral allocation of labor in the integrated equilibrium is

$$\bar{L}(1) = \alpha\bar{L},$$

$$\bar{L}(2) = (1 - \alpha)\bar{L},$$

(see example 3.1 for the equilibrium of a closed economy). Two possible factor price equalization sets, defined by (3.17), are described by the heavy lines in figures 3.3 and 3.4. In the case of a single input our box of factor allocations collapses to a line. The origin of the home country is O, and the origin of the foreign country is O^*. Figure 3.3 describes the case $\alpha < \frac{1}{2}$, figure 3.4 describes the case $\alpha > \frac{1}{2}$. The vector OQ describes $L(1)$ and QO^* describes $L(2)$ using the home country's origin. Similarly O^*Q' describes $L(1)$ and $Q'O$ describes $L(2)$ using the foreign country's origin. If the first industry is located in the home

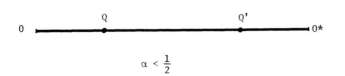

Figure 3.4

country, then factor price equalization requires the endowment point to be between Q and O^*, and if it is located in the foreign country, then the endowment point should be between O and Q'. Hence the factor price equalization sets are represented by the heavy lines.

Now suppose that the endowment lies in OQ in figure 3.3. Then clearly factor price equalization requires that the first industry be located in the foreign country. As we showed in example 3.1, however, there is also an equilibrium in which the increasing returns industry is located in the home country. In this equilibrium $w > w^*$; that is, this is an equilbrium without factor price equalization.

The reason for this possibility is that despite the fact that foreign wages are lower, foreign firms believe themselves to be facing unbounded average costs of production in the first industry as long as $X_1^* = 0$. The result is that domestic firms can produce the good with external economies despite their true cost disadvantage. Although the nonuniqueness result is not confined to the current market structure (given the existence of economies of scale) it seems to be particularly acute in this case because firms identify only a local part of the industry's average cost curve and they operate as if it is horizontal at this level. The drawback of this feature for the uniqueness problem will become clearer in the next chapter.

Finally, we should point out that the relevance of various equilibria depends also on stability properties which we have not discussed (e.g., see Ethier 1982). This is particularly important since even in the simple example that we have just discussed, there exists at E an additional equilibrium in which the foreign country produces both goods and the home country produces only good 1. In this equilibrium there is factor price equalization, but it is different from the integrated equilibrium.

3.9 More on Gains from Trade

The model of country- and industry-specific external economies that we discussed in the last two sections makes gains from trade very likely in the presence of factor price equalization. We showed in example 3.1 that in the case of two countries of equal size there exists an equilibrium with factor price equalization in which both countries gain equally from trade but one country violates conditions (3.9) and (3.10). This happened because, even though the country that specialized in the production of the constant returns good faced a loss in the value of output (at constant prices) when opening to trade, thereby violating (3.9) and (3.10), it gained from trade due to the fall in the price of the good produced with increasing returns to scale, which followed the concentration of its production in the other country in the trading equilibrium. The sufficient conditions for gains from trade do not account for this price decline.

Suppose then that we have a world with country- and industry-specific external economies and that the production functions are the same in every country. Then the following are sufficient conditions for gains from trade:

1. There is factor price equalization.
2. For every $i \in I_E$ good i is produced in only one country.
3. $\sum_{i \in I} c_i(w, X_i^A) X_i^A \geq \sum_{i \in I} c_i(w, \bar{X}_i) X_i^A.$

Proof:
Postulates 1 and 2 imply

$$p_i = c_i(w, \bar{X}_i).$$

Hence

$$p \cdot X^A = \sum_{i \in I} c_i(w, \bar{X}_i) X_i^A.$$

Using this equality and postulate 3, we obtain

$$p \cdot X^A \leq \sum_{i \in I} c_i(w, X_i^A) X_i^A \leq \sum_{i \in I} w \cdot a_i(w^A, X_i^A) X_i^A = w \cdot V = p \cdot X.$$

Hence the autarky consumption vector is affordable in the trading equilibrium.

This result shows that endowments belonging to the factor price equalization set have very desirable welfare properties when the integrated equilibrium is reproduced. Postulate 3 is very likely to be satisfied at such equilibria because all it requires is the *world's* output levels of industries in I_E to be larger on *average* in the trading equilibrium than a country's outputs in autarky.

This result is for the case of factor price equalization. But even without such equalization our analysis suggests that the sufficient condition (3.10) can be substantially weakened by recognizing the gains obtained from cheaper goods in the trading equilibrium. Using the foregoing method of proof, it is straightforward to see that the following is a sufficient condition for gains from trade in the more general case of external effects:

$$\sum_{i \in I} c_i(w, \xi^A) X_i^A \geq \sum_{i \in I} p_i X_i^A. \tag{3.18}$$

Namely a country gains from trade if the cost of producing the autarky consumption vector with autarky external effects and trading equilibrium factor prices is not smaller than the cost of this consumption vector on international markets in the trading equilibrium. The more specialization there is in the trading equilibrium, the more likely is this condition to be satisfied when the external effects are country and industry specific. In example 3.1 both countries satisfy (3.18).

References

Dixit, Avinash, and Norman, Victor. *Theory of International Trade.* Cambridge, England: Cambridge University Press, 1980.

Ethier, Wilfred J. "Internationally Decreasing Costs and World Trade." *Journal of International Economics* 9 (1979): 1–24.

Ethier, Wilfred J. "Decreasing Costs in International Trade and Frank Graham's Argument for Protection." *Econometrica* 50 (1982): 1243–1268.

Graham, Frank D. "Some Aspects of Protection Further Considered." *Quarterly Journal of Economics* 37 (1923): 199–227.

Helpman, Elhanan. "Variable Returns to Scale and International Trade: Two Generalizations." *Economic Letters* 11 (1983): 167–174.

Helpman, Elhanan. "Increasing Returns, Imperfect Markets, and Trade Theory." In *Handbook of International Economics.* Vol. 1. Jones, Ronald W., and Kenen, Peter B. (eds.). Amsterdam: North Holland, 1984a.

Helpman, Elhanan. "The Factor Content of Foreign Trade." *Economic Journal* 94 (1984b): 84–94.

Kemp, Murracy C. and Negishi, Takashi. "Variable Returns to Scale, Commodity Taxes, Factor Market Distortions and Their Implications for Trade Gains." *Swedish Journal of Economics* 72 (1970): 1–11.

Matthews, R.C.O. "Reciprocal Demand and Increasing Returns." *Review of Economic Studies* 37 (1949–1950): 149–158.

Ohlin, Bertil. *Interregional and International Trade.* Cambridge, Mass.: Harvard University Press, 1933.

Vanek, Jaroslav. "The Factor Proportions Theory: The N-Factor Case." *Kyklos* 24 (1968): 749–756.

Varian, Hall R. *Microeconomic Analysis.* New York: Norton, 1978.

4 Contestable Markets

In chapter 3 we incorporated economies of scale into a general equilibrium model by assuming that these economies were wholly external to firms. This assumption is a convenient one because it is consistent with perfect competition and it implies average cost pricing throughout the economy; imperfect competition and monopoly rents are not an issue. And we showed that in certain circumstances the external economies approach leads to a simple and appealing analysis of both the pattern and welfare effects of trade. The immediate question, however, is how general this analysis is. In particular, can it still serve as a useful guide when economies of scale are internal rather than external to firms?

The purpose of this chapter is to introduce the analysis of trade under imperfect competition with a particular market structure; this is the case of *contestable markets*—markets in which the threat of entry forces average cost pricing even though there are products produced by monopolistic firms.

The chapter is in six sections. The first section explains what we mean by a contestable market and defines the basic equilibrium concept. The second section describes the equilibrium of an integrated world economy, where factors of production are perfectly mobile. The third and fourth sections then analyze the nature of international specialization and trade when factors are immobile but trade allows achievement of the integrated equilibrium and equalization of factor prices. The fifth section turns to the analysis of trade patterns when factor price equalization does not occur. Finally, the sixth section analyzes the gains from trade.

In addition this chapter has two appendixes. One of them discusses the issue of existence of equilibrium. The other presents an example of losses from trade.

4.1 The Concept of Market Contestability

The existence of economies of scale internal to firms makes perfect competition impossible. And once markets are imperfectly competitive, there is no reason in general to expect average cost pricing. Recently, however, the work of Baumol, Panzar, and Willig (1982) has suggested that under some circumstances average cost pricing will remain the norm even when economies of scale lead to the presence of only a few firms or even a single firm in a market. They argue that firms will be unable to exploit their market power when the market is *contestable*. By this is meant that there are potential competitors who are able to enter and exit rapidly from the market and that established firms have no cost advantage over these potential competitors.

We will begin by restating the definition of equilibrium for a closed economy. We will then modify the definition to make it applicable to a trading world economy.

Consider then the market for a single product in a closed economy. The demand for the product is a downward sloping function of the price, $D(p)$. There are a number of firms potentially able to produce the product. They all have the same average cost function,

$$c(w, x_\omega),$$

where w is the vector of factor prices and x_ω is the output of firm ω. The function $c(\cdot)$ is decreasing in output; that is, the product is produced with increasing returns to scale.

Now a contestable market equilibrium for the market is defined by three things: the number of firms in the market, m; the output of those firms $(x_1, \ldots, x_m)$; and the market price, p. We have three conditions for this equilibrium. First, we must have market clearing:

$$\sum_{\omega=1}^{m} x_\omega = D(p).$$

Second, the equilibrium must be *feasible* in the sense that no firm is making losses:

$$p \geq c(w, x_\omega), \quad \text{for } \omega = 1, \ldots, m.$$

Third, the equilibrium must be *sustainable* in the sense that no firm can profitably undercut the market price:

for all $p^e \leq p$,

$$p^e \leq c(w, x^e), \quad \text{where } x^e = D(p^e).$$

The implication of this definition of equilibrium is that any good subject to increasing returns must be produced by a single monopolist and priced at average cost. If there were more than one firm, an entrant could undercut the going price and still earn profits because, by producing more than any one

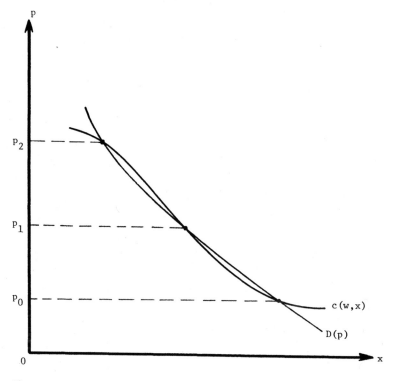

Figure 4.1

incumbent firm, it has lower average costs. If price is above average cost, an entrant can always profitably undercut the incumbent. Thus the outcome must be an average-cost-pricing monopolist.

This is not quite the whole story, however, because there may be more than one level of output at which price equals average cost. Consider figure 4.1, where there are three price-output combinations for $p = c[w, D(p)]$. If this were a model with a Marshallian forward-falling supply curve, one would be tempted to say that there are two stable equilibria here, with prices p_0 and p_2. But with contestable markets prices above p_0 will not be sustainable, because there exists a range of prices from p_0 to p_1 where price exceeds average cost. Clearly then, if there is more than one price where price equals average cost, the contestable markets equilibrium is the *lowest* of these prices. If the condition $p = c[w, D(p)]$ yields a unique answer, of course this is the contestable markets equilibrium price.

There requirement that we choose the lowest price at which price equals average cost becomes important, however, when we move to an international setting. Suppose now that there are $J \geq 2$ countries which need not have the same factor prices. Let w^j be the factor prices of country j. Then our new definition of an equilibrium must involve a vector of numbers of firms,

$$(m^1, \ldots, m^J),$$

where m^j is the number of firms from country j; a "long" vector of outputs,

$$(x^1_1, \ldots, x^1_{m1}; x^2_1, \ldots, x^1_{m2}; \ldots; x^J_1, \ldots, x^J_{mJ})$$

and a world price p. The equilibrium conditions are straightforward extensions of those we have already stated. First, we must have market clearing:

$$\sum_{j \in J} \sum_{\omega=1}^{m} x^j_\omega = D(p),$$

where $D(p)$ is *world* demand.

Second, we require feasibility:

$$p \geq c(w^j, x^j_\omega), \quad \text{for all } j \in J,$$

and

$$\omega = 1, \ldots, m^j.$$

Third, we require sustainability, which takes on the added dimension of international competition:
for all $p^e \leq p$,

$$p^e \leq c(w^j, x^e) \quad \text{for all } j \in J, \text{ where } x^e = D(p^e).$$

As before these conditions imply production by a single firm , and pricing at average cost. And if there is more than one such configuration, the equilibrium is the one with the lowest average cost. In an international context this last consideration can be very significant. Figure 4.2 illustrates a situation where the average cost of production of a good in one country is everywhere lower than in another. Nevertheless, if these were downward-sloping supply schedules due to external economies there would be two possible equilibria. In one of these, at E^2, the low cost foreign country would produce and the high cost home country would not. But if the home country were established in the market and the foreign country were not, then an equilibrium at E^1 would be sustainable. Indeed, such multiple equilibria did appear in the last chapter, raising substantial difficulties in predicting trade patterns.

In the contestable markets case, however, this problem does not arise. Entry will always lead to an equilibrium where price is minimized subject to a break-even constraint; E^1 is not sustainable, and only E^2 is an equilibrium.

In sum, then, the theory of contestable markets implies that every good

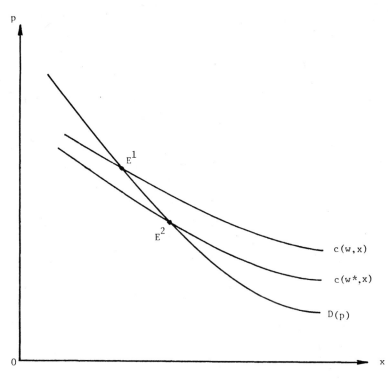

Figure 4.2

subject to increasing returns is produced by a single firm and priced at average cost and that its production is located in whichever country yields the minimum price consistent with zero profits.

4.2 Integrated Equilibrium

The theory of contestable markets yields a simple description of market structure and pricing for an economy in which some goods are produced with internal economies of scale. Each good for which returns to scale are increasing will be produced by a single firm; all goods will be sold at average cost. What we will now do, as in chapters 1 and 3, is to state conditions of equilibrium for a hypothetical construct, the integrated world economy. This construct, the general equilibrium of a world economy with perfectly mobile factors, will serve as the reference point for our analysis of trading equilibria in later sections.

Suppose then that the world economy produces a set of goods I. This set may be partitioned into a subset I_R of goods produced with increasing returns and a subset I_C of goods produced under constant returns. All consumers have identical homothetic preferences for goods. There is a set N of factors of production, which must be fully employed.

The first equilibrium conditions are on pricing. Constant returns goods will simply be priced at average cost:

$$p_i = c_i(w), \quad \text{for all } i \in I_C. \tag{4.1}$$

Each good whose production is characterized by economies of scale will also be priced at average cost and will be produced by a single firm, producing the entire world output $\bar{X}_i$:

$$p_i = c_i(w, \bar{X}_i), \quad \text{for all } i \in I_R. \tag{4.2}$$

We assume for simplicity that there is a unique price consistent with zero profits in each market, so that we need not add an additional condition to ensure that p_i is actually the *minimum* price consistent with the break-even constraint.

Turning to the factor markets, we first need to derive unit factor inputs. These can be derived from the unit cost functions:

$$a_{li}(w) = \frac{\partial}{\partial w_l} c(w), \quad l \in N, i \in I_C,$$

$$a_{li}(w, \bar{X}_i) = \frac{\partial}{\partial w_l} c(w, \bar{X}_i), \quad l \in N, i \in I_R.$$

We can then write our factor market-clearing conditions as

$$\sum_{i \in I_C} a_{li}(w) \bar{X}_i + \sum_{i \in I_R} a_{li}(w, \bar{X}_i) \bar{X}_i = \bar{V}_l, \quad l \in N. \tag{4.3}$$

Finally, each good i receives a share $\alpha_i(p)$ of expenditure, so the conditions of goods market clearing may be written as

$$\alpha_i(p) = \frac{p_i \bar{X}_i}{\sum_{j \in I} p_j \bar{X}_j}, \quad \text{for all } i \in I. \tag{4.4}$$

As in chapters 1 and 3, we can define employment vectors representing the input of factors into each sector i. The allocation of resources in the integrated economy can then be summarized by this set of vectors $\bar{V}(i)$.

4.3 Trading Equilibrium

Suppose now that the world economy is divided into J countries, with each country receiving an endowments V^j of factors of production. For some distributions of endowments the world economy will still be able, through trade, to achieve the same aggregate allocation of resources and output as in the hypothetical case of perfect integration. When this occurs, factor prices will be equalized, and we can analyze the trade pattern in a very simple way.

First, we need to specify the set of distributions of world resources under which factor prices can be equalized. As in chapter 3's case of industry- and country-specific economies of scale, to reproduce the integrated economy, the trading economy must *concentrate* production of each sector subject to increasing returns in one country. (Here production is concentrated in the hands of a single firm as well.) In addition production must be allocated in such a way as to employ fully each country's resources using the integrated economy techniques of production. Thus the set of distributions of world resources consistent with factor price equalization is

$$\text{FPE} = \left\{ (V^1, \ldots, V^J) | \exists \lambda_{ij} \geq 0, \sum_{j \in J} \lambda_{ij} = 1 \quad \text{for all } i \in I, \ \lambda_{ij} \in \{0, 1\} \right.$$

$$\left. \text{for all } i \in I_R, \text{ and } j \in J, \text{ such that } V^j = \sum_{i \in I} \lambda_{ij} \overline{V}(i) \text{ for all } j \in J \right\}. \tag{4.5}$$

This definition, which is identical to (3.17), differs from (1.4) only in imposing integer constraints on the allocation of increasing returns sectors. These constraints make the set of factor price equalization smaller. In particular, FPE has full dimensionality only if I_C, the number of constant returns sectors, is at least as large as the number of factors.

The implications of (4.5), and the implications for trade if factor prices are in fact equalized, can be illustrated with a two-factor, two-country, three-good example. Suppose there are three goods. Good 1 is produced with increasing returns, and goods 2 and 3 are produced with constant returns. In figure 4.3, OQ_1 and O^*Q_1' represent $\overline{V}(1)$, the inputs into sector 1 in the integrated equilibrium; Q_1Q_2 and $Q_1'Q_2'$ represent $\overline{V}(2)$; Q_2O^* and $Q_2'O$ represent $\overline{V}(3)$. Our conditions for factor price equalization require that we allocate these vectors to countries in such a way as to employ fully all resources *and* that we concentrate production of good 1 in only one country.

Clearly, if we concentrate production of 1 in the home country, we can still fully employ resources for any endowment point in $Q_1Q_2O^*\tilde{Q}_2$. If we concentrate production of 1 in the foreign country, we can fully employ resources for any point in $O\tilde{Q}_2'Q_1'Q_2'$. So the set FPE consists of the union of these two parallelograms. The region is smaller than in the constant returns case of chapter 1 by the shaded areas, which reflect the integer constraint imposed by the requirement of concentrated production (compare to figure 3.2).

If the endowment point lies in the factor price equalization set, there are three main points we can easily see from this example:

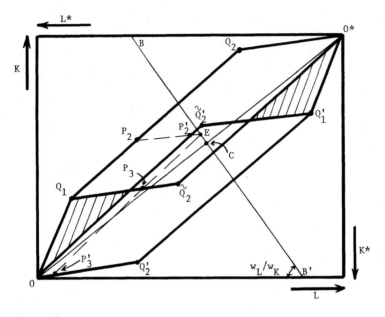

Figure 4.3

1. There may easily be more than one set of allocations λ_{ij} of world production that satisfies (4.5). Consider the allocation point E in figure 4.3. The following are two possible patterns of production. The home country could produce good 1, devoting resources OQ_1 to that purpose and then $Q_1 P_2$ and $Q_1 P_3$ to the production of goods 2 and 3, respectively. Alternatively, the foreign country could produce good 1; in this case the home country devotes resources OP'_2 and OP'_3 to the production of the other two goods. This shows that the pattern of international specialization and trade is in general not fully determinate.

2. Though trade in goods may not be fully determined, we can predict net trade in factor services. In figure 4.3 we draw through the point E an income line BB', which has a slope $-w_L/w_K$. We know that the home country's share in world income is $\overline{OC}/\overline{OO^*}$, where C is the intersection of BB' with the diagonal OO^*. It follows from homotheticity of preferences that OC represents the vector of factor services embodied in home country consumption. So net trade in factor services is always represented by EC, even though there are two possible patterns of specialization. More generally, as long as factor prices are equalized we will continue to have a "Vanek chain" in which a country will be a net exporter of the services of factors with which it is relatively abundantly endowed.

3. Exchange of factor services is not the only reason for trade in goods. Even if E lay on the diagonal, so that there was no net trade in factor services, the requirement that production of good 1 be concentrated would lead to specialization and trade.

This analysis is very simple and appealing. It depends, however, on the assumption that trade leads to a reproduction of the integrated equilibrium. Our next task is to answer two questions. First, what assurance do we have that factor prices will be equalized, even if the distribution of endowments lies in FPE? Second, can we say anything about trade when endowments lie outside FPE? The next two sections take up these questions in turn.

4.4 Robustness of Factor Price Equalization

We know that as long as the endowment point lies in the set FPE, there is an equilibrium of the trading world economy with equalized factor prices, which reproduces the equilibrium of the integrated economy. But is this the *only* equilibrium? In chapter 3 we gave an example showing that when economies of scale were external to firms, there could be other equilibria with unequal factor prices. Though we have not made a general analysis for the case of contestable markets, it seems clear that there is a stronger presumption for factor price equalization than in the case of external effects. In particular, in an example corresponding to that given in the previous chapter, the nonfactor price equalization equilibrium can be ruled out in a world of contestable markets.

As in example 3.1, then, consider a world of two countries, home and foreign, with only one factor of production, labor, producing two goods, X and Y. Good Y is produced with constant returns; good X is produced with increasing returns, with the cost function

$$c_X(w, x) = wx^{-\zeta}, \quad 0 < \zeta < 1.$$

We assume Cobb-Douglas preferences, with a share $\alpha < \frac{1}{2}$ of expenditure falling on X.

Figure 4.4, which reproduces figure 3.4, shows the allocation of resources in the world economy. OO^* represents the world supply of labor. OQ represents the labor devoted to production of X in the integrated economy and is equal to $Q'O^*$. QO^* represents the allocation of resources to Y in the integrated economy and equals OQ'. We must have $\overline{OQ/OO}^* = \alpha$, $\overline{QO}^*/\overline{OO}^* = 1 - \alpha$.

As drawn, figure 4.4 embodies the assumption that $\alpha < \frac{1}{2}$, shown by the fact that Q is to the left of Q'. In this case any endowment point is consistent with

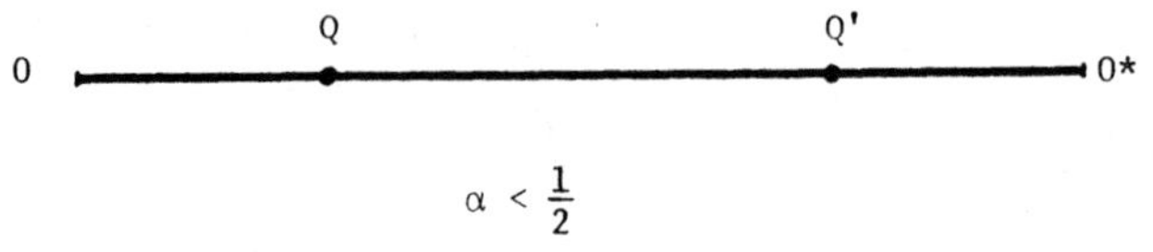

$$\alpha < \frac{1}{2}$$

Figure 4.4

factor price equalization. For points in OQ, good X must be produced in the foreign country to allow the same scale as in the integrated economy. For points in $Q'O^*$, X production must be concentrated in the home country. For points in QQ', either country can produce X.

Now the question is whether there is a sustainable equilibrium with a different specialization pattern. Can we have world equilibrium with an endowment point in OQ, but with X produced in the home country? (There is a symmetrical case with the endowment in $Q'O^*$ and X produced in the foreign country.)

If the endowment lies in OQ and the home country specializes in X, we must have a relative wage in the home country

$$\frac{w}{w^*} = \frac{\alpha}{1-\alpha} \frac{L^*}{L} > 1.$$

But given the higher wage in the home country, a firm would find it profitable to produce X in the foreign country. Thus this equilibrium is not sustainable.

In the external effects model of chapter 3 this equilibrium *was* sustainable because firms viewed their average costs as dependent on industry output, which they could not affect. If no X is produced in the foreign country, firms considering entry would find themselves at a productivity disadvantage relative to those in the home country which outweighed the wage differential. In the contestable markets case, however, competition comes from firms that contemplate taking over the whole market, and they see that the wage differential gives them a potential cost advantage.

Some readers may notice that the definition of a sustainable equilibrium under contestable markets can give rise to some problems about existence of equilibrium that are special to a trading world. These problems are discussed briefly in the appendix to this chapter.

Our example suggests then that the concept of a factor price equalization equilibrium which reproduces the integrated economy is at least as useful when we have internal economies of scale and contestable markets as when we have external economies and perfect competition.

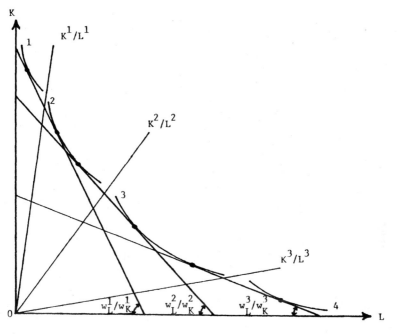

Figure 4.5

4.5 Unequal Factor Rewards

Many of our results on trade patterns in this book depend on the assumption that factor prices are equalized or that production functions are homothetic. In the case of contestable markets, however, we can pursue an analysis parallel to that in section 1.6, to derive results for the case of unequal factor rewards.

Figure 4.5 illustrates technology and cost relationships for a two-factor, three-country, four-good world. It is identical in appearance to figure 1.8, but with a difference in interpretation. What are illustrated are not isoquants in the usual sense. Instead, they are curves constructed by taking the isoquants for the *actual* world output $\bar{X}_i$ of each good and shrinking them by a factor $1/p_i\bar{X}_i$. Thus these curves represent alternative input combinations *per dollars' worth of output*. Also for each country j the ray K^j/L^j represents the capital/labor ratio of its endowment, and the downward-sloping lines with slope w^j_L/w^j_K are unit cost lines.

It is intuitively apparent that w_L/w_K is increasing in K/L. This can be provided either directly from the diagram by derivation of an appropriate GDP function or by defining a world factor price frontier. We will simply assert that this must in fact be the case.

In the example shown in the figure, the first country can produce the actual world output of 1 more cheaply than any other. The world output of good 2 can be produced equally cheaply in countries 1 and 2; that of good 3 equally cheaply in 2 and 3. World output of good 4 can be produced most cheaply in country 3. Thus there is a chain of comparative advantage. Country 1, the most capital abundant, produces 1 and 2; country 2 produces 2 and 3; country 3 produces 3 and 4. The capital intensity of the goods that countries produce corresponds to their capital abundance. (Note that capital intensity is evaluated at the *actual* level of output. This means that the result is not dependent on homotheticity of production functions.) Now, since a dollar worth of output is produced with more capital and less labor in a country with a higher capital/labor ratio, the factor content of bilateral trade flows reflects cross-country differences in factor endowments.

In general, let T^{jk} be the vector of commodity imports by country j from country k. Then the factor content of this import vector will be

$$T_V^{jk} = \sum_{i \in I_C} a_i(w^k) T_i^{jk} + \sum_{i \in I_R} a_i(w^k, \bar{X}_i) T_i^{jk}. \tag{4.6}$$

Now we know that for any good produced in k under constant returns,

$$c_i(w^j) \geq c_i(w^k) = w^k \cdot a_i(w^k), \quad \text{for all } i \in I_C. \tag{4.7}$$

Otherwise, the good would be cheaper to produce in j. With contestable markets a similar condition holds for goods in I_R:

$$c_i(w^j, \bar{X}_i) \geq c_i(w^k, \bar{X}_i) = w^k \cdot a_i(w^k, \bar{X}_i), \quad \text{for all } i \in I_R. \tag{4.8}$$

But we also know that the following inequalities hold:

$$c_i(w^j) \leq w^j \cdot a_i(w^k), \tag{4.9}$$

$$c_i(w^j, \bar{X}_i) \leq w^j \cdot a_i(w^k, \bar{X}_i), \tag{4.10}$$

because the choice of production technique in k does not minimize costs for j's factor prices.

Putting these together, we have

$$(w^j - w^k) \cdot T_V^{jk} \geq 0, \tag{4.11}$$

which is the same result as (1.15). It says that when we examine bilateral trade flows, we will find that a country on average exports goods whose factor content is large in factor services that are relatively cheap in that country, and it imports goods whose factor content is large in factor services that are expensive in that country.

4.6 Gains from Trade

We conclude the main body of this chapter by analyzing the welfare impacts of trade. Gains from trade are *not* ensured under contestable markets. We give an example of losses in the appendix. However, we can state a sufficient condition for gains that looks quite mild and suggests a strong presumption of gains.

Our sufficient condition for gains from trade is the following: *a country gains from trade if*

$$\sum_{i \in I} c_i(w, \bar{X}_i) X_i^A \leq \sum_{i \in I} c_i(w, X_i^A) X_i^A,$$

where w is the country's post-trade vector of factor prices, X_i^A is the country's *autarky* output of good i, and $\bar{X}_i$ is the *world* output of i after trade (for $i \in I_C$ average costs are independent of X_i).

The proof follows the same lines as that in chapter 3, but we no longer require factor price equalization. First, with contestable markets no good's price can exceed the average cost of producing the current world output in our country; otherwise, a domestic firm would enter and take over the market. So we have

$$p_i \leq c_i(w, \bar{X}_i), \quad \text{for all } i \in I.$$

Thus our condition implies

$$\sum_{i \in I} p_i X_i^A \leq \sum_{i \in I} c_i(w, X_i^A) X_i^A.$$

Next let w^A be autarky factor rewards. We know that

$$c_i(w, X_i^A) \leq w \cdot a_i(w^A, X_i^A), \quad \text{for all } i \in I,$$

because the autarky choice of technique is not cost minimizing at post-trade factor prices.

Finally, since factors were fully employed in autarky, we have

$$\sum_{i \in I} a_i(w^A, X_i^A) X_i^A = V,$$

where V is the country's factor endowment.

Putting these inequalities together, our condition for gains from trade implies

$$\sum_{i \in I} p_i X_i^A \leq w \cdot V = \text{GDP};$$

that is, the country's income after trade allows it to purchase its pretrade output, so it must have gained from trade.

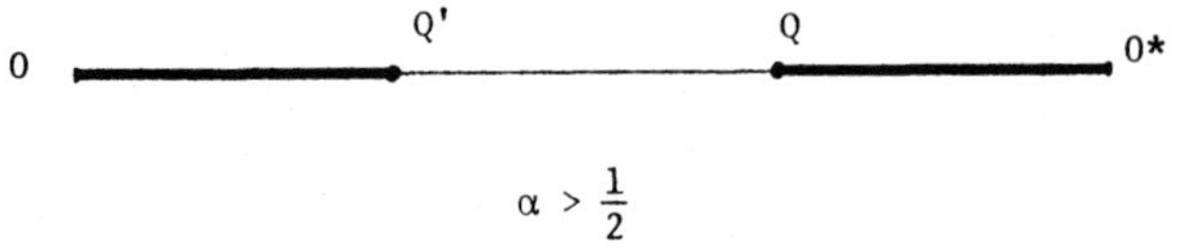

Figure 4A.1

Now the important point about the sufficient condition for gains is that it compares *national* outputs before trade with *world* outputs after trade. All that we require is that on average the trading world economy have larger production of goods subject to increasing returns than our economy alone would have had in autarky. The traditional concern that countries might lose from trade emphasizes the possibility of a decline in the national output of sectors with increasing returns, something that does not seem too unlikely. But in our analysis the scale of production in our country is not important, and losses seem much less likely. The example given in the appendix demonstrates that losses are possible, but it is a heavily contrived case. In general, the contestable markets model suggests a strong presumption of gains from trade.

Appendix 4A: Existence of Equilibrium

Under certain conditions a sustainable equilibrium in the sense we have defined it may not exist. The possibility of nonexistence may not be a serious problem, for reasons to be discussed in a moment. For completeness, however, the possibility deserves some discussion.

Consider again the example discussed in section 4.4, where there are two goods, two countries, and only one factor of production. Suppose now that the share of expenditure falling on the increasing returns sector is $\alpha > \frac{1}{2}$.

The allocation of resources in the world economy can be analyzed using figure 4.A1. OO^* represents the world endowment of labor. OQ represents the employment of labor in the production of X in the integrated equilibrium; $\overline{OQ} = \overline{Q'O}\,^*$, and $\overline{OQ}/\overline{OO}^* = \alpha$. QO^* and OQ' represent the employment of labor in the production of Y. The difference from figure 4.4 is of course that Q' now lies to the left of Q.

The region FPE now consists of two disjoint sets, OQ' and QO^*. If the endowment point lies in either of these line segments, we have no problems: there is a contestable markets equilibrium with X produced in the larger country.

Suppose, however, that the endowment point lies in $Q'Q$. Then no contestable markets equilibrium exists. The definition of such an equilibrium given in section 4.1 required that any good subject to increasing returns be produced by a single firm in whichever location has the lowest cost. But if we attempt to concentrate production when the endowment lies in $Q'Q$, the relative wage of the country specializing in X must rise—a condition that would lead to entry by a firm in the other country. So no equilibrium exists. The difficulty with existence that arises here is special to a world with many countries because it stems from the fact that factor markets are segregated while goods markets are integrated. In convex economies these features do not pose existence problems.

It is possible to argue that the correct lesson to draw from this example is that we need to reformulate our concept of equilibrium. Our inclination is, however, not to pursue the issue further. The problem of nonexistence here is a consequence of the fact that the share of expenditure falling on a single good is so large that shifting that good's location of production has an important effect on factor prices. In a more realistic model with many goods, the problem would be less serious, although it will not disappear.

Appendix 4B: Losses from Trade

There is a presumption of gains from trade under contestable markets, but losses from trade are possible. In this appendix we given an example. The example involves asymmetries of tastes and technology between countries. These are not necessary to produce losses from trade, but the examples we have been able to construct without asymmetries are extremely intricate.

Consider then a world of two countries, Home and Foreign. There is only one factor of production, labor, in each country. There are three goods. Home can produce only goods 1 and 3; Foreign only goods 2 and 3.

Good 1 is produced with increasing returns; we can summarize this by a unit labor requirement:

$$a_{L1}(X_1),$$

which is decreasing in output. Good 2 is produced in Foreign at a constant unit labor input a^*_{L2}. Good 3 is produced in both countries at constant returns; we choose units so that the unit labor input is one is both countries.

On the demand side Home tastes are assumed to take a very special form:

$$U(D_1, D_2, D_3) = \beta_1 \min [D_1, \bar{D}_1] + \beta_2 \min [D_1 + D_2, \bar{D}_2] + D_3, \qquad (4.\text{B}1)$$

$$\text{where } \bar{D}_2 > \bar{D}_1.$$

This can be interpreted as follows. There is a "primary" segment of demand in

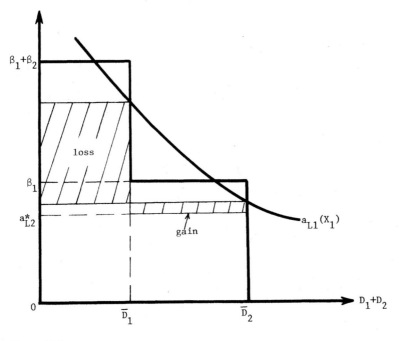

Figure 4B.1

which good 1 is superior to good 2; and a "secondary" segment in which they are equally good. Foreign has simple tastes: only good 3 is demanded.

Let us first consider autarky equilibrium. In Foreign this is simple: good 3 is produced, at a price of one. Autarky equilibrium in Home is illustrated by figure 4.B1. There the demand for good 1 is expressed as a function of its price in terms of good 3; it is a step function, defined by (4.B1), since good 2 is unavailable. Also shown is the cost of producing good 1 in terms of good 3 which, given our choices of units, is simply the unit labor requirement. The particular way we have drawn it implies $\beta_2 < a_{L1}(\bar{D}_1) < \beta_1 + \beta_2$, $a_{L1}(\bar{D}_2) < \beta_i$, $i = 1, 2$.

Now suppose the two countries open trade. We will assume that both countries continue to produce good 3, so that wages are equalized. And we assume that a^*_{L2} is less than $a_{L1}(\bar{D}_2)$.

The result is illustrated in the figure. Because it is cheaper, good 2 takes over the "secondary" market, in which it is equally desirable, from good 1. The loss of that market reduces the scale of production of good 1, raising the price of good 1 in the "primary" market. The two shaded rectangles represent Home's gain from lower prices in the secondary market and its offsetting loss in the primary market. The gain can be arbitrarily small relative to the loss: good 1 will lose the secondary market even if good 2 is only marginally cheaper. Thus it is possible, as in the figure, for Home to lose as a result of trade.

It should be clear how what is happening here relates to our general analysis. We showed that gains from trade are ensured when on average the scale of production of increasing returns sectors is larger in the trading world economy than in our own country in autarky. Here only one good is produced with increasing returns, and we have managed to construct a case where that good's production falls. Even with only one good and two countries this is hard to contrive. In a many good, many country world this would surely be a curiosum.

Reference

Baumol, William J., Panzar, John C., and Willig, Robert D. *Contestable Markets and the Theory of Industry Structure.* New York: Harcourt Brace Jovanovich, 1982.

5   Oligopoly

In this chapter we pursue an approach complementary to that adopted in chapters 3 and 4. In those chapters we explored the impact of economies of scale on trade by adopting assumptions that ruled out oligopolistic complications: purely external economies and perfect competition in chapter 3, limit-pricing monopoly in chapter 4. What we do in this chapter is the reverse: we focus on the implications of oligopoly.

There is of course no general model of oligopoly. Small numbers of firms may engage in explicit or tacit collusion, and we do not know how to predict whether this happens or what follows if it does. Even with noncooperation the outcome of competition depends on numerous details, especially the choice variables of firms (e.g., prices or outputs) and the nature of conjectures about other firms' responses. So it is not possible to provide any sort of general analysis of the impact of oligopoly on trade.

Even where a general model is not available, however, study of special cases can still yield useful insights. In recent years a number of researchers have developed interesting and suggestive analyses of trade using the oldest and simplest approach to industrial structure: Cournot's assumption that firms take each other's output as given. It is difficult to give a real-world justification for this assumption; in practice firms seem to compete in prices more than in quantities. And indeed, there are important circumstances where the choice of decision variables has significant implications (e.g., Eaton and Grossman 1983). Even though the assumption of Cournot behavior is itself hard to justify, however, using this assumption often seems to lead to intuitively plausible conclusions. The reason for this is probably that it implies oligopolies that behave in a way intermediate between perfect competition and monopoly. Furthermore the results usually vary systematically with the number of firms, becoming more competitive as the number of firms increases.

In this chapter we use the Cournot approach to examine two ways in which industrial structure can exert an influence on trade patterns independently of and perhaps in opposition to other factors. The first is through the impact of *seller concentration* on trade, and vice versa. Suppose that the number of firms competing to produce a good in one country is smaller than the number in another. Other things equal, we would expect the first country to have a higher relative price of the good in the absence of trade and to import the good if trade is possible. If other things are not equal, the difference in concentration will be a separate influence that can actually cause trade to run the "wrong" way from the point of view of relative costs of production or autarky prices.

At the same time trade itself has a direct effect on concentration. By allowing trade in a good, two countries in effect create an industry less concentrated than either national industry would have been in autarky. This increase in competition can be a source of gains from trade—or more precisely, gains from the possibility of trade, since it is potential competition that matters, and this can make a difference even where little or no trade actually results (see Helpman 1984).

The second way in which imperfect competition can affect trade is through *market segmentation*. If transport costs or other barriers to trade allow firms to charge different f.o.b. prices to different customers, they will have an incentive to price discriminate—in particular, to offer low prices in markets in which their market share, and therefore their incentive to restrict sales to support the price, are low. This price discrimination can alter the pattern of trade, and, most strikingly, can lead to "cross hauling"—two-way trade in the same product (see Brander and Krugman 1983).

5.1 Seller Concentration: Partial Equilibrium

Many of the implications of seller concentration for trade can be brought out in a partial equilibrium analysis. Consider a single good produced in two countries with cost functions $C(w, x)$ and $C^*(w^*, x)$, respectively. Let there be m consumers in the first country, m^* in the second, and let all of the consumers have the same per capita demand function:

$$D = D(p). \tag{5.1}$$

For some reason, we assume, there is no free entry into this industry. This can result from government regulation or from other natural barriers. Instead, there are exogenously fixed numbers of firms n and n^*.

Equilibrium without Trade

Suppose we consider one of these countries in isolation. The industry demand curve will be the sum of individual demands, so that

$$X = mD(p),$$ (5.2)

where X is industry output. The inverse demand is

$$p = D^{-1}\left(\frac{X}{m}\right) = \tilde{D}\left(\frac{X}{m}\right).$$

Firms maximize profit. They are assumed to take other firms' outputs as given, implying the first-order condition that expresses the equality of marginal cost to marginal revenue:

$$p + \frac{x}{m}\tilde{D}'[D(p)] = C_x(w, x),$$ (5.3)

where x is the output of a representative firm and $C_x(\cdot)$ is its marginal cost. The left-hand side represents marginal revenue. But since all firms are alike

$$x = \frac{X}{n} = \frac{mD(p)}{n}.$$ (5.4)

This gives us our basic equilibrium condition:

$$p\left[1 - \frac{1}{n\sigma(p)}\right] = C_x\left[w, \frac{D(p)m}{n}\right],$$ (5.5)

where $\sigma(p)$ is the elasticity of demand.

The Competitive Effect of Trade

Suppose now that the possibility of trade is opened up. It is useful to begin with the case where the countries are completely symmetric: $C(\cdot)$ and $C^*(\cdot)$ are the same, and $w = w^*, m = m^*, n = n^*$. In this case the countries will have had equal prices in autarky. In a competitive model this would imply no effect from trade. In this case, however, the possibility of trade has the effect of increasing competition. After trade the marginal revenue of a representative firm becomes

$$\mathrm{MR} = p\left[1 - \frac{1}{(n + n^*)\sigma(p)}\right].$$ (5.6)

It is immediately apparent that at the pretrade price $\mathrm{MR} > C_x$ because the elasticity of demand faced by a firm increases, so firms expand their output and the price falls. Since the countries remain symmetric, no actual trade in this good results: each country's output and consumption of the good remain equal. But the possibility of trade, by increasing competition, nevertheless has mattered (see also Markusen 1981).

The Direction of Trade

If the countries are not symmetric, there may be trade in this product. But the direction of trade cannot, as in a purely competitive model, be determined simply by a comparison of costs or of pretrade prices. There are three sets of variables here—costs, market sizes, and numbers of firms—and all must be taken into account.

First, let us drop the assumption of equal numbers of firms. If $C(\cdot)$ and $C^*(\cdot)$ remain the same, $w = w^*$, and $m = m^*$, but $n \neq n^*$, then whichever country has the larger number of firms will be a net exporter of the good. The logic is simple. Since all firms produce the same output in equilibrium, the home country's share in world output is $n/(n + n^*)$. But its share of world demand is $m/(m + m^*) = \frac{1}{2}$ in this case. So the country will be a net exporter if $n/(n + n^*) > \frac{1}{2}$, and conversely.

If one country has a larger number of firms, it will also have a lower pretrade price than the other country, which seems to suggest that there will at least be a normal relationship between autarky prices and trade flows. This relationship need not hold, however, when other elements of symmetry are removed. Suppose, for example, that market sizes are different. Then it is immediately apparent from our discussion that the direction of trade depends on whether n/m is greater or less than n^*/m^*. On the other hand, by combining (5.5) with MR = MC, it can be seen that relative pretrade prices depend on a comparison of total numbers of firms as well as numbers of firms per capita. Thus there are combinations of these values at which the first country will have a lower pretrade price for the good yet be a net importer in a trading equilibrium.

Finally, consider the effect of differences in costs. It is a feature of Cournot models that high cost firms may continue to produce. If, for example, marginal costs are higher in the home country in the trading equilibrium, then condition (5.4) requires that $x < x^*$ but not necessarily that $x = 0$. In equilibrium, high cost firms must have lower market shares than their lower cost competitors but may continue to produce precisely because a lower market share implies a higher perceived elasticity of demand and thus a higher marginal revenue. Other things equal, the lower cost country will tend to export this good, but other things need not be equal and the lower cost country could end up being a net importer.

5.2 Seller Concentration: General Equilibrium Trade Patterns

The effect of seller concentration is to drive a wedge between price and marginal revenue. It is very difficult to derive the extent of this wedge in a full general equilibrium model, unless the model has some very special features; one of the product differentiation models of part II is an example of the kind of special structure needed. It is easier, however, to describe the *effects* of the monopoly wedge on the trade pattern and the gains from trade.

In an imperfectly competitive setting firms will hire factors of production up to the point where their marginal revenue product equals their price. If there are no market failures other than imperfect competition and no intermediate inputs, the economy will lie on its production possibility frontier, but at the "wrong" point because resources will be allocated on the basis of marginal revenues rather than prices.

Can we still predict the trade pattern from a knowledge of technology and factor endowments? The answer is basically yes if the shadow prices determining output, the marginal revenues perceived by firms are the same in all countries.

If, on the other hand, the ratio of marginal revenue to price differs between countries, the conventional supply-oriented determinants of comparative advantage will not be a reliable guide to the direction of trade.

These points may be illustrated quite simply for the case of constant returns to scale. In that case the economy in fact *maximizes* the value of output measured in terms of *marginal revenues*, because marginal revenues are equated to marginal costs (see Helpman 1984). Let R_i be the ratio of price to marginal revenue for good i as perceived by firms in some country. Then the country's economy will allocate resources in a way that maximizes $\Sigma R_i^{-1} p_i X_i$. But if all countries perceive the same "wedge" $1 - R_i^{-1}$ for each i, then differences in their output vectors will depend solely on differences in supply, that is, on differences in factor endowments when technologies are identical. By contrast, if marginal revenues are not the same across countries, differences in output vectors may depend on the R_i's as well as or instead of differences in factor endowments, leaving us unable to predict trade patterns from factor endowments alone.

But what determines R? From (5.2), (5.4), and the definition of R, we have

$$R = \left(1 - \frac{x}{\bar{X}} \cdot \frac{1}{\sigma}\right)^{-1},$$

where x is the output of a particular firm, $\bar{X}$ is world output of the good that firm produces, and σ is the world elasticity of demand for that good. So if R is to be the same in all countries, all firms producing a good must have the same output. As we saw in the partial equilibrium discussion, this will in turn happen only if all firms have the same marginal cost schedules. The only case where this is likely to happen is if factor prices are equalized—something that we will show remains possible if there are sufficiently many goods produced with constant returns in competitive markets.

Factor Price Equalization

In investigating the possibility of factor price equalization in a Cournot approach, we use the same basic method as in chapter 1 and in the contestable markets approach in chapter 4: factor prices will be equalized if it is possible to reproduce through trade the production of a hypothetical integrated world economy in which factors of production are costlessly tradable.

As a first step we need to describe the integrated equilibrium. We can divide industries into a set of oligopolistic sectors, I_O, and the remaining competitive sectors I_C. In each imperfectly competitive industry the degree of monopoly power, the ratio of price to marginal cost, equals

$$R_i(p, \bar{n}_i) = \left[1 - \frac{1}{\bar{n}_i \sigma_i(p)} \right]^{-1}, \quad \text{for all } i \in I_O, \tag{5.7}$$

where p is the vector of commodity prices, $\bar{n}_i$ the number of firms in the industry, and $\sigma_i(p)$ the *market* elasticity of demand, assuming homothetic preferences. The representative firm faces the elasticity of demand $\bar{n}_i \sigma_i(p)$.

The first equilibrium condition is on pricing. For oligopolistic industries the pricing rule that arises from equating marginal cost to marginal revenue can be written as

$$\frac{R_i(p, \bar{n}_i)}{\theta_i(w, x_i)} = \frac{p_i}{c_i(w, x_i)}, \quad \text{for all } i \in I_O, \tag{5.8a}$$

where $\theta_i(\cdot)$ is the inverse of the elasticity of cost with respect to output, and it serves as our measure of the degree of economies of scale. Thus MC = MR is equivalent to the statement that the ratio of the degree of monopoly power to the degree of economics of scale equals the rate of markup of price over average cost.

For competitive industries, we simply have pricing at average cost:

$$p_i = c_i(w), \quad \text{for all } i \in I_C. \tag{5.8b}$$

Next factor market clearing requires

$$\sum_{i \in I_C} a_{li}(w) \bar{X}_i + \sum_{i \in I_O} a_{li}(w, x_i) \bar{X}_i = \bar{V}_l, \quad l \in N, \tag{5.9}$$

where $a_{li}(\cdot)$ is the unit input requirement of factor l into industry i; this depends only on factor prices for competitive industries but may also depend on output per firm in oligopolistic sectors. $\bar{X}_i$ is industry output; $X_i = \bar{n}_i x$ in oligopolistic industries.

Finally, we need goods market-clearing conditions. With homothetic preferences each will receive a share of expenditure $\alpha_i(p)$, that is, depending on relative prices; so we have the condition

$$\alpha_i(p) = \frac{p_i \bar{X}_i}{\sum_{j \in I} p_j \bar{X}_j}, \quad i \in I. \tag{5.10}$$

Given these equilibrium conditions for the integrated economy, the question now becomes whether countries can in fact reproduce this equilibrium through trade. We begin with an illustrative example and then develop the general condition.

As in chapter 4 consider first the example of a two-country, two-factor, three-good world, where one of the goods, say good 1, is produced by imperfectly competitive firms. Let n be the number of such firms in one country, n^* be the number in the other, and let us define $s_n = n/(n + n^*)$ as the share of the home country in the total number of firms. If factor prices are equalized, each firm will have the same marginal costs. It will therefore have the same marginal revenue in equilibrium, and thus all firms will produce at the same output level x. Given industry output in the integrated economy $\bar{X}_1$, then with factor price equalization we must have country outputs

$$X_1 = s_n \bar{X}_1 \quad \text{and} \quad X_1^* = s_n^* \bar{X}_1,$$

where $s_n^* = 1 - s_n$.

What this implies for factor price equalization is illustrated in figure 5.1. The vectors OQ_1, $Q_1 Q_2$, and $Q_2 O^*$ describe the integrated equilibrium employment vectors $\bar{V}(1)$, $\bar{V}(2)$, and $\bar{V}(3)$, respectively, relative to the origin of the home country. If all goods were produced with constant returns to scale in competitive industries, then $OQ_1 Q_2 O^* Q_1' Q_2'$ would become the factor price equalization set. However, given that sector 1 is oligopolistic with a *given* number of firms in each country, the factor price equalization set is smaller. The line segments $O\tilde{Q}_1$ and $O^*\tilde{Q}_1'$ represent the allocation of factors to the first industry in each country; they equal $s_n \bar{V}(1)$ and $s_n^* \bar{V}(1)$, respectively. Once we have made this allocation, we can use $\tilde{Q}_1$ and $\tilde{Q}_1'$ as origins for the allocation of resources into the other two industries. The line segments $\tilde{Q}_1' \tilde{Q}_2'$ and $\tilde{Q}_1 \tilde{Q}_2$ correspond to $\bar{V}(2)$, the factor input into industry 2 in the integrated equilibrium; $\tilde{Q}_2 \tilde{Q}_1'$ and $\tilde{Q}_2' \tilde{Q}_1$ correspond to $\bar{V}(3)$. Production in these industries can be allocated freely between the countries. Thus any endowment point in the shaded parallelogram is consistent with equal factor prices.

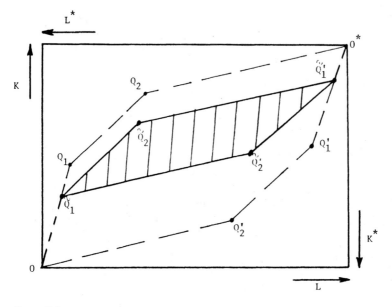

Figure 5.1

Suppose we were to vary the allocation of firms across countries by putting more firms in the home country and fewer in the foreign, or vice versa. Then the allocation of industry one's production between countries would change, that is, the relative length of $O\tilde{Q}_1$ and $O^*\tilde{Q}'_1$. Thus the factor price equalization region would slide back and forth along the broken lines. The entire area enclosed by broken lines is the conventional Heckscher-Ohlin zone of factor price equalization.

The general statement of the condition for factor price equalization is similar to, but somewhat stricter than, the condition with contestable markets. Let I_0 be the set of oligopolistic industries, and let s^j_{ni} be country j's share of the number of firm's in industry i. As before let $\overline{V}(i)$ be the allocation of factors to industry i in the integrated economy. Then the factor price equalization set is

$$\text{FPE} = \left\{ (V^1, \ldots, V^J) | \exists \lambda_{ij} \geq 0, \sum_{i \in I} \lambda_{ij} = 1 \text{ for all } i \in I, \right.$$
$$\left. \lambda_{ij} = s^j_{ni} \text{ for } i \in I_0, \text{ and } V^j = \sum_{i \in I} \lambda_{ij} \overline{V}(i) \text{ for all } j \in J \right\}. \quad (5.11)$$

This set obviously has full dimensionality only if the number of perfectly competitive industries is at least as large as the number of factors. It differs from the conventional case in that it places additional constraints on the factor allocations, much as if there were additional factors of production, which will turn out to be one useful way of viewing the problem.

What can we say about trade if factor prices are equalized? We can once again use the technique from chapter 1: since tastes are homothetic, we can predict net trade in factor services. Let s^j be country j's share of world *spending*. Then the vector of factor services consumed by the country is $s^j \bar{V}$, and its vector of net imports of embodied factor services is

$$t^j_V = s^j \bar{V} - V^j.$$

Thus the country will tend to be an exporter of the services of factors of which it has a relatively high share of the world's endowment and an importer of those for which it has a relatively low share.

There is, however, an important difference here from the contestable markets case. We no longer have average cost pricing—so GDP is no longer simply the sum of factor incomes— and trade in factor services need not be balanced even when trade in goods is balanced. In particular, it is possible that a country will be a net importer or exporter of the services of *all* factors while having balanced trade in goods.

Consider the following example. Suppose that a country's relative factor endowments are identical to those of the world as a whole, but it has more than its pro-rata share of firms in all imperfectly competitive industries. Then because of the monopoly rents it earns, the country's share of world GDP will exceed its share of world factor endowments:

$$s^j > \frac{V^j_1}{\bar{V}_1} = \frac{V^j_2}{\bar{V}_2} = \cdots = \frac{V^j_N}{\bar{V}_N}.$$

This implies that the country is a net importer of all factors' services.

This possibility need not cause us too much concern, however. It still remains true that we have a "Vanek chain" of comparative advantage, which lets us rank services so that all exported services are ranked higher than all imported services for every country. The monopoly rents alter the location of the "cut" between exported and imported services but do not change the ranking. This is similar to the case of imbalanced trade discussed in chapter 1. With constant returns to scale imbalanced trade makes spending exceed factor income, and a deficit country may end up importing all factor services.

These points are illustrated in figures 5.2 and 5.3. The factor price equalization set is the parallelogram $\tilde{Q}_1 \tilde{Q}_2 \tilde{Q}'_1 \tilde{Q}'_2$ as in figure 5.1. Let E be the endowment point; the home country is relatively capital rich. Then the line BB' describes factor income, and $OC'/C'O^*$ is the ratio of home to foreign

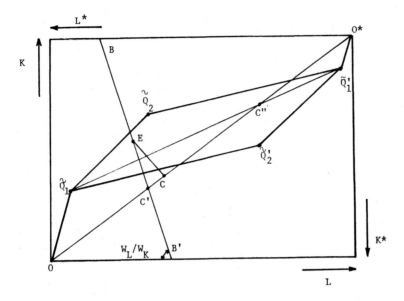

Figure 5.2

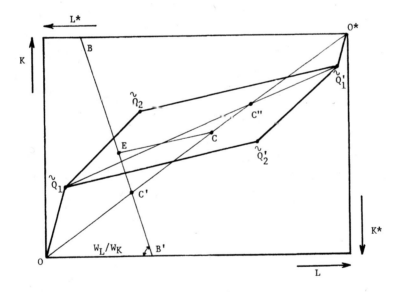

Figure 5.3

factor income. This is equal to the GDP ratio in the absence of profits. However, in the current case there are profits, and each country appropriates a share of world profits in proportion to the number of firms that it has in the oligopolistic industry. The home country's profits share is s_n, and the foreign country's share is s_n^*. The distribution of profits is represented by point C'', where C'' is the intersection point between the diagonal OO^* and $\tilde{Q}_1 \tilde{Q}'_1$. The ratio OC''/C'' O^* equals s_n/s_n^*. Since GDP consists of factor income plus profits, point C on the diagonal OO^* that corresponds to relative GDP levels is located between C' and C''. The larger are profits relative to factor income, the closer is C to C''. Assuming balanced trade, the vector of the factor content of trade is represented by EC.

At point E (in both figures) the home country has a number of firms in the oligopolistic industry that exceeds its pro-rata share as measured by factor income; that is, $s_n > s$. In this case the home country exports good 1, just as in the partial equilibrium model discussed in the previous section. Figure 5.2 shows a situation where the home country is a net exporter of capital services and a net importer of labor services (C is to the southeast of E), which is the "normal" prediction. Figure 5.3 shows a situation where the home country imports *both* labor and capital services (C is to the northeast of E) despite the existence of balanced trade. It pays for these services with oligopolistic profits.

We can restore the full view of indirect trade in factor services with a simple device: by defining fictitious factors to absorb monopoly rents. Let us call these imaginary set of factors "entrepreneurs," specific to industries, and redefine technology so that one entrepreneur is needed for every imperfectly competitive firm. Since profits per firm are equalized across countries, so is the reward to "entrepreneurs." Monopoly profits now become the payments to the entrepreneur, and our expanded definition of factor payments accounts for all of GDP. Balanced trade in factor services is restored when trade in goods is balanced, with trade in entrepreneurial services as the balancing items. This reinterpretation of course makes no difference to our results. This reinterpretation of course makes no difference to our results. It is, however, useful in thinking about trade patterns and the welfare effects of trade.

It is important to understand that our use of the fictitious factor is different from its common use in economies with diminishing returns. There it restores constant returns to scale; it does not do so in our case. In fact in our case it introduces an element of increasing returns to scale, because "entrepreneurs" are used in fixed amounts and therefore generate fixed costs from the point of view of the firm. In some applications these fixed costs can be usefully interpreted as entry barriers.

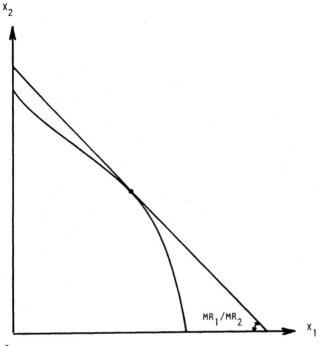

Figure 5.4

5.3 Seller Concentration: Welfare

Our partial equilibrium analysis suggested that the possibility of trade will have a procompetitive effect, leading to a reduction of monopoly distortions and thus to gains from trade over and above those of competitive models. We can formulate two sufficient conditions for gains from trade that hinge roughly on the economywide sign of this effect on competition.

In an imperfectly competitive economy firms will hire factors of production up to the point where their marginal revenue product equals their cost. Thus in the absence of intermediate inputs the economy will always produce at a point on its production possibility frontier where the marginal rate of transformation between any two goods equals the ratio of marginal revenues.

The simpler case is if there are constant returns to scale or increasing returns that are not too large relative to the convexifying effects of differences in factor intensities. In this case we will have the situation illustrated in figure 5.4 where the economy acts as if it were maximizing the value of output using marginal revenues rather than world prices as shadow prices. Thus, if MR_i is the marginal revenue earned on good i after trade, we know from (5.4) or (5.8a) that (see Helpman 1984)

$$\sum_{i \in I} MR_i(X_i - X_i^A) \geq 0. \tag{5.12}$$

But what we want for gains from trade is to kno.v that after trade the economy can still afford its pretrade consumption; namely

$$\sum_{i \in I} p_i(X_i - X_i^A) \geq 0. \tag{5.13}$$

We can rewrite (5.13) to separate off the piece in (5.12):

$$\sum_{i \in I} p_i(X_i - X_i^A) = \sum_{i \in I} p_i - MR_i + MR_i)(X_i - X_i^A)$$

$$= \sum_{i \in I} (p_i - MR_i)(X_i - X_i^A) + \sum_{i \in I} MR_i(X_i - X_i^A).$$

This immediately implies a sufficient condition for gains from trade:

A country gains from trade if

$$\sum_{i \in I} (p_i - MR_i)(X_i - X_i^A) \geq 0.$$

Since $(p_i - MR_i)$ is an index of monopoly distortion, this says that a sufficient condition for gains is that on average the economy expands it output of imperfectly competitive industries, or more loosely, that for the economy as a whole the procompetitive effect dominates. Alternatively, since $MR_i = MC_i$ (marginal revenue equals marginal cost), it states that on average output increases in industries where the willingness to pay p_i exceeds the opportunity cost MC_i.

A slightly more complex case arises if increasing returns are more important. In this case we could have an equilibrium allocation of resources like that pictured in figure 5.5, where the value of output in terms of marginal revenue is minimized, or an equilibrium like that in figure 5.6, where a local but not a global maximimum is chosen. This invalidates the line of reasoning just followed. Yet it is possible to pursue a different approach.

Recall that in our discussion of the trade pattern we suggested the idea of defining artificial factors, "entrepreneurs," one of whom is needed to run each imperfectly competitive firm. What we can do now is pursue that idea. In each imperfectly competitive industry we define a pseudo technology—call it the "hat" technology—that adds to the true technology the requirement of a fixed input of one industry-specific entrepreneur for each imperfectly competitive firm. Corresponding to the hat technology is a "hat" average cost function

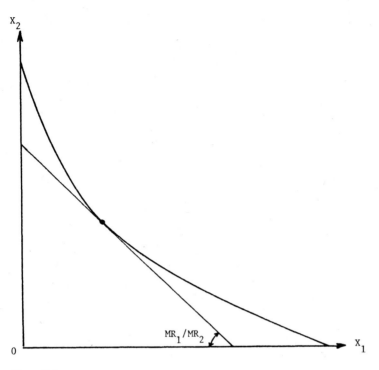

Figure 5.5

$\hat{c}_i(\hat{w}, x_i)$,

where the vector of factor prices $\hat{w}$ is extended to include the imputed returns to entrepreneurs which are set equal to the monopoly profits.

The hat cost function will exhibit economies of scale even if the original technology exhibits constant returns to scale. These economies will be measured by

$$\hat{\theta}_i(\hat{w}, x_i) = \frac{\hat{c}_i(\hat{w}, x_i)}{\hat{C}_{ix}(\hat{w}, x_i)}.$$

But *marginal* cost is unaffected by defining the new pseudotechnology, and *average* cost is by construction equal to price. So

$$\hat{\theta}_i(\hat{w}, x_i) = \frac{p_i}{MC_i} = R_i(p, \bar{n}_i).$$

In effect then with our technology monopoly power *equals* economies of scale.

We are now in a position to state our sufficient condition for gains from trade, one that applies even if the production set is not convex.

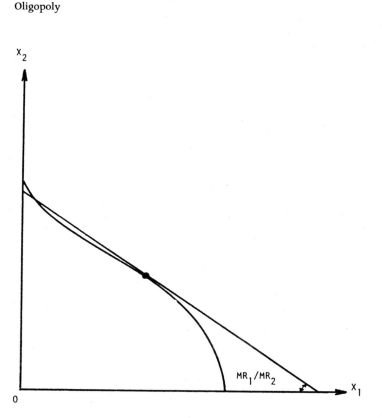

Figure 5.6

A country gains from trade if

$$\sum_{i\in I} \hat{c}_i(\hat{w}, x_i)X_i^A \le \sum_{i\in I} \hat{c}_i(\hat{w}, x_i^A)X_i^A.$$

This says that gains from trade are ensured if on average output per firm tends to expand in industries where the hat technology exhibits economies of scale. But we have shown that the construction of the hat technology creates a correspondence between economies of scale and monopoly power. So the condition in fact requires that on average output per firm rises in industries with substantial monopoly power, or more loosely that trade has a generally procompetitive effect.

The condition looks very similar to the sufficient condition advanced in chapter 3 and may be proved in the same way. First, because of the definition of $\hat{c}(\cdot)$, we must have price equal to average hat cost:

$$p_i = \hat{c}_i(\hat{w}, x_i), \quad \text{for all } i \in I_0.$$

Next the average hat cost at post-trade factor prices of producing autarky output per firm is less than the cost of the autarky inputs, since these were chosen at different factor prices:

$$\hat{c}_i(\hat{w}, x_i^A) \leq \hat{w} \cdot \hat{a}_i(\hat{w}^A, x_i^A).$$

By full employment, autarky inputs sum to the national endowment, which includes "entrepreneurs":

$$\sum_{i \in I} \hat{a}_i(\hat{w}^A, x_i^A) X_i^A = \hat{V}.$$

Putting these together, we have

$$\sum_{i \in I} p_i X_i^A \leq \hat{w} \cdot \hat{V} = \text{GDP}.$$

In other words, the condition implies that a country is still able to purchase its autarky consumption basket. Both of our conditions therefore say that trade is beneficial if on average the output of highly monopolized industries expands.

We would argue for a mild presumption that this sufficient condition is likely to be met. As the partial equilibrium analysis suggested, a procompetitive effect, with monopolistic industries expanding, is expected from trade. It is of course possible to construct examples where trade reduces welfare, but our analysis suggests that extra gains from increased competition are probably more likely.

5.4 Free Entry

We have shown that we can say a good deal about both the pattern of trade and its welfare effects even when seller concentration is allowed to enter as an additional variable. One might question, however, whether seller concentration should be regarded as a primary variable in the same way as tastes, technology, and factor endowments. It might be hoped that by making concentration endogenous we can strengthen our results, and this is in fact the case.

To introduce entry into the Cournot approach, it is necessary to add an assumption. The new assumption we need is a characterization of the decision to enter. In the previous chapter we hypothesized that potential entrants assume that the industry price will not be affected by their entry. Here we adopt a very different and hopefully more realistic assumption: that potential entrants correctly calculate what their postentry profits will be and enter if these expected profits are positive. If one ignores (as we will) the fact that the number of firms must be an integer, this implies that entry proceeds until profits are driven to zero.

Partial Equilibrium Analysis

Let us first return to the partial equilibrium model of section 5.1, where we now assume that there is free entry, and a cost function $C(x)$ characterized by economies of scale. In the absence of trade the number of firms, output per firm, price, and average cost (equal to price) will depend on the size of the market, m. With mild additional restrictions on the model, an increase in m will lead to increases in both the number of firms and output per firm and to a fall in price and average cost.

If trade is opened between two countries where potential entrants have the same cost functions, the effect is the same as if each country simply had a larger market. The integrated world market will have more firms than either national market before trade (although less than the two combined); since output per firm is increased, average cost falls.

Suppose, however, that costs are not the same across countries. In particular, let the average cost curves for firms in one country lie everywhere below those in the other. Then the result is obvious: entry that drives profits in the lower cost country to zero must lead to a complete cessation of production in the other country. So with free entry a simple relation between costs and the direction of trade—a relation that need not hold when the number of firms is arbitrarily given—is restored.

General Equilibrium

The partial equilibrium discussion seems to suggest that a straightforward relationship between comparative advantage and trade may be restored even with Cournot competition if entry drives monopoly profits to zero. And in two fairly general cases this can be shown to be true.

In the first case production technologies are homothetic. As we showed in chapter 2, this lets us write average cost functions in the separable form:

$$c(w, x) = \frac{\tilde{c}(w)}{\bar{c}(x)},$$

where $\tilde{c}(w)$ is the cost of "factor input" and is linearly homogeneous. The cost functions of firms will be proportional to the price of this factor input, which can be regarded as a sort of implicit intermediate good. But we have just seen from our partial equilibrium analysis that neither of two countries' firms can have a uniformly higher average cost if each is to produce a good under free entry. So as long as countries are not specialized, the implicit intermediate goods price must be equalized.

From this point we can apply our usual analysis. Each economy will in effect allocate resources so as to maximize the value of its output of intermediate goods valued at their implicit prices. Since all countries will face the same implicit prices, differences in relative production can be predicted from factor endowments.

The alternative case where free entry restores standard comparative advantage is when factor endowments are sufficiently similar to permit factor price equalization. The criterion for factor price equalization is the same as always, namely it must be possible to produce through trade the outputs that would occur if there were costless trade in factors of production.

The equilibrium conditions for the integrated economy are the same as in (5.8)–(5.10), except for one thing. The number of firms in each industry is now free to vary, but free entry imposes average cost pricing, implying the additional conditions

$$\frac{R_i(p, n_i)}{\theta_i(w, x_i)} = 1, \quad \text{for all } i \in I_O.$$

As before factor prices will be equalized if trade allows us to reproduce the integrated equilibrium.

This is, however, more likely if we have free entry. The reason is that the distribution of imperfectly competitive firms across countries can now shift to accommodate differences in factor endowments. In terms of the analysis of the previous section, the imperfect industry shares s_{ni}^j become free to vary. Thus the factor price equalization region expands to fill the whole hexagon in figure 5.1. The set of factor price equalization is

$$\text{FPE} = \left\{ (V^1, V^2, \ldots, V^J) \mid \exists \lambda_{ij} \geq 0, \sum_{j \in J} \lambda_{ij} = 1 \text{ for all } i \in I, \text{ such that} \right.$$

$$\left. V^j = \sum_{i \in I} \lambda_{ij} \overline{V}(i) \text{ for all } j \in J \right\}.$$

If factor prices are equalized, we need not assume homotheticity in production. Instead, we compute the scale of production and factor proportions in the hypothetical integrated equilibrium. We are then able to compute the factor services embodied in each country's consumption. If countries have identical homothetic preferences, country j's consumption of factor services is $s^j \overline{V}$, where s^j is its share in world income; with free entry we have no profit, so all income is factor income. And the country's net imports of factor services are therefore

$$t^j_V = s^j \bar{V} - V^j.$$

So the country imports services of factors in which it is relatively scarce and exports services of factors in which it is relatively abundant.

If we have neither homothetic production technology nor factor price equalization, it need no longer be true that the scale of production is the same in all countries. Suppose, for example, that production becomes more capital intensive at larger scales. Then in some industries one might find coexistence of large firms from capital-rich countries and small firms from capital-poor countries, both earning zero profits. Obviously in such a case predicting trade from factor endowments will be much more complex than in our simpler cases.

It remains true, however, that in some fairly important situations free entry can restore a simple factor proportions story of the trade pattern.

Trade and Welfare

With free entry we will have true average cost pricing, rather than the pseudo-average-cost pricing we defined for the case of restricted entry. It will therefore be possible to write a simple sufficient condition for gains from trade:

A country gains from trade if

$$\sum_{i \in I} c_i(w, x_i) X_i^A \leq \sum_{i \in I} c_i(w, x_i^A) X_i^A.$$

In effect a country will gain if on average the scale of production in decreasing-cost industries rises. The proof that this is sufficient is similar in form to that developed in chapters 3, 4, and earlier in this chapter.

The problem with this criterion for gains from trade is that it is likely to be violated when free entry drives domestic firms out of some oligopolistic industries, because then $x_i = 0$ and average cost might be extremely high (it might even be unbounded), thereby violating this condition (compare it to the discussion in the last section of chapter 3). The country, however, may be gaining despite this loss of competitiveness if the prices that it has to pay for such goods is low in the trading equilibrium. It is therefore helpful to consider a weaker condition. Using the now standard method of proof it can be shown that *a country gains from trade if*

$$\sum_{i \in I} p_i X_i^A \leq \sum_{i \in I} c_i(w, x_i^A) X_i^A.$$

Namely it gains if the post-trade value of the autarky consumption vector does not exceed its cost of production with autarky output levels per firm, when costs are evaluated with post-trade factor prices.

We would argue that the presumption for gains from trade is stronger with free entry than where numbers of firms are fixed. In the no-entry case the only force working toward higher output per firm and lower prices in imperfectly competitive sectors was the procompetitive effect of trade. In this case, as illustrated by our example, there is an additional effect. Increased competition leads to exit of firms, so the world economy will typically have fewer firms than the sum of what individual countries would have had in autarky. This *rationalizing* effect strengthens the presumption that the scale of output per firm increases and the price falls and therefore that there are gains from trade.

5.5 Market Segmentation

The discussion of the Cournot model may seem to suggest that this market structure, whatever its implications for the welfare effects of trade, has fairly conventional implications for the pattern of trade. It is possible to show, however, that in the presence of transport costs segmenting national markets a Cournot oligopoly produces some results quite different from competitive models.

Integrating transport costs into a general equilibrium trade model is a messy affair even with constant returns and perfect competition. The main point of the analysis can, however, be made in a partial equilibrium approach, and it is to this that we restrict ourselves. The general conclusion that emerges from this analysis is discussed at the end of the section.

The Model

Consider a good produced in two countries. Assume that the cost function is linear and identical in the two countries. However, we now make a distinction between output delivered to the domestic market and exported output. Let X_i be the output of a domestic firm delivered to the home market and X_1^* be its deliveries to the foreign market; then we will let costs be

$$C_1 = F + cX_1 + (c + t)X_1^*, \tag{5.14a}$$

where t is a constant per unit transportation cost.

Similarly for a foreign firm we let X_2^* be deliveries to its own market, X_2 be its deliveries to our market, and assume that its costs are

$$C_2 = F + cX_2^* + (c + t)X_2. \tag{5.14b}$$

Demand in the two countries will be assumed to be identical; we summarize its properties by the inverse demand function:

$$p = D^{-1}(X) = \tilde{D}(X), \tag{5.15}$$

where X is total deliveries to the domestic market. It is useful to impose a condition on $\tilde{D}(\cdot)$ beyond that of negative slope; this condition is that marginal revenue declines with sales:

$$\tilde{D}'(X_1 + X_2) + X_1\tilde{D}''(X_1 + X_2) < 0, \quad \text{for all } X_1, X_2 \geq 0, \tag{5.16}$$

within the relevant range. This is obviously satisfied by linear demand.

Now the crucial assumption of this model is that each firm treats the two markets it serves as *segmented*; that is, instead of simply producing and allowing others to transport if it is profitable, each firm makes a decision on how much to ship to each market. Furthermore each firm regards not just the output of other firms but their choices about where to ship that output as unaffected by its own actions. Thus the firm plays separate Cournot games in each market, linked only by the cost of production.

The Two-Firm Case

The basic peculiarities of this situation can be brought out in a restricted-entry setting. Suppose, in particular, that there are only two firms, one in each country.

The linearity of the cost function makes this analysis very simple: since marginal costs are constant, we can analyze what happens in each market separately. In fact, given the symmetry of the setup, we need only analyze the domestic market, since the foreign market will be its mirror image.

Total deliveries of the good to the domestic market will be the sum of shipments from the domestic firm X_1, and shipments from the foreign firm X_2. Thus price will be

$$p = \tilde{D}(X_1 + X_2). \tag{5.17}$$

Each firm will set its marginal revenue equal to its marginal cost, yielding the two conditions

$$MR_1 = \tilde{D}(X_1 + X_2) + X_1\tilde{D}'(X_1 + X_2) = c, \tag{5.18}$$

$$MR_2 = \tilde{D}(X_1 + X_2) + X_2\tilde{D}'(X_1 + X_2) = c + t. \tag{5.19}$$

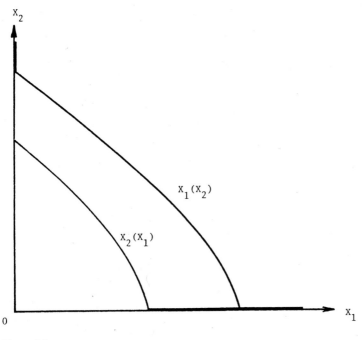

Figure 5.7

These conditions implicitly define reaction functions for the two firms; the condition (5.16) assures that these reaction functions are downward sloping because it ensures that an increase in either firm's shipments reduces the other firm's marginal revenue. It is also straightforward to show that if the reaction functions intersect at all, the function defined by (5.18) is steeper than that defined by (5.19).

But do these functions intersect? Not necessarily. Figures 5.7 and 5.8 illustrate the two possibilities. In figure 5.7, X_2 is driven to zero. In figure 5.8 a positive level of X_2 results even though the foreign firm must pay a transport cost to enter the market. Which case results depends on a simple criterion: X_2 will be positive if and only if in the absence of foreign competition the home firm would charge a price $p > c + t$. This will induce foreign entry because, in the vicinity of $X_2 = 0$, marginal revenue MR_2 equals the price p. To put the result another way, there will be positive imports if the autarky monopoly markup of price over marginal cost exceeds transport costs.

But now notice that what happens in the foreign market is a mirror image of what happens in the domestic market. So if $X_2 > 0$, $X_1^* = X_2 > 0$. Thus in this case we get *two-way trade in the same product*. This trade occurs despite the fact that there are transport costs and neither country has a cost advantage.

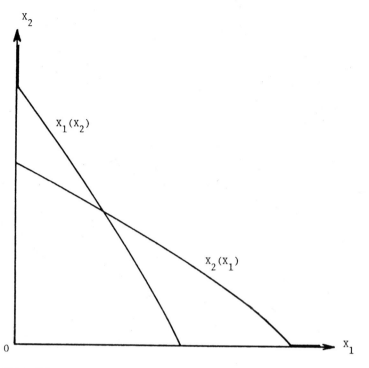

Figure 5.8

What sustains this trade is the fact, noted in section 5.1, that in Cournot markets, low cost producers need not drive out higher cost competitors. Each firm is a low cost shipper to its own market, a high cost shipper to the other market. It must have a smaller market share in the foreign market (unless transport costs are zero, in which case market shares are equal); this lower market share means a lower perceived elasticity of demand and hence a higher marginal revenue. In equilibrium this higher marginal revenue exactly offsets transportation costs.

This difference in perceived elasticity of demand means that the two firms are in effect price discriminating, or "dumping," into one another's markets, so this model can be described as one of "reciprocal dumping" as a cause of trade (see Brander and Krugman 1983).

Welfare Analysis

In the partial equilibrium framework it is natural to analyze welfare effects by looking at the sum of consumer and producer surplus. In general, the effect of

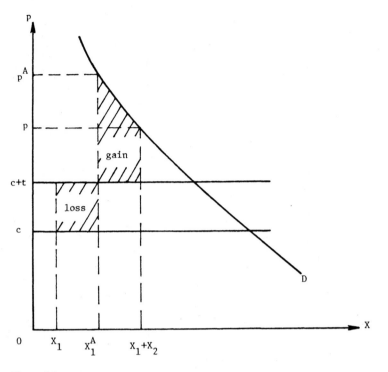

Figure 5.9

trade on this sum is ambiguous, as illustrated by figure 5.9. Trade has a procompetitive effect: each firm's exports do not displace an equal volume of shipments from the other firm to its home market, so total output and consumption rise and the price falls. That part of exports which is additional to autarky output X_1^A adds to total surplus. On the other hand, part of the exports displaces domestic shipments. Since this involves shifting to a higher cost source, it represents a loss. These two effects, *output creation* and *output diversion*, create an ambiguity about the welfare effects of trade.

It is possible to shed some light on the cases where trade brings a gain or loss by considering how welfare varies with the transportation cost t. If transport costs exceed $\bar{t} = p^A - c$, they will be prohibitive of trade. Thus we are concerned with the range $0 \le t < \bar{t}$.

Suppose $t = 0$. Then there are no costs to cross-hauling—pointless though it may be—and trade is unambiguously beneficial. So we know that for sufficiently low t, trade is beneficial.

But this does not mean that lowering transport costs always raises welfare. A small reduction in t has three effects, illustrated in figure 5.10. It produces a

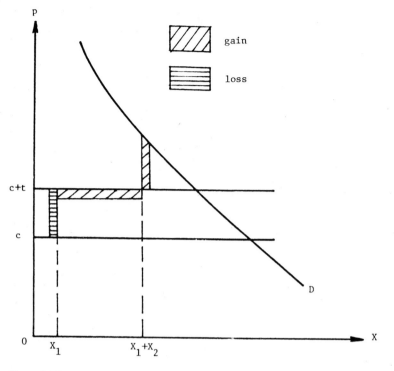

Figure 5.10

direct gain from reduced transport costs, $-X_2 dt$. It also produces a gain from that part of increased exports which represents a net addition to production, $(p - c - t)(dX_1 + dX_2)$. But that part of exports which substitutes for domestic shipments is a loss, $t dX_1$.

In general, the sum of these three effects is ambiguous. At the two extremes of our range, however, we know the sign. At $t \simeq 0$, the loss term drops out, so higher transport costs reduce welfare when they are initially low. At $t \simeq \bar{t}$, on the other hand, $p - c \simeq t$ and $X_2 \simeq 0$, so the two gains drop out, and *lowering* transport costs reduces welfare. This suggests that the sum of consumer and producer surplus will vary with t in the way suggested by figure 5.11. Trade will reduce welfare when transport costs are sufficiently close to prohibitive and increase it when they are sufficiently low.

Free Entry

Suppose now that we allow free into the industry. As in section 5.4, we disregard the integer constraint so that profits are driven to zero. Perhaps

welfare

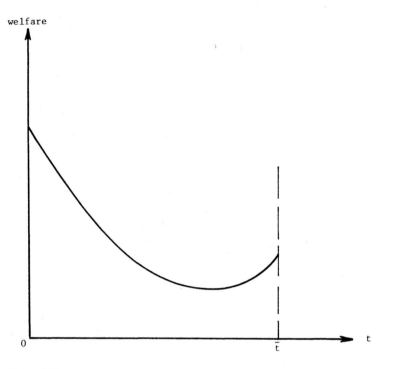

Figure 5.11

surprisingly, this does not eliminate the possibility of two-way trade. This possibility depends on a wedge between price and marginal, not average cost. As long as $p^A - c > t$ in autarky, which always be true for sufficiently low t, we will still have two-way trade in the same product.

Free entry and exit will, however, eliminate for this particular model the possibility of losses from trade. The argument is stated fully in Brander and Krugman (1983).

We should also note that although we have analyzed a partial equilibrium example, the possibility of two-way trade in identical products is not eliminated in general equilibrium. General equilibrium does nothing to prevent the markup of price over marginal cost from exceeding transport costs, which is all that is needed to yield our results.

The important point to be learned from the market segmentation analysis is that although oligopoly may sometimes yield results similar to those of competitive models, it is very different from perfect competition. Price may be driven to average cost by competition but never to marginal cost. And a difference between price and marginal cost can make behavior very different from that in a perfectly competitive model.

References

Brander, James, and Krugman, Paul R. "A 'Reciprocal Dumping' Model of International Trade." *Journal of International Economics* 15 (1983): 313–321.

Eaton, Jonathan, and Grossman, Gene M. "Optimal Trade and Industrial Policy under Oligopoly." Working Paper No. 1236, NBER (1983).

Helpman, Elhanan. "Increasing Returns, Imperfect Markets, and Trade Theory." In *Handbook of International Economics*. Vol. 1. Jones, Ronald W., and Kenen, Peter B. (eds.). Amsterdam: North Holland 1984.

Markusen, James R. "Trade and Gains from Trade with Imperfect Competition." *Journal of International Economics* 11 (1981): 531–551.

III   Differentiated Products

In this part of the book we analyze in depth one particular approach to the modeling of trade in the presence of increasing returns that has proved to be a highly flexible way of investigating a variety of problems. This is the *differentiated products* approach. It is based on the assumption that imperfectly competitive firms are able to differentiate their products so that their outputs become imperfect substitutes.

We begin, in chapter 6, with an exposition of two alternative models of the process of product differentiation. This chapter is a difficult one, and many readers may wish to accept its results without going through the details. In chapters 7, 8, and 9 we use the differentiated products approach to develop a theory of trade. Chapter 7 lays out the basic analysis and describes the pattern of trade in a world with product differentiation. Chapter 8 turns to the volume and composition of trade, with particular attention to ability of the theory to explain the empirical observations that are much of the motivation for this book. Chapter 9 then turns to the welfare effects of trade.

Chapters 10 and 11 develop extensions of the basic approach. In chapter 10 the concern is with the effects of transport costs; the analysis helps shed some light on both the motivations for factor movements and the role of the size of the domestic market in determining trade patterns. Chapter 11 extends the analysis to allow for differentiated intermediate goods; the analysis leads to a discussion of interindustry linkages and the reasons for the formation of national industrial complexes that consist of several linked sectors.

6 Demand for Differentiated Products

In the first part of this book we laid out three alternate approaches to modeling trade in the presence of increasing returns: external affects, contestable markets, and Cournot oligopoly. For most of the rest of the book we will concern ourselves with a fourth approach: monopolistic competition. This approach turns out to be a very useful one for many purposes. As we will see in later chapters, the strategic simplifications involved in the monopolistic competition approach will allow us to cut through many complexities, to develop simple yet illuminating models of a number of different features of the international economy.

The key to the approach take in later chapters is the assumption that goods have a natural hierarchical classification: there are a limited number of "products," each of which can be divided into many differentiated "varieties." In the context of such a world it seems reasonable to impose more structure on preferences than in a general model with many goods. The structure we impose on preferences in turn induces a relatively simple form of demand functions faced by individual firms.

The purpose of this chapter is to show how to go from a formulation of preferences to the demand curves faced by firms. Although the results of this exercise are crucial to much that happens later in the book, the derivations are not; readers who are either familiar with or uninterested in the details of product differentiation may wish to accept our results on faith and proceed to chapter 7.

6.1 The General Formulation

We imagine an identifiable sectoral stucture of commodities. Thus a pencil is a well-defined object and so is a refrigerator, a personal computer, a restaurant meal, and a haircut. Each one of these goods is a differentiated product, however, in the sense that there are many varieties of it available in the market and many more varieties that could potentially be produced. There are red and yellow pencils, soft and hard pencils, white and green refrigerators, small and large refrigerators, 16K memory personal computers and 128K memory personal computers, Chinese meals and French meals, short style and long style haircuts, and so on.

Since products can be differentiated in many dimensions and no workable general theory of preferences for differentiated products is available, we will follow other authors by specializing the preference structure in order to capture a small number of elements that are associated with product differentiation, thereby generating manageable demand functions. Such preferences can be represented by a two-level utility functions:

$$U = U[u_1(\cdot), u_2(\cdot), \ldots, u_I(\cdot)], \tag{6.1}$$

where $u_i(\cdot)$ is the subutility derived from the consumption of product i and $U(\cdot)$ is the upper tier utility function that translates all sectoral subutility levels into an overall welfare level. For our purposes it will be assumed that $U(\cdot)$ is increasing and homothetic in its arguments. If a product i is a homogeneous product, we take $u_i(\cdot)$ to depend only on the quantity consumed D_i, and in particular, we choose $u_i(D_i) \equiv D_i$. If, on the other hand, product i is a differentiated product, then $u_i(\cdot)$ depends on the quantity of each variety being consumed.

A taste for variety can arise in one of two ways. On one hand, there are some products, like meals, that an individual likes to have in many varieties. In a period of, say, one month a typical consumer may like to eat in Chinese, French, Italian, and Hungarian restaurants, each time going out to a different restaurant. His welfare level would be significantly reduced if he had to eat only Chinese food during a single month. This is an example of a taste for variety. On the other hand, an individual might like a particular style for his hair and he would not like to change the style each time he goes to the barber. In this case the individual has a most preferred variety, and he will normally not mix several varieties in his consumption choice. Nevertheless, if the population is composed of individuals with different preferences of the most desired variety, there will be a taste for variety in the population at large. For many purposes it does not matter which of these stories account for product differentiation; all that we need is the existence of a taste for variety in the aggregate.

In the remaining part of this chapter we present in more detail various specification of the subutility functions $u_i(\cdot)$ and their implications for the demand structure.

6.2 Love of Variety Approach

One way to introduce preferences for differentiated products is to assume that there are commodities that individuals like to consume in many varieties, so that variety is valued in its own right. Beginning with the work of Spence (1976) and Dixit and Stiglitz (1977), it has become customary to specify preferences for varieties of such commodities by means of a concave and *symmetrical* subutility function $u_i(D_{i1}, D_{i2}, \dots)$, where $D_{i\omega}$ is the quantity of variety ω that is being consumed. The number of varieties that are potentially available can be infinitely large. However, given the existence of some fixed costs in production, the finiteness of resources puts a finite upper bound on the number of varieties that are supplied in equilibrium. The symmetry and concavity assumptions imply that individuals would normally choose to consume a large number of varieties, provided the varieties do not differ too much in price. In the limiting case where all varieties of product i are equallly priced, an individual chooses to consume all available varieties in equal quantities.

The CES Subutility Function

A particularly useful form of $u_i(\cdot)$ is the symmetrical constant elasticity of substitution function, which can be represented by

$$u_i(D_{i1}, D_{i2}, \dots) \equiv \left(\sum_\omega D_{i\omega}^{\beta_i} \right)^{1/\beta_i}, \quad \beta_i = \left(1 - \frac{1}{\sigma_i} \right), \quad \sigma_i > 1, \tag{6.2}$$

where σ_i is the elasticity of substitution. The requirement for an elasticity of substitution larger than one is dictated by the need to have a demand elasticity that is larger than one in order to make sense of monopolistic competition (if the elasticity of demand with respect to price is smaller than one, marginal revenue is negative). However, since σ_i is the elasticity of substitution between pairs of varieties of the same product, we expect it to be large, and assuming that it is larger than one does not seem to be a severe restriction.

The subutility function (6.2) has the convenient property that every pair of varieties is equally well substitutable for each other. Moreover the degree of substitutability of a pair of varieties does not depend on either the consumption levels of the two being considered or those of any other variety. It also captures clearly the notion that variety is valued per se. For suppose that n_i varieties of product i are available to consumers and they are equally priced at p_i (a variety not available can be considered to have an infinite price). Then whatever spending level E_i is allocated to product i, it is optimal to purchase all varieties in equal quantities. Hence the subutility level achieved from an expenditure level E_i is

$$u_i\left(\frac{E_i}{n_i p_i}, \frac{E_i}{n_i p_i}, \ldots, \frac{E_i}{n_i p_i}, 0, 0, \ldots\right) = n_i^{1/(\sigma_i - 1)} \frac{E_i}{p_i}. \qquad (6.2')$$

Hence, for a given level of spending on the product and a given price for the available varieties, welfare increases as the number of varieties becomes larger. This is the sense in which variety is valued per se.

Demand Functions

Due to the weak separability of preferences imposed by (6.1) (which seems quite natural in the context of differentiated products) and linear homogeneity imposed by (6.2), it is clear that the consumer's problem of utility maximization subject to a budget constraint can be solved in two stages. First, for a given allocation of spending across products $(E_1, E_2, \ldots, E_I)$ maximize $u_i(\cdot)$ subject to total spending E_i on product i, $i \in I$. In the second stage, choose the expenditure allocation so as to maximize overall welfare subject to the overall budget constraint.

For the subutility function (6.2) the first-stage maximization yields the following demand functions (e.g., see Dixit and Stiglitz 1977):

$$D_{i\omega} = \frac{p_{i\omega}^{-\sigma_i}}{\displaystyle\sum_{\omega' \in \Omega_i} p_{i\omega'}^{1-\sigma_i}} E_i, \quad \omega \in \Omega_i, \qquad (6.3)$$

where $p_{i\omega}$ is the price of variety ω and Ω_i is the set of available varieties (with a finite price).[1]

Elasticity of Demand

Now, when we discuss an industry i that is occupied by many firms producing different varieties of the product, it seems natural to assume that a single firm

---

1. The problem $\max \{u_i(\cdot) | \sum_{\omega \in \Omega_i} p_{i\omega} D_{i\omega} \leq E_i\}$ has the following first-order condition for an interior solution:

$$D_{i\omega}^{-1/\sigma_i} u_i(\cdot) = \lambda p_{i\omega}, \quad i \in I,$$

where λ is the Lagrangian multiplier of the constraint. Hence $D_{i\omega} = (\lambda/u_i)^{-\sigma_i} p_{i\omega}^{-\sigma_i}$, and using the budget constraint, $E_i = \sum_{\omega \in \Omega_i} p_{i\omega} D_{i\omega} = (\lambda/u_i)^{-\sigma_i} \sum_{\omega \in \Omega_i} p_{i\omega}^{1-\sigma_i}$.

Solving for (λ/u_i) from the last equation and substituting the result into the first-order conditions yields (6.3).

considers the expenditure level E_i to be independent of its actions. In this case the price elasticity of demand faced by the firm that produces variety ω is

$$\sigma_i + \frac{p_{i\omega}^{1-\sigma_i}}{\sum\limits_{\omega' \in \Omega_i} p_{i\omega'}^{1-\sigma_i}}(1 - \sigma_i).$$

It has, however, often been assumed that when the number of varieties is large, the firm disregards the second component of the elasticity term and so considers σ_i to be the elasticity of demand that it faces. For example, when all varieties are equally priced, the second term equals $(1 - \sigma_i)/n_i$, and it goes to zero as n_i approaches infinity. The σ_i approximation is precise when the set of potential varieties is a continuum and the set of varieties Ω_i is of nonzero measure.

Thus, if we represent potential varieties by all points of the real line, the subutility defined in (6.2) is replaced by the functional:

$$u_i(D) \equiv \left\{ \int_{\omega \in \Omega_i} [D_i(\omega)]^{\beta_i} d\omega \right\}^{1/\beta_i},$$

which yields the demand functions

$$D_i(\omega) = \frac{p_i(\omega)^{-\sigma_i}}{\displaystyle\int_{\omega \in \Omega_i} [p_i(\omega')]^{1-\sigma_i} d\omega'} E_i, \quad \omega \in \Omega_i.$$

The price elasticity of demand for variety $\omega \in \Omega_i$ is precisely σ_i as long as Ω_i is of positive measure. The measure of Ω_i represents the number of available varieties.

For the analysis of cases that use the preferences discussed in this section, we will assume that a firm in industry i considers σ_i to be the elasticity of demand that it faces, so that its perceived demand function is

$$D_{i\omega} = k_i p_{i\omega}^{-\sigma_i}, \quad \omega \in \Omega_i, \tag{6.4}$$

where $k_i = E_i / \sum_{\omega \in \Omega_i} p_{i\omega}^{1-\sigma_i}$.

These demand functions have been derived from preferences that exhibit love for variety and for what might be termed horizontal differentiation of products. Horizontal differentiation can be contrasted with vertical differentiation, where the latter refers to the existence of a quality ranking which is common to all consumers. We will not deal with vertical differentiation (e.g., see Gabszewicz et al. 1981); we will, however, deal with another form of horizontal differentiation in the next section.

Expenditure Shares

We close this section with a derivation of cross-sectoral spending patterns in the case where all varieties of a given product are equally priced. These results are needed for future purposes. In this case, using (6.1) and (6.2'), the consumer's decision problem reduces to

$$\max_{D_1, D_2, \ldots, D_I} U[n_1^{1/\beta_1} D_1, n_2^{1/\beta_2} D_2, \ldots, n_I^{1/\beta_I} D_I] \quad \text{subject to} \quad \sum_{i \in I} p_i n_i D_i \leq E,$$

(6.5)

where D_i is the consumption level of a representative variety of product i and E is the aggregate spending level ($E_i = p_i n_i D_i$). Since $U(\cdot)$ is homethetic, the demand functions that are derived from this problem have the following separable form:

$$D_i = \phi_i(p, n)E, \quad i \in I,$$

where $p = (p_1, p_2, \ldots, p_I)$, $n = (n_1, n_2, \ldots, n_I)$, and the elasticities of substitution are built into the functions $\phi_i(\cdot)$.

This implies that the share of spending allocated to product i is

$$\alpha_i(p, n) \equiv p_i \phi_i(p, n), \quad i \in I,$$

(6.6)

which has the important property that it depends only on the number of varieties available to consumers and on their prices.

6.3 Ideal Variety Approach

Contrary to the characterization of preferences for varieties in the previous section, suppose now that an individual prefers a particular variety of product i, which we will call his "ideal" variety. Generally speaking, one can imagine varieties being distinguished by a number of attributes. However, we choose a one-dimensional representation, similar to the one-dimensional representation employed in the previous section, and we will not dwell on the details of the more general approach; the interested reader is referred to Lancaster (1979, chapter 2) who is the originator of this modeling strategy.

Suppose then that varieties of product i can be represented by points on the circumference of a circle, with the circumference being of unit length. Each point represents a different variety (the circumference of a circle can also be used to represent varieties in the continuum representation discussed in the pevious section). In this case the ideal product of our individual is also represented by a point on this circumference. The meaning of the ideal variety is that when the individual is offered a well-defined quantity of the good but is

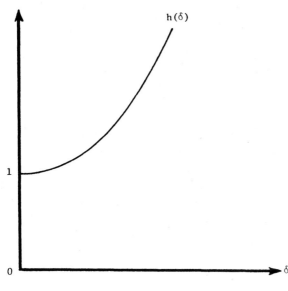

Figure 6.1

free to choose any potentially possible variety, he will choose the ideal variety independently of the quantity offered and independently of the consumption level of other goods. Moreover, when comparing a given quantity of two different varieties, it is assumed that the individual prefers the variety that is closest to his ideal product, where closeness is measured by the shortest arc distance on the circumference of the circle.

In particular, assume that the subutility of product i for a consumer whose ideal variety is $\tilde{\omega}$ has the following separable form:

$$u_i[D_i(\omega), \omega, \tilde{\omega}] \equiv \frac{D_i(\omega)}{h_i[\tilde{\delta}(\omega, \tilde{\omega})]} \tag{6.7}$$

where $D_i(\omega)$ is the consumption level of variety ω, $\tilde{\delta}(\omega, \tilde{\omega})$ is the shortest arc distance on the circumferences of the circle between ω and $\tilde{\omega}$, and $h_i(\delta)$ is Lancaster's compensation function. This function is so named because it can be interpreted as describing the compensation in the consumed quantity that is required in order to maintain a given subutility level when switching consumption to varieties that are further away from the ideal product.

It is assumed that $h_i(\delta)$ is a convex function with $h_i(0) = 1$, $h_i'(0) = 0$, and $h_i'(\delta) > 0$ for $\delta > 0$. A typical compensation function is drawn in figure 6.1. The requirement of a unit value at $\delta = 0$ is a convenient normalization, and the convexity requirement, which amounts to assuming rising marginal compensation with the distance from the ideal product, helps to exclude minor ambiguities. Finally, the flatness requirement at $\delta = 0$ will imply that the elasticity of aggregate demand goes to infinity as the number of available varieties becomes infinitely large.

Given our normalization $h_i(0) = 1$, it is convenient to think of $D_i(\omega)/h_i[\tilde{\delta}(\omega, \tilde{\omega})]$ as the ideal product $\tilde{\omega}$ equivalent quantity embodied in the consumption of $D_i(\omega)$ units of variety ω. Under this interpretation $h_i[\tilde{\delta}(\omega, \tilde{\omega})]$ represents the quantity of variety ω that is equivalent from the point of view of the consumer to a single unit of the ideal product $\tilde{\omega}$.

It is now easy to see how one can generalize the subutility function (6.7) in order to allow for consumption of many varieties; one converts the quantity of every variety into its ideal product equivalent and adds up the ideal product equivalent units. For example, if Ω_i represents a finite set of available varieties, then

$$u_i(\cdot) = \sum_{\omega \in \Omega_i} \left\{ \frac{D_i(\omega)}{h_i[\tilde{\delta}(\omega, \tilde{\omega})]} \right\}. \tag{6.8}$$

It is clear from this linear form that when a Shekel worth of variety ω' provides more ideal unit equivalents than a Shekel worth of any other variety, then the consumer will specialize in consuming ω'. This is indeed at the heart of the first-stage decision process that is described next.

Two-Stage Budgeting

As in the previous section, decompose the consumer maximization problem into two stages. For a given allocation of spending $(E_1, E_2, \ldots, E_I)$, the subutility levels $u_i(\cdot)$ are maximized. Then, taking account of the first-stage solution, spending is allocated across sectors so as to maximize overall welfare. Given (6.8), the first-stage maximization process for product i is

$$\max \sum_{\omega \in \Omega_i} \left\{ \frac{D_i(\omega)}{h_i[\tilde{\delta}(\omega, \tilde{\omega})]} \right\}$$

subject to $\sum_{\omega \in \Omega_i} p_i(\omega) D_i(\omega) \leq E_i$.

Clearly a solution to this problem is

$$D_i(\omega') = \frac{E_i}{p_i(\omega')}, \quad D_i(\omega) = 0 \text{ for } \omega \neq \omega', \tag{6.9}$$

where

$$\omega' \in \arg \left\{ \min p_i(\omega) h_i[\tilde{\delta}(\omega, \tilde{\omega})] \mid \omega \in \Omega_i \right\}. \tag{6.10}$$

In other words, $p_i(\omega)h_i[\tilde{\delta}(\omega, \tilde{\omega})]$ is the effective price of a unit of the ideal product $\tilde{\omega}$ when variety ω is being purchased. It is therefore worth spending everything that has been allocated to product i on the variety that embodies the lowest effective price of the ideal product. If there is more than one available variety that provides the lowest effective price, the mixing of consumption of these varieties is possible, but this will not affect our results.

It is important to note that the current specification implies that a consumer chooses the variety independently of his income or his intersectoral preferences as represented by the upper tier utility function [see (6.10)]. His choice depends only on prices of available varieties and the distance of the available varieties from his ideal product.

Given the variety choice, the second-stage maximization problem can now be solved. Generally, one can allow preferences for some goods to be of the type described in this section; for others, they can be of the type described in the previous section, and some goods can be homogeneous products. For simplicity consider the case where all goods are differentiated with preferences as described in this section (homogeneous products can be considered to be a special case). Then given the variety choices ω'_i according to (6.10), the combination of (6.7) and (6.9) enable us to write the second-stage decision problem as

$$\max U(\tilde{D}_1, \tilde{D}_2, \ldots, \tilde{D}_I) \tag{6.11}$$

$$\text{subject to} \quad \sum_{i \in I} \tilde{p}_i(\omega'_1, \tilde{\omega})\tilde{D}_i \leq E,$$

where

$$\tilde{D}_i = \frac{D_i(\omega'_i)}{h_i[\tilde{\delta}(\omega'_i, \tilde{\omega}_i)]}$$

$$\tilde{p}_i(\omega'_i, \tilde{\omega}_i) = p_i(\omega'_i)h_i[\tilde{\delta}(\omega'_i, \tilde{\omega}_i)];$$

a subscript i has been added to variety symbols. The variable $\tilde{p}_i(\cdot)$ represents the effective price of a unit of the ideal i product.

Assume that $U(\cdot)$ is homothetic, we obtain the following form of demand functions:

$$\tilde{D}_i = \phi_i[p(\omega', \tilde{\omega})]E, \quad i \in I,$$

where $\tilde{p}(\omega', \tilde{\omega}) = [\tilde{p}_1(\omega'_1, \tilde{\omega}_1), \tilde{p}_2(\omega'_2, \tilde{\omega}_2), \ldots, \tilde{p}_I(\omega'_I, \tilde{\omega}_I)]$, and $\phi_i(\cdot)$ has all the properties of a demand function with respect to prices. This implies that the demand functions for varieties ω'_i are

$$D_i(\omega'_i) = \phi_i[\tilde{p}(\omega', \tilde{\omega})]h_i[\tilde{\delta}(\omega'_i \tilde{\omega}_i)]E, \quad i \in I. \tag{6.12}$$

Aggregation

We turn now to the aggregation of individual demand functions in order to derive the demand function faced by a producer of a given variety. An important difference between the demand functions that arises from the current specification and the specification described in the previous section is that in the latter case we can use a representative consumer to derive the market demand function, whereas in the former case this cannot be done because not all consumers choose to purchase the same variety. We have seen that a consumer chooses the variety that suits him best, given prices of available varieties. It is therefore expected that under these circumstances a price increase by a firm that produces a particular variety will drive some customers away from it, and those who remain will buy less. Hence the demand curve faced by the firm is downward sloping, with the sizes of the slope depending on both the usual price effect and the additional effect associated with the size of the clientele.

In order to avoid technical problems that arise in the calculation of aggregate demand functions for a given distribution function of ideal products in the population $F(\tilde{\omega}_1, \tilde{\omega}_2, \ldots, \tilde{\omega}_I)$, we restrict the derivation of aggregate demand functions to the case where there exists only one differentiated product [our results do not change significantly in the more general case if every $\tilde{\omega}_i$ is independently distributed; i.e., if the density of $F(\cdot)$ has the form $f_1(\tilde{\omega}_1) f_2(\tilde{\omega}_2)$ $\ldots f_I(\tilde{\omega}_I)$ and $F(\cdot)$ describes a uniform distribution for all i].

We assume that preferences for the ideal product are uniformly distributed over the unit length circumference of the circle and the population density on the circumference is equal to L (hence due to the fact that the circumference is of unit length, L is both the density and the size of the population). All individuals are assumed to have the same utility function and the same endowment, so they end up having the same income and spending level E as well as the same demand function. Denoting by $\bar{p}$ the price vector of the homogeneous products $i = 2, \ldots, I$, and by $\tilde{p}(\omega', \tilde{\omega})$ the price of variety ω' of the differentiated product, the demand function for variety ω' that is selected by an individual whose ideal product is $\tilde{\omega}$ can be represented by

$$D_1(\omega') = \phi_1[\tilde{p}(\omega', \tilde{\omega}), \bar{p}]h[\tilde{\delta}(\omega', \tilde{\omega})]E, \tag{6.13}$$

where we have dropped the subscript $i = 1$ from the compensation function [see (6.12)].

Consider figure 6.2; there the unit length circumference of the circle represents all potential varieties. We want to derive the demand function for a firm producing variety ω, with competitors ω_l and ω_r, where the prices charged by these competitors are $p(\omega_l)$ and $p(\omega_r)$, and $p(\omega)$ is the price of ω.

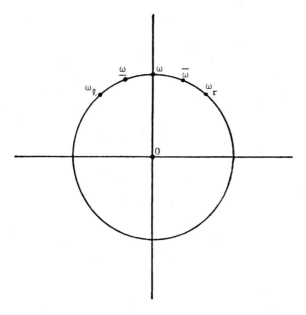

Figure 6.2

The first step is to find out how large the firm's clientele is. In figure 6.2 the firm's market width is indicated by the range from the lower bound $\underline{\omega}$ to the upper bound $\overline{\omega}$. Figure 6.3 shows how these bounds are determined. On the horizontal axis is $\tilde{\omega}$, the ideal variety of consumers. On the vertical axis is $\tilde{p}(\omega', \tilde{\omega})$, the effective price paid by a consumer with ideal variety $\tilde{\omega}$. The effective price of any variety ω' is higher, the further a consumer's ideal variety is from ω'. Consumers with $\tilde{\omega}$ between ω_l and ω_r will choose variety ω if and only if

$$p(\omega)h[\tilde{\delta}(\omega, \tilde{\omega})] \le \min\{p(\omega_l)h[\tilde{\delta}(\omega_l, \tilde{\omega})], p(\omega_r)h[\tilde{\delta}(\omega_r, \tilde{\omega})]\}.$$

What is clear from the figure is that this means that the set of consumers choosing variety ω will be a compact set ranging from $\underline{\omega}$ to $\overline{\omega}$, where $\underline{\omega}$ and $\overline{\omega}$ are the locations of consumers who are just indifferent between variety ω and varieties ω_l and ω_r, respectively. The values of $\underline{\omega}$ and $\overline{\omega}$ are implicitly defined by

$$p(\omega_l)h[\tilde{\delta}(\omega_l, \underline{\omega})] = p(\omega)h[\tilde{\delta}(\omega, \underline{\omega})], \tag{6.14a}$$

$$p(\omega_r)h[\tilde{\delta}(\omega_r, \overline{\omega})] = p(\omega)h[\tilde{\delta}(\omega, \overline{\omega})]. \tag{6.14b}$$

Let $d^* = \tilde{\delta}(\omega_l, \omega_r)$ be the distance between ω_l and ω_r. It is convenient to identify varieties with their distance from ω_l. Thus ω may be represented by d

$\tilde{p}[\omega'(\overset{\sim}{\omega}),\overset{\sim}{\omega}]$

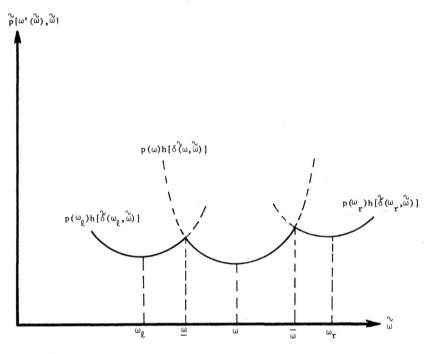

Figure 6.3

$= \widetilde{\delta}(\omega_l, \omega)$, $\underline{\omega}$ may be represented by $d - \underline{d}$, where $\underline{d} = \widetilde{\delta}(\underline{\omega}, \omega)$, and $\overline{\omega}$ may be represented by $d + \overline{d} = \widetilde{\delta}(\omega_l, \overline{\omega})$, where $\overline{d} = \widetilde{\delta}(\omega, \overline{\omega})$. Using this notation, (6.14) can be rewritten as

$$p(\omega_l)h(d - \underline{d}) = p(\omega)h(\underline{d}), \tag{6.15a}$$

$$p(\omega_l)h(d^* - d - \overline{d}) = p(\omega)h(\overline{d}). \tag{6.15b}$$

By inverting the implicit relationships defined in (6.15), we obtain the boundaries of the firm's clientele (or its market width) as functions of its closest competitors' varieties (as measured by the distance between them d^*), their pricing, and the firm's pricing $p(\omega)$ and variety choice (as measured by d):

$$\underline{d} = \underline{\delta}[p, d; p(\omega_l), p(\omega_r), d^*], \tag{6.16a}$$

$$\overline{d} = \overline{\delta}[p, d; p(\omega_l), p(\omega_r), d^*], \tag{6.16b}$$

where p stands now for the price charged by the firm [i.e., $p = p(\omega)$].

Finally, using (6.13), we add up the demand functions of all the consumers that choose to purchase the firm's product in order to obtain the demand function faced by the firm:

$$
D[p, d; \bar{p}, p(\omega_l), p(\omega_r), d^*, E] \equiv \left\{ \int_0^{\underline{\delta}(\cdot)} \phi_1[ph(\delta), \bar{p}]h(\delta)d\delta + \right.
$$
$$
\left. \int_0^{\overline{\delta}(\cdot)} \phi_1[ph(\delta), \bar{p})h(\delta)d\delta \right\} E,
$$

(6.17)

where the functions $\underline{\delta}(\cdot)$ and $\overline{\delta}(\cdot)$ are defined in (6.16). Since $\phi_1(\cdot)$ is declining in p and so are $\underline{\delta}(\cdot)$ and $\overline{\delta}(\cdot)$, the two sources of decline in demand as a result of a price increase are apparent from (6.17); the decline in the quantity demanded due to the depth effect is reflected in the decline of $\phi_1(\cdot)$, and the decline in demand due to the narrowing of the width of the market is reflected in the decline of $\underline{\delta}(\cdot)$ and $\overline{\delta}(\cdot)$.[2]

Properties of the Aggregate Demand Function

Since we will consider market structures in which firms play a noncooperative game, choosing a variety and its price and taking as given the variety choice and pricing strategy of their rivals, we are interested in the price elasticity of the demand function (6.17) and in its response to a specification of its variety as reflected in d. In particular, since we will be considering symmetrical equilibria in which all varieties are equally priced and equally distributed on the circumference of the circle, we restrict our discussion to the case

$$
p(\omega_l) = p(\omega_r) = p_1
$$

and evaluations of the elasticity of demand and the response of demand to changes in product specification at

$$
p = p_1 \quad \text{and} \quad d = \frac{d^*}{2}.
$$

2. Implicit differentiation of (6.15a) and (6.15b) yields [using $p = p(\omega)$]:

$$
\frac{\partial \underline{\delta}(\cdot)}{\partial p} = -\frac{h(d)}{p(\omega_l)h'(d - \underline{d}) + ph'(\underline{d})} < 0
$$

and

$$
\frac{\partial \overline{\delta}(\cdot)}{\partial p} = -\frac{h(\overline{d})}{p(\omega_r)h'(d^* - d - \underline{d}) + ph'(\overline{d})} < 0.
$$

At this point $\underline{\delta}(\cdot) = \overline{\delta}(\cdot) = d*/4$, and

$$\frac{\partial D(p_1, d*/2; \overline{p}, p_1, p_1, d*, E)}{\partial d} = 0. \tag{6.18}$$

The elasticity of demand with respect to price, which is negative, is equal in absolute value to a function $\sigma(p_1, \overline{p}, n)$, where $n = 2/d*$. The choice of $n(= 2/d*)$ as the relevant variable is convenient for future use because in a symmetrical equilibrium it equals the number of firms in the industry, which equals in turn the number of varieties available to consumers.

Two things are worth noting about properties of the demand function (6.17). First, observe that due to (6.18), $d*/2$ is an extremum of the quantity demanded with respect to product specification. It can be verified [by examining $\partial^2 D(\cdot)/\partial d^2$ at this point] that this extremum is a maximum. This means that when the firm prices its variety according to the pricing of its closest rivals, the "middle" choice of product specification maximizes the quantity that it can sell. This stems from the fact that a change in specification that brings it closer to, say, ω_r, brings in new customers who switch from ω_r to ω and brings about a loss of customers who switch from ω to ω_l (this is known in the marketing literature as brand switching). The customers who remain loyal to ω do not change their aggregate purchases (although every type changes its purchase level), and the new customers buy precisely the quantity that was bought by the departing customers. Hence aggregate sales are not affected.

Second, it can be shown (e.g., see Helpman 1981) that the elasticity of demand $\sigma(p_1, \overline{p}, n)$ is larger than one and that

$$\lim_{n \to +\infty} \sigma(p_1, \overline{p}, n) = +\infty.$$

Finally, consider the spending shares in a symmetrical equilibrium. Using (6.17), which represents demand for a single variety being consumed by a share $1/n$ of the population, the share of spending allocated to the differentiated product is

$$\alpha_1(p, \overline{p}, n) \equiv 2np \int_0^{1/2n} \phi_1[ph(\delta), \overline{p}]h(\delta)d\delta. \tag{6.19}$$

Similarly the share of spending allocated to homogeneous product i is

$$\alpha_i(p, \overline{p}, n) = 2np_i \int_0^{1/2n} \phi_i[ph(\delta), \overline{p}]d\delta, \quad i = 2, 3, \ldots, I. \tag{6.20}$$

Hence the share of spending allocated to a product depends on commodity prices and the number of varieties available to consumers.

Cobb-Douglas Preferences

In some applications we will assume that the upper tier utility function $U(\cdot)$ is Cobb-Douglas (C-D). This is a useful function because it implies an elasticity of demand $\sigma(p, \bar{p}, n)$ that does not depend on prices but only on the available number of varieties.

In order to see this property, observe that for the C-D case (6.11) implies

$$\phi_i[\tilde{p}(\omega', \tilde{\omega})] \equiv \frac{\alpha_i}{\tilde{p}_i(\omega'_i, \tilde{\omega}_i)} = \frac{\alpha_i}{p_i(\omega'_i)h_i[\tilde{\delta}_i(\omega'_i, \tilde{\omega}_i)]},$$

where α_i is the exponential of $\tilde{D}_i$; $\alpha_i > 0$, $\sum_{i \in I} \alpha_i = 1$. Hence the multiproduct equivalent of (6.17) is independent of the distribution of preferences for ideal products, and

$$D_i[p_i, d_i; p_i(\omega_l), p_i(\omega), d_i^*, E] = \frac{\alpha_i[\tilde{\delta}_i(\cdot) + \bar{\delta}_i(\cdot)]E}{p_i}.$$

In a symmetrical equilibrium the elasticity of the bracketed term on the right-hand side of this equation does not depend on prices. Hence the elasticity of $D_i[\cdot]$ with respect to p_i, evaluated at a symmetrical equilibrium, depends only on d_i^*, or the number of available varieties n_i, thereby showing that with C-D upper tier preferences, the elasticity of demand $\sigma_i(\cdot)$ depends only on n_i; that is, $\sigma_i = \sigma_i(n_i)$.

References

Dixit, Avinash, and Stiglitz, Joseph E. "Monopolistic Competition and Optimum Product Diversity." *American Economic Review* 67 (1977): 297–308.

Gabszewicz, Jaskold, Shaked, Avner, Sutton, John, and Thisse, J. F. "International Trade in Differentiated Products." *International Economic Review* 22 (1981): 527–535.

Helpman, Elhanan. "International Trade in the Presence of Product Differentiation, Economies of Scale and Monopolistic Competition: A Chamberlin-Heckscher-Ohlin Approach." *Journal of International Economics* 11 (1981): 305–340.

Lancaster, Kelvin. *Variety, Equity, and Efficiency.* New York: Columbia University Press, 1979.

Spence, Michael E. "Product Selection, Fixed Costs, and Monopolistic Competition." *Review of Economic Studies* 43 (1976): 217–236.

Varian, Hall R. *Microeconomic Analysis.* New York: Norton, 1978.

7   Trade Structure

Economies of scale provide an incentive for specialization and trade over and above such reasons as international differences in factor endowments. Thus in a world where scale economies are important it is natural to expect to find countries exchanging goods produced with quite similar factor proportions. If we were to aggregate groups of products into sectors defined by similarity of factor proportions, we would expect to find substantial amounts of two-way intrasectoral trade.

In this chapter and the next we will use the specification of preferences for differentiated products developed in chapter 6 as a basis for a model in which this idea is given a particularly strong form. The monopolistic competition model uses as a simplifying device the assumption that there are sectors or "industries" consisting of many products produced with the same production function. This sort of model obviously lends itself to a view of trade in which comparative advantage drives specialization at the aggregative, sectoral international level but economies of scale cause specialization at the level of individual products. Or to use a terminology that has become widely accepted, we can have a Heckscher-Ohlin view of *inter*industry specialization but a scale economy view of *intra*industry trade.

The basic logic of this model is quite simple. Imagine a sector whose product is differentiated. Suppose that every variety is produced with increasing returns to scale. Also assume that these economies of scale are relatively small so that the industry can accommodate many producers, each one producing a different variety. Then, following Chamberlin (1933), it is natural to expect in this industry a market structure known as monopolistic competition; that is, every firm chooses a variety and its pricing so as to maximize profits, taking as given the variety choice and pricing strategy of the other producers in the industry. In this case every firm ends up producing a different variety of the product.

Now imagine a demand structure within which there is a taste for variety.

This may arise either because people like variety or because every person likes a particular product but different people like different products. Then for every pair of countries that actively produce varieties of the good, we should expect to observe intraindustry trade. Under monopolistic competition, which is the natural market structure under these circumstances, each country will produce different varieties of the product, while every variety is demanded in both countries. Hence differentiated products provide a simple explanation of intraindustry trade. We need, however, to go beyond this straightforward explanation in order to develop a theory that contains this ingredient but also generates additional predictions consistent with other features of observed trade structures.

7.1 Behavior of Firms

Consider a firm in a differentiated product industry that has to choose a variety and its pricing so as to maximize profits. The firm takes as given the variety choice and pricing strategies of other firms in the industry. We assume that every variety of the product is produced with the same production function and also enters into demand in the same way. This is a strong assumption, but it fits well into the approach taken in this study which abstracts from intraindustry heterogeneity. Given these assumptions, we can focus on a representative firm, whose decision problem is

$$\max_{[\omega, p(\omega)]} \{p(\omega)D(\cdot) - C[(w, D(\cdot)] | \omega \in \overline{\Omega}\}, \tag{7.1}$$

where $D(\cdot)$ is the relevant demand function that depends on the structure of preferences, $\overline{\Omega}$ is the set of varieties from which the firm has to choose, $C(\cdot)$ is the cost function (the same for every variety), and w is the vector of input prices. Industry subscripts are omitted in this discussion of a single firm.

The cost function is assumed to be derived from an increasing returns to scale technology, so that average costs are declining in output (it is also possible to allow for a U-shaped average cost curve), and $C(\cdot)$ has the usual properties of cost functions (see Varian 1978, chapter 3). When preferences are of the Spence-Dixit-Stiglitz type, a single producer competes equally with every other producer, and he derives the same profit level for any variety choice that is not supplied by others. If he were to choose a variety that is already supplied by another firm, he would have to share the market for this variety, thereby ending up with profits lower than those he could attain by adopting some other variety. Therefore no variety will be produced by more than one firm.

When preferences are of the Lancaster type, the relevant demand function is taken from (6.17). In this case demand depends on the variety choice in two important ways. First, since a firm competes mainly with only two producers—those that produce the closest substitute on both sides of its variety—its variety choice determines its two immediate rivals. These rivals do not change for choices within a certain range of products. Second, within the range of products for which the immediate rivals do not change, variety choice determines which one of the two is the closest competitor. In this case (7.1) can be solved in two stages. For every subset of $\overline{\Omega}$ within which the two closest competitors remain the same, solve (7.1) using the demand function derived in section 6.3. Then compare the maximal profits on each subset, and choose one with the highest profits.

Now whatever variety is selected, it is clear from (7.1) that profit-maximizing pricing requires equating marginal revenue to marginal cost. Hence

$$p(\omega)\left[1 - \frac{1}{\sigma(\cdot)}\right] = C_x[w, D(\cdot)] \quad \text{for optimal } \omega, \tag{7.2}$$

where $C_x(\cdot)$ stands for the marginal cost and $\sigma(\cdot)$ is the elasticity of demand. As usual, marginal revenue equals the price times one minus one over the elasticity of demand. In the case of S-D-S (Spence-Dixit-Stiglitz) type of preferences $\sigma(\cdot)$ is a constant, whereas in the Lancaster case it is a function of arguments that appear in the demand function except for the expenditure level (due to homotheticity). In the S-D-S case the variety choice reduces to choosing any ω that is not supplied by others. In the Lancaster case the precise choice of ω, conditional on the subset defined by the two closest competitors, is reduced to the choice of d in the demand function (6.17). Choosing d so as to maximize (7.1) yields

$$\{p(\omega) - C_x[w, D(\cdot)]\} \frac{\partial D(\cdot)}{\partial d} = 0,$$

where ω is implicitly defined by $d = \tilde{\delta}(\omega_l, \omega)$ [recall that ω_l is the variety produced by the "left-side" competitor and $\tilde{\delta}(\cdot)$ measures the distance between varieties on the circumference of the circle]. As long as the elasticity of demand $\sigma(\cdot)$ is larger than one, a firm that equates marginal revenue to marginal cost ends up charging a price that exceeds marginal cost [see (7.2)]. Therefore for such a firm the condition of optimal variety choice reduces to

$$\frac{\partial D(\cdot)}{\partial d} = 0. \tag{7.3}$$

The point is that since all product specifications have the same cost structure, then as long as the price exceeds the marginal cost, changes in product specification that increase sales increase also profits. Hence product specification should be chosen to maximize sales, which is implicit in condition (7.3) (second-order conditions of course have to be satisfied also, and they are discussed in Lancaster 1979, chapter 6).

It is useful to rewrite condition (7.2) in a form that is more revealing in various applications. We have discussed in chapter 2 measures of the degree of economies of scale. We have seen that the ratio of average to marginal cost,

$$\theta(w, x) \equiv \frac{C(w, x)/x}{C_x(w, x)},$$

is a useful measure.

Analogously to the degree of scale economies, we have a measure of monopoly power, $R(\cdot)$, which equals to the ratio of average to marginal revenue:

$$R(\cdot) \equiv \frac{p}{MR(\cdot)} = \left[1 - \frac{1}{\sigma(\cdot)}\right]^{-1}. \tag{7.4}$$

It is therefore a function of the arguments of the elasticity of demand function. When this measure is larger than one, which happens in the presence of monopoly power, average revenue declines with output. Clearly for profit-maximizing producers we never observe it taking values smaller than one.

Using the measures of economies of scale and monopoly power, condition (7.2), which describes equality of marginal revenue to the marginal cost, can be rewritten as

$$\frac{R(\cdot)}{\theta[w, D(\cdot)]} = \frac{p(\omega)D(\cdot)}{C[w, D(\cdot)]} \quad \text{for optimal } \omega. \tag{7.5}$$

Hence, when marginal revenue equals marginal cost, the ratio of the degree of monopoly power to the degree of economies of scale equals one plus the markup rate on average costs. Also, when profits are driven down to zero, the degree of monopoly power equals the degree of economies of scale. This is similar to the oligopolistic structure discussed in chapter 5.

7.2 Integrated Equilibrium

In this section we construct a two-sector, two-factor model and describe its equilibrium for a closed economy. This will serve as a model of an *integrated* economy. For concreteness we refer to one good as food, which we take to be a homogeneous product, and we refer to the other good as manufactures, which we take to consist of many differentiated products. We also refer to one factor of production as labor and to the other as capital.

The food industry Y produces with constant returns to scale. Its unit cost function is $c_Y(w_L, w_K)$, where w_L is the wage rate and w_K is the rental rate on capital. The unit cost function represents marginal and average costs. Competition in the food industry brings about marginal (equals average) cost pricing. Choosing food as the numeraire, we set $p_Y = 1$, and the pricing condition becomes

$$1 = c_Y(w_L, w_K). \tag{7.6}$$

In the manufacturing sector every variety is produced with the same increasing returns to scale production function. For current purposes suppose that the number of firms in this industry is equal to $\bar{n}$, with each firm producing a different variety. Consider a candidate equilibrium in which every firm charges the same price p for its product. If preferences are of the Lancaster type, then firms are also equally spaced on the circumference of the circle in terms of their variety choice. We have seen in chapter 6 that in this case the elasticity of demand for every variety depends on commodity prices and the number of available varieties; that is, $\sigma = \sigma(p, \bar{n})$, and condition (7.3) of optimal product selection is also satisfied. If preferences are of the S-D-S type, the elasticity of demand is a given constant. In either case the pricing strategy of a representative firm in the industry, which is characterized by equality of marginal revenue to marginal cost, brings about equality of output levels across firms. Using (7.5), the pricing condition in the manufacturing sector is represented by

$$\frac{R(p, \bar{n})}{\theta(w_L, w_K, x)} = \frac{p}{c(w_L, w_K, x)}, \tag{7.7}$$

where $c(\cdot)$ is the average cost function and x is the output level of a single representative firm.

The factor market-clearing conditions take the usual form, and we can represent them by exploiting the properties of the cost functions. Since

$$a_{iY}(w_L, w_K) \equiv \frac{\partial c_Y(w_L, w_K)}{\partial w_i}, \quad i = L, K,$$

is the demand for factor i per unit output in the food industry, and

$$A_{iX}(w_L, w_K, x) \equiv \frac{\partial C(w_L, w_K, x)}{\partial w_i}, \quad i = L, K,$$

is the demand for factor i by a representative firm in the manufacturing sector, then aggregate demand for factor i is

$$a_{iY}(w_L, w_K)\,\overline{Y} + A_{iX}(w_L, w_K, x)\overline{n}, \quad i = L, K,$$

where $\overline{Y}$ is the output level of food. Aggregate demand for a factor of production consists of the demand by the food sector, which equals perunit output use of the input times the output level, plus the demand in the manufacturing sector, which consists of per firm use times the number of firms in the industry. As usual, the number of firms in the constant returns to scale sector is not uniquely determined.

Using this representation of the demand for factors of production, the factor market-clearing conditions can be written as

$$a_{LY}(w_L, w_K)\overline{Y} + A_{LX}(w_L, w_K, x)\overline{n} = \overline{L} \,, \tag{7.8}$$

$$a_{KY}(w_L, w_K)\overline{Y} + A_{KX}(w_L, w_K, x)\overline{n} = \overline{K} \,, \tag{7.9}$$

where $\overline{L}$ is the size of the labor force and $\overline{K}$ is the capital stock.

It remains to specify the equilibrium conditions in commodity markets. Due to Walras's law, it is sufficient to specify a clearing condition for food only. We have seen in chapter 6 that with homothetic upper tier preferences the share of spending allocated to a particular commodity is a function of commodity prices and the number of varieties available to consumers. Hence, taking $\alpha_Y(p, \overline{n})$ to be the share of spending allocated to food, the condition for clearing of the food market can be represented by

$$\alpha_Y(p, \overline{n}) = \frac{\overline{Y}}{\overline{Y} + px\overline{n}}. \tag{7.10}$$

In words, the share of food in spending is equal to its share in gross domestic product.

Conditions (7.6)–(7.10) represent five equilibrium conditions that implicitly define equilibrium values for factor rewards (w_L, w_K), the price and output of every variety of the manufactured product (p, x), and output of food $(\overline{Y})$. The number of firms in the manufacturing sector has been so far taken as given. Thus, for example, if $\overline{n}$ is exogenously determined by entry regulation, then the solution to this system is a viable equilibrium if it entails non-negative profits in the manufacturing sector. If profits are negative, some firms will be driven out from the industry until the remaining firms do not lose money. In this case $\overline{n}$ is not a binding constraint.

Alternatively, if there are no impediments to entry and exit in the manufacturing sector, then the number of firms is endogenously determined. In particular, if the number of firms is large enough so as to make it possible to treat $\bar{n}$ as a continuous variable rather than an integer, then we expect entry and exit to lead to zero profits; namely

$$p = c(w_L, w_K, x). \tag{7.11}$$

In this case (7.6)–(7.11) are the equlibrium conditions and $\bar{n}$ is added to the list of variables whose equilibrium value is implicitly defined by the system. Observe that in this case (7.7) can be replaced by the simpler condition $R(\cdot)$ $= \theta(\cdot)$; that is, the degree of monopoly power equals the degree of economies of scale.

It is useful to pause at this stage in order to clarify the equilibrium determination of the number of firms in the manufacturing sector. To be rigorous, we should treat this number as an integer. In the case of free entry and exit, an equilibrium number of firms can be defined as an integer $\bar{n}$ such that (7.6)–(7.10) implies non-negative profits [i.e., $p \geq c(w_L, w_K, x)$] and such that maximal profits derived by $\bar{n} + 1$ firms facing these equilibrium factor rewards would be negative. This is a suitable description when a firm that considers entry believes that its entry will not change factor rewards, which is a reasonable assumption when $\bar{n}$ is large or the manufacturing sector is small relative to the economy (the last requirement of course makes more sense in a multisector formulation). However, when $\bar{n}$ is a large number, an approximation to the true equilibrium is obtained by means of (7.6)–(7.11).

For future use, it is convenient to rewrite the system (7.6)–(7.11) in a somewhat different form. Using the average cost function, define the demand for factor i per unit output of the differentiated product as

$$a_{iX}(w_L, w_K, x) = \frac{\partial c(w_L, w_K, x)}{\partial w_i}, \quad i = L, K.$$

Clearly $a_{iX}(\cdot) \equiv A_{iX}(\cdot)/x$.

Now let $\bar{X} = \bar{n}x$ be the output level of the manufacturing sector. This is a well-defined quantity that aggregates heterogeneous products; it is meaningful to add up two blue pencils and three green pencils and to state that there are five pencils. (One should be careful in using this aggregative variable, however.) Then we can rewrite conditions (7.6)–(7.11) as follows:

$$1 = c_Y(w_L, w_K), \tag{7.12}$$

$$p = c(w_L, w_K, x), \tag{7.13}$$

$$R(p, \bar{n}) = \theta(w_L, w_K, x), \tag{7.14}$$

$$a_{LY}(w_L, w_K)\bar{Y} + a_{LX}(w_L, w_K, x)\bar{X} = \bar{L}, \tag{7.15}$$

$$a_{KY}(w_L, w_K)\bar{Y} + a_{KX}(w_L, w_K, x)\bar{X} = \bar{K}, \tag{7.16}$$

$$\alpha_Y(p, \bar{n}) = \frac{\bar{Y}}{(\bar{Y} + p\bar{X})}, \tag{7.17}$$

$$\bar{X} = \bar{n}x. \tag{7.18}$$

Condition (7.12) is the same as (7.6). Condition (7.13) replaces (7.11), and (7.14) replaces (7.7), taking into account the long-run zero profit condition (7.13). The other correspondences are self-explanatory. One should only bear in mind that the equilibrium conditions (7.12)–(7.18) apply to an economy in which entry and exit in the manufacturing sector brings about zero profits; this is Chamberlin's large group case. In order to deal with cases of restricted entry, in which the number of firms does not bring profits down to zero, one has to use conditions (7.6)–(7.10). Equations (7.12)–(7.18) implicitly define equilibrium values for factor rewards, the output level and pricing of a single variety, the output level of food and manufacturing products, and the number of varieties.

It should be observed that the last system of equilibrium conditions represents a proper generalization of the traditional two-sector model presented in chapter 1. The conditions under which our model reduces to the standard one are easily specified. First, let the production function in the manufacturing sector exhibit constant returns to scale. Then the average cost function $c(w_L, w_K, x)$ is independent of output x and so are the per unit output factor demand functions $a_{iX}(w_L, w_K, x)$, $i = L, K$. Hence conditions (7.12)–(7.13) and (7.15)–(7.17) become the standard conditions of the two-sector model.

Now consider (7.14). Clearly with constant returns to scale in the manufacturing sector the degree of scale economies $\theta(\cdot)$ is identically equal to one. If preferences are of the S-D-S type, then we should interpret them as having an infinite elasticity of substitution, which amounts to saying that all the varieties are perfect substitutes in consumption. In this case the degree of monopoly power $R(\cdot)$ is also identically equal to one and (7.14) is satisfied. Observe, however, that under these circumstances the equilibrium number of varieties is irrelevant, because consumers do not care how many varieties are available. On the other hand, the output level of manufactured products, which is of concern to consumers, is well determined.

If preferences are of the Lancaster type, two interpretations are possible. The first one is similar to that advanced for the S-D-S type preferences; that is all varieties are perfect substitutes in consumption. This amounts to assuming that the compensation function $h(\cdot)$ is flat (or identically equal to one); no one has an ideal product. It is easy to see that when $h'(\cdot)$ tends to zero, the elasticity of demand tends to infinity, implying $R(\cdot) = 1$. Hence in this case too (7.14) is satisfied, and the preceeding discussion of the equilibrium number of varieties applies.

For the Lancaster-type preferences there is also another interpretation. Suppose that there are constant returns to scale and the compensation function is not identically equal to one, but remember that $h'(0) = 0$. Then, because of constant returns to scale, in equilibrium *all* the varieties are produced, and everyone consumes his ideal product; goods are custom made. In this case the elasticity of demand become, infinite, implying $R(\cdot) = 1$, so that (7.14) holds.[1]

We close the discussion of this section with the observation that conditions (7.12)–(7.13) and (7.15)–(7.16) are isomorphic to the equilibrium conditions in production for a two-sector constant returns to scale economy when x is treated as a parameter (compare with Jones 1965 and see Helpman and Razin 1983 for a discussion of this point). The economic logic behind this interpretation is that when x is kept constant, output expansion of manufactured products is achieved via an increase in the number of firms with all of them looking alike, thereby generating constant returns at the industry level.

From these production conditions we obtain the maximal level of gross domestic product function:[2]

$$GDP = \Pi(p, \bar{L}, \bar{K}, x), \tag{7.19}$$

which has the usual properties with respect to $(p, \bar{L}, \bar{K})$. The individual firm output level x plays here the role of a productivity variable, similar to our interpretation of the external effects in chapter 3.

---

1. This interpretation, which requires all varieties to be produced, cannot be applied to the S-D-S-type preferences when the potential variety set $\overline{\Omega}$ is taken to be the set of integers. For in this case infinitely many varieties are produced, making unbounded the subutility level $u_x(\cdot)$. However, when $\overline{\Omega}$ is taken to be a finite length interval or the circumference of a circle, then this interpretation can also be applied to this class of preferences.

2. The implicit industry production function embedded in this structure is obtained as follows. Let $f(v)$ be the production function for a single variety, and consider the equation $x = f(V/n)$, where V is aggregate employment of factors of production in the industry and n is the number of firms. Invert this equation to obtain $n = \xi(V, x)$. Clearly $\xi(\cdot)$ is positively linear homogeneous in V, given x. Now define $F(V, x) \equiv x\xi(V, x)$ as the industry's implicit production function. $F(\cdot)$ is positively linear homogeneous in V, and for $V = (L, K)$ it has the unit cost function $c(w_L, w_K, x)$ used in (7.12)–(7.17). Letting $F_Y(L_Y, K_Y)$ be the production function of food, the economy's gross domestic product function is

$$\Pi(p, \bar{L}, \bar{K}, x) \equiv \max\{F_Y(L_Y, K_Y) + pF(L_X, K_X, x)|L_Y + L_X \leq \bar{L}, K_Y + K_X \leq \bar{K}\}.$$

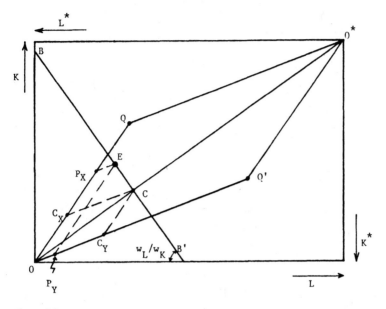

Figure 7.1

7.3 Trade Patterns: Free Entry

We can now discuss trade patterns that emerge in a two-country world where every country has access to the same technologies and is populated by the same types of individuals. Technologies and preferences are those used in the previous section.

We begin with the equilibrium of the integrated world economy described by (7.12)–(7.18). Then we divide the world into two countries by means of a division of the resources—labor and capital—and we investigate how the pattern of trade depends on this division. We will show that the intersectoral pattern of trade is determined by the cross-country difference in relative factor endowments but that there will also be intraindustry trade when countries do not differ too much in the composition of factor endowments.

Consider figure 7.1, which describes the intersectoral allocation of labor and capital in the integrated equilibrium. The vector OQ describes employment in the manufacturing sector, and the vector OQ' describes employment in the food industry. The vector OO^* describes aggregate employment which equals $(\bar{L}, \bar{K})$. We assume that in this equilibrium the manufacturing sector uses more capital per worker than the food sector, and this assumption is reflected in the figure by the fact that OQ is steeper than OQ'. We choose to measure output in units for which $\overline{OQ} = \bar{X}$ and $\overline{OQ'} = \bar{Y}$.

Now suppose that there are two countries, a home and a foreign country. Let

O be the origin of the home country and O^* be the origin of the foreign country. Take an allocation point above the diagonal but in the parallelogram OQO^*Q', say point E. For this allocation point we can find sectoral employment levels of labor and capital in each country that ensure full employment with the techniques of production that prevail in the integrated equilibrium. This is seen in the figure by drawing a parallelogram between O and E to obtain points P_X and P_Y. In this representation $\overline{OP_Y} = Y$ and $\overline{OP_X} = X$, whereas $\overline{P_YQ'} = Y^*$ and $\overline{P_XQ} = X^*$. Hence the integrated equilibrium factor rewards, commodity prices, and output per firm in the manufacturing sector, make the two-country economy described by E supply precisely the aggregate output levels $(\overline{Y}, \overline{X})$. In this two-country allocation the home country produces $n = X/x$ varieties of the differentiated product, and the foreign country produces $n^* = X^*/x$ varieties, where

$$n + n^* = \bar{n} = \frac{\overline{X}}{x}.$$

By construction these supply levels match the demand levels. A similar equilibrium can be constructed for every allocation point in the parallelogram OQO^*Q'. Hence, as in the standard model discussed in chapter 1, OQO^*Q' describes the factor price equalization set. Moreover in the present context apart from factor rewards, output levels per firm in the manufacturing sector are also equalized.

In order to identify the pattern of trade, draw through E a negatively sloped line with slope w_L/w_K (line BB' in figure 7.1). This line describes every country's GDP level because it represents factor income which is the only source of income (there are no pure profits). The intersection point of BB' with the diagonal OO^* at point C identifies relative country size as measured by GDP. Thus $\overline{OC}/\overline{O^*C}$ is the relative size of the home country. We can in fact choose units of measurement of commodity prices such that in these units $\overline{OO^*}$ equals world GDP. Then $\overline{OC}$ will be equal to the gross domestic product of the home country and $\overline{O^*C}$ will be equal to the gross domestic product of the foreign country.

Since every country spends the same budget share on food and on manufactured products, and we take all income to be spent, aggregate consumption of the home country is obtained in figure 7.1 by constructing a parallelogram between O and C to obtain points C_Y and C_X. Hence $\overline{OC_Y}$ equals home consumption of food, and $\overline{OC_X}$ equals home consumption of manufactured products. It is now easy to see by comparing the production points (P_Y, P_X) with the consumption points (C_Y, C_X), that in this equilibrium the home country imports food and it is a *net* exporter of manufactured products.

The emphasis on "net" in the description of manufactured trade flows stems from the fact that home consumption of manufactured products consists of n varieties that are domestically produced and n^* varieties that are imported. Then, if s stands for the share of the home country in world income, we have

$$D_X = s(nx + n^*x) \tag{7.20a}$$

because home residents consume a proportion s of the output of every variety. Similarly foreign residents consume a proportion $s^* = 1 - s$ of the output of every variety, and

$$D_X^* = s^*(nx + n^*x). \tag{7.20b}$$

This means that the quantity sn^*x of manufactured goods is imported to the home country and the quantity s^*nx is exported by the home country. Hence net exports, represented in the figure by $\overline{C_X P_X}$, are equal to

$$s^*nx - sn^*x.$$

We have identified then an equilibrium with intraindustry as well as with interindustry trade. The same pattern of trade emerges for all allocation points within the factor price equalization set. The home country, which is relatively capital rich, is a net exporter of manufactured products, which are relatively capital intensive, and an importer of food. The foreign country, which is relatively labor rich, exports the relatively labor-intensive food products, and it is a *net* importer of the relatively capital-intensive manufactured products. Despite the existence of intraindustry trade the interindustry pattern of trade is determined by the cross-country difference in relative factor endowments, just as in the Heckscher-Ohlin model.

It is straightforward to see from this analysis that if food was also a differentiated product produced with increasing returns to scale, with its degree of monopoly power being a function of commodity prices and the number of varieties available to consumers [we allow in this case $R_i(p, \bar{n}_Y, \bar{n}_X)$, $i = Y, X$], then our prediction of the intersectoral pattern of trade would remain the same. Obviously in this case we would have intraindustry trade in both sectors. In particular, at the points on the diagonal representing the same compositions of factor endowments in both countries there is intraindustry trade in both sectors and *no* interindustry trade.

Finally, note that C represents the factor content of consumption. Therefore the factor content of trade is represented in figure 7.1 by the vector EC; the (home) capital-rich country is a net importer of labor services and a net exporter of capital services.

7.4 Unequal Factor Rewards

If figure 7.1 were representing the standard homogeneous products constant returns to scale two-sector model, then we would be able to predict that for factor allocations above OQO^* the home country has a higher equilibrium wage rate and a lower equilibrium return to capital than the foreign country. Clearly in this equilibrium relative commodity prices and employed techniques of production are not the same as in the equilibria with factor price equalization, and at least one country specializes in production (see chapter 1).

This reasoning does not carry over directly to economies with product differentiation and economies of scale. If output per firm in the manufacturing sector is always the same in both countries, unless one of them does not produce, then we can apply the preceding argument from chapter 1 to the GDP function $\Pi(p, \bar{L}, \bar{K}, x)$, where x is the relevant level of output per firm in the manufacturing sector, in order to argue that for allocations above OQO^* the wage rate is higher in the home country and the return to capital is higher in the foreign country. Then we can also conclude that in this set the home country is a net exporter of manufactured products and an importer of food, with the home country possibly specializing in the production of manufactured products and the foreign country in the production of food (we cannot exclude at this stage factor price equalization for allocations above OQO^*). However, we cannot be sure of this, unless manufactures are produced with a homothetic technology.

The assumption of homotheticity seems to be too strong a requirement for technologies with economies of scale that are internal to the firm, because it implies that the relative factor intensity in activities that generate fixed costs are the same as in activities that generate variable costs. Thus it does not allow the existence of inputs, like buildings, sights, large-scale equipment (e.g., furnaces), and top management, which generate mainly fixed costs and contribute negligibly to variable costs.

With a homothetic production function the cost function is separable, and average cost can be written as

$$c(w_L, w_K, x) \equiv \frac{\tilde{c}(w_L, w_K)}{\bar{c}(x)}, \tag{7.21}$$

where $\tilde{c}(\cdot)$ has the properties of a unit cost function and $\bar{c}(\cdot)$ is increasing in x. In this case, depending on whether $\tilde{c}(w_L, w_K) \gtreqless \tilde{c}(w_L^*, w_K^*)$, average costs of producing manufactures are higher in the home country for every output level, lower in the home country for every output level, or they are equal in both countries for every output level. Clearly the country with the lower cost will produce manufactures, and if they have the same cost structure, there will be a symmetrical equilibrium in the manufacturing sector where x is the same in both countries.

Observe, however, that in the absence of homotheticity there might exist allocations above OQO^* with an equilibrium in whivh $w_L < w_L^*$, $w_K > w_K^*$ with $x > x^*$, provided that given factor rewards the cost-minimizing capital/labor ratio rises with output (we do not know how to exclude such equilibria). In this case the intersectoral pattern of trade might be different from what we have described.

7.5 Many Goods and Factors

The logic of the two-sector analysis developed in section 7.3 generalizes to multisector and multifactor economies. In order to abstract from cases where the precise combinations of available varieties play a significant role in equilibrium, assume that in symmetric equilibria the degree of monopoly power functions can be represented as follows:

$$R_i = R_i(p, \bar{n}), \quad i \in I,$$

where $p = (p_1, p_2, \ldots, p_I)$ is the vector of commodity prices and $\bar{n} = (\bar{n}_1, \bar{n}_2, \ldots, \bar{n}_I)$ is the vector of the number of varieties available in every sector. We treat homogeneous product sectors that produce with constant returns to scale as a special case, according to the procedures described in section 7.3. These monopoly power functions are constants when preferences are of the S-D-S type. For preferences of the Lancaster type the existence of these type of monopoly power functions requires an assumption of independence across sectors in the distribution of preferences for ideal products, unless the upper tier utility function is of the Cobb-Douglas type. In the latter case $R_i = R_i(\bar{n}_i)$ as we have shown in chapter 6.

In the multisector, multifactor case the equilibrium conditions for the integrated world economy, which are the generalization of (7.12)–(7.18), can be written as follows:

$$p_i = c_i(w, x_i), \quad i \in I, \tag{7.22}$$

$$R_i(p, \bar{n}) = \theta_i(w, x_i), \quad i \in I, \tag{7.23}$$

$$\sum_{i \in I} a_{li}(w, x_i)\bar{X}_i = \bar{V}_l, \quad l \in N, \tag{7.24}$$

$$\alpha_i(p, \bar{n}) = \frac{p_i \bar{X}_i}{\sum\limits_{j=1}^{I} p_j \bar{X}_j}, \quad i \in I, \tag{7.25}$$

$$\bar{n}_i = \frac{\bar{X}_i}{x_i}, \quad i \in I. \tag{7.26}$$

The equations are self-explanatory and need no comment. We begin with the values of (w, p, x) and $(\bar{X}, \bar{n})$ that emerge from this equilibrium and consider trading equilibria that arise from the distribution of $\bar{V}$ across J countries. Let $\bar{V}(i)$ be the vector of resources allocated to sector i in the integrated equilibrium. Clearly $\bar{V}(i) = a_i(w, x_i)\bar{X}_i$.

Define the following set:

$$\text{FPE} = \Big\{(V^1, V^2, \ldots, V^J) | \exists \lambda_{ij} \geq 0, \sum_{j \in J} \lambda_{ij} = 1, \text{ for all } i \in I,$$

$$\text{such that } V^j = \sum_{i \in I} \lambda_{ij} \bar{V}(i), \text{ for all } j \in J \Big\}.$$

This is the factor price equalization set when we ignore the integer constraint on the number of firms in differentiated product industries. It is defined by the cross-country factor allocation vectors $(V^1, V^2, \ldots, V^J)$, which exhaust the world's input vector $\bar{V}$ and enable full employment of resources in every country, when it uses the techniques of production of the integrated world equilibrium.

Following the arguments from section 7.3, we can construct an equilibrium with factor price equalization, and the cross-country equalization of the output levels x_i, for every factor endowment allocation in FPE. In this equilibrium country j imports n_i^k varieties of good i from country k, and it exports to it n_i^j varieties of this good, provided good i is a differentiated product. Since there is a multiplicity of goods and factors of production, we cannot precisely predict net exports of every sector for a given country, but in line with the general factor proportions theory outlined in chapter 1, we can predict the *factor content* of net trade flows. Thus the factor content of country j's *net* imports is

$$t_V^j = s^j \bar{V} - V^j,$$

where s^j is the share of country j in world spending. If we renumber factors of production so that

$$\frac{V_1^j}{\bar{V}_1} < \frac{V_2^j}{\bar{V}_2} < \ldots < \frac{V_m^j}{\bar{V}_m} < s^j < \frac{V_{m+1}^j}{\bar{V}_{m+1}} < \ldots < \frac{V_N^j}{\bar{V}_N},$$

then country j is a net exporter of services of factors 1 to m and a net importer of services of factors $m + 1$ to N. Thus country j exports services of those factors of production with which it is relatively well endowed.

It is clear from this discussion that within the bounds of factor price equalization, defined by the set FPE, we have the standard prediction of the intersectoral pattern of trade despite the existence of intraindustry trade. The set FPE is nonempty if there exists a symmetrical equilibrium for the integrated world economy, because in this case factor allocations that assign the same composition to every country belong to it. However, the dimensionality of FPE depends on the relationship between the number of industries and the number of factors or production. As usual FPE has full dimensionality if the number of industries is at least as large as the number of factors of production, and if in the integrated equilibrium there exist N industries with independent production techniques.

7.6 Restricted Entry

So far we have examined Chamberlin's large group case: the case where the number of competitors in a differentiated product industry is endogenously determined by entry and exit up to the point at which profits are driven down to zero. The question taken up in this section is whether our predictions of trade patterns apply only to Chamberlin's large group case. We show that in the small group case we can also predict the intersectoral pattern of trade from differences in factor proportions and the existence of intraindustry trade.

First, consider the case where the integrated 2×2 world economy can accommodate $\bar{n}$ firms in the manufacturing sector. This may result from the fact that with $\bar{n}$ firms every firm makes positive profits, which are driven below zero when an additional firm enters the industry, or that there are sunk costs associated with entry and $\bar{n}$ firms have already entered (they also already may have commited themselves to varieties that are equally spaced on the circumference of the circle). For current purposes we need not specify precisely the concept of equilibrium that is being used, particularly in terms of the profit opportunities perceived by a potential entrant. All we require is a well-defined concept that makes $\bar{n}$ determinate and is consistent with symmetry.

In this case the relevant equilibrium conditions for the integrated economy are given by (7.6)–(7.10). Given $\bar{n}$, this system implicitly defines equilibrium values for (p, x, w_L, w_K, Y). The equilibrium allocation of labor and capital to the food industry and the manufacturing sector is described by the vectors OQ and OQ', respectively, in figure 7.2. The vector OA represents employment by a representative firm in the manufacturing sector, so that $\overline{OQ/OA}$ is equal to $\bar{n}$.

Now consider a two country world with the endowment point E which is above the diagonal OO^* (i.e., the home country is relatively capital abundant) but in the set of factor price equalization. The line BB' describes *factor income*

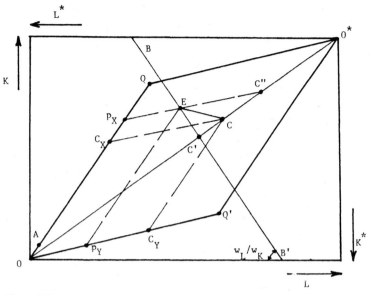

Figure 7.2

of every country. However, since firms in the manufacturing sector are now making positive profits, point C' (i.e., the intersection point of BB' with OO^*) no longer describes relative GDP levels, *unless* the ratio of aggregate profits to factor income is the same in every country. Yet for all endowment points above OO^* this ratio is higher in the home country than in the foreign country. By drawing through E a line that is parallel to O^*Q and denoting its intersection point with OO^* by C'', we obtain a representation of relative home country profits by the ratio $\overline{OC''}/\overline{C''O}^*$. Since C'' is to the right of C', it means that the ratio of profits to factor income is higher in the home country. This procedure also allocates firms to countries in a way that is consistent with the integrated equilibrium. An alternative is discussed in the sequal.

It is clear from our discussion that relative incomes are represented by a point to the right of C' and to the left of C'', say point C. Point C also represents the factor content of consumption. Hence the vector EC represents the factor content of *net* trade; the home country is seen to be a net importer of labor services and a net exporter of capital services. By constructing parallelograms between E and O as well as between C and O we see that the home country imports food (the difference between C_Y and P_Y) and is a net exporter of manufactures (the difference between P_X and C_X). There is of course intraindustry trade in manufactures. This is the trade pattern that emerged also in the large group case.

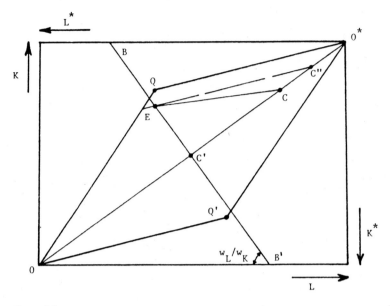

Figure 7.3

A new possibility that arises with profit-making firms is for the home country to be a net importer of both labor and capital services (see also chapter 5). This happens when profits are large relative to factor income and the home country has much more capital per worker than the foreign country. Under these circumstances point C is close to point C'', and the vector EC is upward sloping, as described in figure 7.3. Observe, however, that even in this case the home country imports food and exports a higher value of manufacturers than it imports. The factor content of its exports consists of a higher capital/labor ratio than the factor content of its imports.

This structure of factor content trade flows is best understood by following the suggestion made in chapter 5 to consider this model to be a *three*-factor model—with the third factor called, say, enterpreneurship—absorbing profits. Thus, using the Vanek ordering, the home country may have the highest comparative advantage in enterpreneurship, the second highest comparative advantage in capital, and the lowest comparative advantage in labor. It may therefore end up having a factor content trade pattern in which it exports enterpreneurship services and imports capital and labor services. This is the nature of equilibrium described in figure 7.3.

Second, consider the case where the number of firms $\bar{n}$ in the manufacturing sector is so small that we can no longer abstract from the integer problem (recall that in the previous analysis, and in the construction of figures 7.2 and

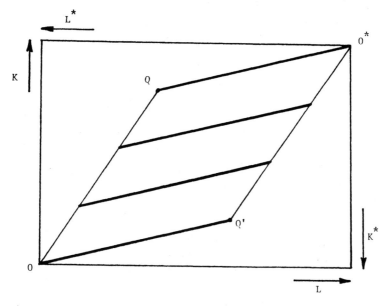

Figure 7.4

7.3, we have treated the number of firms as prefectly divisible so that, say, $\overline{OP}_X/\overline{OA}$ in figure 7.2 can be considered to be the number of firms in the manufacturing sector of the home country). If there are only two sectors, the factor price equalization set that takes explicit account of the indivisibility of firms consists of a finite number of lines parallel to QO^*, each line representing a given number of firms in the home and foreign country. An example of such a set for $\bar{n} = 3$ is represented by the four heavy lines in figure 7.4. Clearly in this case the factor price equalization set is of measure zero in factor space and not very interesting, because it is very unlikely that the endowment point will belong to it. However, if there exist at least two sectors in *addition* to the manufacturing industry, with algebraically independent techniques of production (more generally, if there exist a number of sectors additional to the number of *restrictive* sectors equal at least to the number of factors of production), then the set of factor price equalization has full dimensionality.

An example is given in figure 7.5. The vector OQ_1 represents employment in a manufacturing sector that can accommodate only three firms. The vectors O_1Q_2 and Q_2O^* represent employment in two unrestricted sectors (which may also produce differentiated products). The vector OA_1 describes employment in a representative firm in the manufacturing sector, and OA_2 describes employment by two firms in the manufacturing sector. The parallelogram drawn between Q_1 and O^* describes the factor price equalization set when all

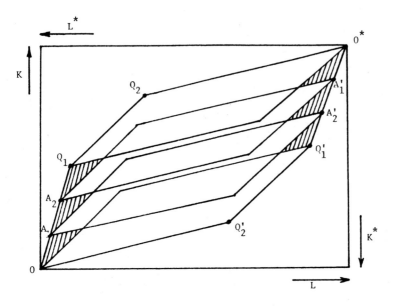

Figure 7.5

manufactured products are produced in the home country; the parallelogram drawn between A_2 and A'_1 describes the factor price equalization set when the home country has two firms in the manufacturing sector and the foreign country has a single firm; the parallelogram drawn between A_1 and A'_2 describes the factor price equalization set when the home country has a single firm in the manufacturing sector and the foreign country has two; and the parallelogram drawn between O and Q'_1 describes the factor price equalization set when all manufactured products are produced in the foreign country. The union of these sets, which is the set $OQ_1Q_2O^*Q'_1Q'_2$ exclusive of the shaded triangles, is *the* set of factor price equalization. For every point in this set we have a trade pattern similar to the one described for the 2 × 2 × 2 model, in which no account was taken of the integer problem concerning the number of firms, except that in the current case there might exist more than one allocation of the number of firms to countries (which stems from the usual difficulty when the number of sectors exceeds the number of factors of production).

Finally, consider the case where the integer problem can be disregarded, but now not only $\bar{n}$, is given, n and n^* $(n + n^* = \bar{n})$ are also given. Namely the number of firms in the manufacturing sector is given for every country. This may result either from the history of entry in each country or from government regulation. Assuming that there are two sectors in addition to the manufacturing industry, the set of factor price equalization is described by

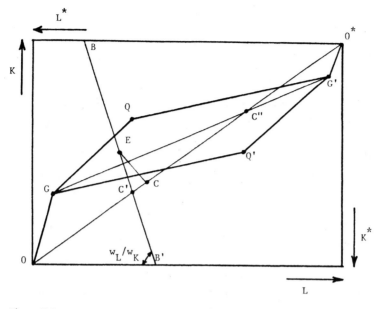

Figure 7.6

$GQG'Q'$ in figure 7.6. Here the vector OG describes employment in manufacturing in the home country, O^*G' describes employment in manufacturing in the foreign country, GQ describes employment in one of the other sectors in the integrated equilibrium, and QG' describes employment in the third sector in the integrated equilibrium ($OG + O^*G'$ is employment in manufacturing in the integrated equilibrium).

Let E be the endowment point. Then C' describes relative factor income, and C'' describes relative profits ($\overline{OC'}/\overline{C'O}^*$ and $\overline{OC''}/\overline{C''O}^*$, respectively), where C' is the intersection point of BB' with the diagonal OO^* and C'' is the intersection point with the diagonal OO^* of the line connecting G and G'. Hence relative GDP and the factor content of consumption is represented by a point C on OO^* between C' and C''. The trade pattern is again similar to that described by figures 7.2 and 7.3 when the other two sectors are aggregated to represent the counterpart of the food industry.

7.7 Predictors of the Intersectoral Pattern of Trade

In the traditional Heckscher-Ohlin model there are three predictors of the pattern of trade: relative commodity prices, relative factor rewards, and relative factor endowments. It is well known that under the standard assumptions, which include no factor-intensity reversal and identical homothetic preferences, all three are valid Thus, if the home country is relatively labor abundant, then its autarky relative price of the labor-intensive good and the wage/rental ratio are lower than in the capital-rich country, and all three predictors suggest that in the presence of international trade the home country will be an exporter of the labor-intensive good. In this section we investigate the extent to which relative commodity prices and relative factor rewards can provide valid predictions in the Chamberlin-Heckscher-Ohlin model.

The fact that relative factor endowments provide a valid prediction of the intersectoral pattern of trade was established in this chapter. It remains therefore to consider relative commodity prices and relative factor rewards. Relative commodity prices are not very useful for this purpose, because in the presence of economies of scale a country's size affects its pretrade relative commodity prices. The larger a country is, the better advantage it can take of the economies of scale, thereby having lower prices of manufactured products. Hence, if we observe two countries in autarky that are identical except for size, we may expect the larger country to have a relatively lower price of manufactured goods. However, if trade opens, there will be no intersectoral trade between these countries—all trade will be intraindustry trade (there is "false comparative advantage" in the terminology of Lancaster 1980).

This raises the following question: Is there a way to adjust prices for the scale effect so as to obtain scale-adjusted prices that provide a valid prediction of the pattern of trade? There is an interesting special case where this can be done: if the upper tier utility function is Cobb-Douglas and manufactured goods are produced with a homothetic production function. In this case relative factor rewards also provide a valid prediction of the intersectoral pattern of trade. In what follows we discuss this case in the framework of the $2 \times 2 \times 2$ model and also the difficulties that arise in more general frameworks.

Let the production function of manufactures be homothetic. Then the average cost function is given by (7.21). In this case the measure of economies of scale $\theta(\cdot)$ is independent of factor rewards, and factor use per unit output is decomposable as follows:

$$a_{lX}(w_L, w_K, x) = \frac{\tilde{a}_{lX}(w_L, w_K)}{\overline{c}(x)}, \quad l = L, K, \tag{7.27}$$

where $\tilde{a}_{lX}(w_L, w_K) = \partial \tilde{c}(w_L, w_K)/\partial w_l$. We assume that the degree of economies of scale declines with output.

Let the upper tier utility function be Cobb-Douglas. Then for Lancaster-type preferences the degree of monopoly power depends only on n (see chapter 6).

We assume that $R(n)$ is a declining function. Combining this information with (7.27), the equilibrium conditions (7.12)–(7.18) can be rewritten as

$$1 = c_Y(w_L, w_K), \tag{7.28}$$

$$\tilde{p} = \tilde{c}(w_L, w_K), \tag{7.29}$$

$$R(\bar{n}) = \theta(x), \tag{7.30}$$

$$a_{LY}(w_L, w_K)\bar{Y} + \tilde{a}_{LX}(w_L, w_K)\bar{Z} = \bar{L}, \tag{7.31}$$

$$a_{KY}(w_L, w_K)\bar{Y} + \tilde{a}_{KX}(w_L, w_K)\bar{Z} = \bar{K}, \tag{7.32}$$

$$\alpha_Y = \frac{\bar{Y}}{(\bar{X} + \tilde{p}\bar{Z})}, \tag{7.33}$$

$$p = \frac{\tilde{p}}{\bar{c}(x)}, \tag{7.34}$$

$$\bar{n}x = \bar{Z}\bar{c}(x), \tag{7.35}$$

where $\bar{Z}$ is the output level of an artificial intermediate input.

Observe that conditions (7.28), (7.29), (7.31), (7.32), and (7.33) constitute an independent system of equilibrium conditions for a standard two-sector model with outputs $\bar{Y}$ and $\bar{Z}$, where $\tilde{p}$ is the price of $\bar{Z}$ (see Jones 1965). Hence they uniquely determine $(w_L, w_K, \tilde{p}, \bar{Y}, \bar{Z})$. This is seen as follows. The first four conditions can be solved for the relative supply $\bar{Z}/\bar{Y}$ as a function $\psi(\cdot)$ of $\tilde{p}$ and $\bar{K}/\bar{L}$. This is plotted as an upward-slopping curve in figure 7.7. Taking $\tilde{\Pi}(\tilde{p}, \bar{L}, \bar{K})$ to be the GDP function associated with these four supply conditions, the function $\psi(\cdot)$ is defined by

$$\psi\left(\tilde{p}, \frac{\bar{K}}{\bar{L}}\right) = \frac{\tilde{\Pi}_p(\tilde{p}, 1, \bar{K}/\bar{L})}{\tilde{\Pi}(\tilde{p}, 1, \bar{K}/\bar{L}) - \tilde{p}\tilde{\Pi}_p(\tilde{p}, 1, \bar{K}/\bar{L})}.$$

Condition (7.33) is plotted as the downward-slopping curve in figure 7.7. The intersection between these two curves determines the equilibrium values of $\tilde{p}$ and $\bar{Z}/\bar{Y}$. Equilibrium factor rewards are given by

$$w_L = \frac{\partial\tilde{\Pi}(\tilde{p}, \bar{L}, \bar{K})}{\partial\bar{L}}, \tag{7.36}$$

$$w_K = \frac{\partial\tilde{\Pi}(\tilde{p}, \bar{L}, \bar{K})}{\partial\bar{K}}, \tag{7.37}$$

and other variables are also easily recovered.

Now suppose that there are two identical countries, a home country and a foreign country, except that $L^* = \lambda C$, $K^* = \lambda K$, $\lambda > 1$. Hence both countries

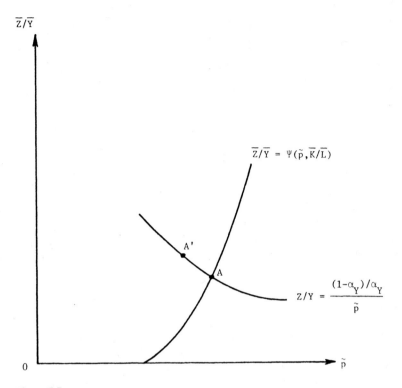

$$\overline{Z}/\overline{Y}$$

$$\overline{Z}/\overline{Y} \ = \ \Psi(\tilde{p}, \overline{K}/\overline{L})$$

$$Z/Y \ = \ \frac{(1-\alpha_Y)/\alpha_Y}{\tilde{p}}$$

Figure 7.7

have the same factor proportions, but the foreign country is larger. We want to compare autarky equilibria. Since they have the same factor proportions, they have the same equilibrium values of $\tilde{p}$ and Z/Y. By (7.36)–(7.37) factor rewards are also the same. In addition $Y^* = \lambda Y$ and $Z^* = \lambda Z$; that is, the output levels (Y, Z) are proportionately higher in the foreign country.

Now let us compare (n, x) with (n^*, x^*). Equation (7.30) implies that both points lie on the upward-sloping curve in figure 7.8, and equation (7.35) implies that (n, x) lies on the lower downward-sloping curve and (n^*, x^*) lies on the higher downward-sloping curve in this figure. Hence Q and Q^* describe the corresponding equilibrium points; the larger country produces more varieties and has a larger output per firm. Using (7.34)–(7.35) this implies that the relative price of manufactures is lower in the larger country and that its output of manufactures is more than proportionally larger.

To summarize, we have seen that

1. factor prices in terms of food are the same in both countries;

2. the larger country produces more varieties, with a higher output per firm;

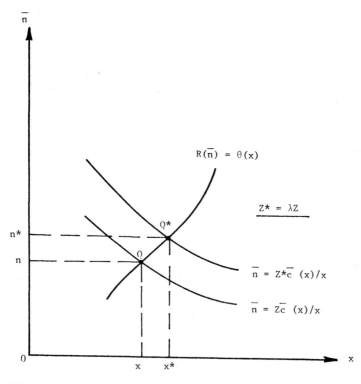

Figure 7.8

3. the relative price of manufactured products is lower in the larger country, and its output of manufactures is more than proportionally larger.

In autarky both countries have the same relative factor rewards and use therefore the same techniques of production. Since they also have the same factor proportions, the larger country employs in each sector more labor and capital in direct proportion to its relative size. This results in a proportionately higher output of food and, due to the economies of scale, a more than proportionately higher output of manufactured products, with the higher output of manufactured products being composed of more varieties and a higher output per firm. The relatively larger supply of manufactures makes their relative price lower in the larger country.

If we were to use pretrade relative commodity prices to predict the pattern of trade, we would predict that the large country will be a net exporter of manufactured products and an importer of food. However, it is clear from our discussion in section 7.3 that identical factor compositions will cause all international trade to be intraindustry trade within the manufacturing sector and that every country will produce its own consumption of food. It is therefore clear that in this case autarky relative commodity prices do not serve as reliable predictors of the pattern of trade.

Moreover the very same economic factors that lead to an autarky relatively lower price of manufactured products in the larger country (when both countries have the same factor proportions) make the post-trade relative price of manufactured products lower than the relative price of manufactured products in either one of the countries prior to trade. This stems from the fact that the introduction of international trade combines both countries into an integrated economy. Hence autarky relative commodity prices do not provide the usual bounds on post-trade relative commodity prices, for we have just seen that the post-trade relative price of manufactured goods will be outside (and to the left of) the bounds determined by autarky relative prices of these goods. If countries have different factor proportions, the location of pretrade relative commodity prices depends on the scale effect previously mentioned and the usual Heckscher-Ohlin effect. Clearly, if factor proportions do not differ by much, the scale effect dominates.

How useful then are autarky prices in predicting the pattern of trade? Observe that the autarky values of $\tilde{p}$ do predict the intersectoral pattern of trade. Suppose the foreign country has a higher capital/labor ratio. Then its equilibrium point in figure 7.7 is on a downward-sloping curve to the left of A, say at A'. This is so because manufactured products are relatively capital intensive; therefore the foreign country's upward-sloping curve is above the upward-sloping curve of the home country (the Rybczynski effect). In this case the foreign country will have a lower $\tilde{p}$, which via (7.36)–(7.37) means a higher wage rate and a lower rental rate in terms of food. Hence the country with the lower $\tilde{p}$ will be a net exporter of manufactured products. But $\tilde{p}$ can be considered to be the scale-adjusted relative price of manufactures, which is the index we have been looking for.

The implication of all this is quite simple. Since $\tilde{p} = p\bar{c}(x)$, then in order to predict the pattern of trade, we need to know both pretrade relative commodity prices and the scale of operation of manufacturing firms in each country. In addition we need to have an estimate of $\bar{c}(x)$, which is a component of the cost function. This information can be used to calculate the scale-adjusted relative price of manufactured products in each country in order to predict the intersectoral pattern of trade.

Now let us consider the predictive power of factor rewards. We have seen that countries with identical factor proportions have the same factor rewards in terms of food. Hence they have the same wage/rental ratio. In such cases the Heckscher-Ohlin prediction is no active trade. In the present model there is no active intersectoral trade under these circumstances, but there will be intrain-dustry trade. Since the Heckscher-Ohlin theory is concerned with intersectoral trade, it is fair to argue that its factor-rewards-oriented prediction remains valid if we can also show that differences in factor proportions imply that the capital-rich country has a higher wage/rental ratio in autarky. In the special case considered so far this relationship holds, as we have shown before. Hence relative scale-adjusted commodity prices and relative factor rewards provide a valid prediction of the intersectoral pattern of trade.

What happens when upper tier preferences cannot be represented by a Cobb-Douglas utility function? Then, even with homothetic production functions, neither factor rewards nor the index of scale-adjusted relative prices predict properly the pattern of trade. The reason for this difficulty stems from the fact that whenever the elasticity of substitution in consumption does not equal one (unlike the Cobb-Douglas case), aggregate relative demand depends not only on relative commodity prices but also on the number of varieties available to consumers. For example, if the utility function has constant elasticity of substitution and the elasticity of substitution is larger than one, it can be shown that the relative demand for manufactured products increases as the number of varieties increases, or alternatively that the share of income spent on food declines as the number of varieties increases. In addition, a nonunitary elasticity of substitution implies that $R(\cdot)$ depends on relative commodity prices in a rather complex way. As a result the simple links that we have presented here break down. In particular, size differences can lead to differences in relative factor rewards and scale-adjusted relative commodity prices. The pattern of trade therefore cannot be predicted from price information but only from information about relative factor endowments (see Helpman 1981 for more details).

References

Chamberlin, Edward H. *The Theory of Monopolistic Competition*. Cambridge, Mass.: Harvard University Press, 1933.

Dixit, Avinash, and Norman, Victor. *Theory of International Trade*. Cambridge, England: Cambridge University Press, 1980.

Helpman, Elhanan. "International Trade in the Presence of Product Differentiation, Economics of Scale and Monopolistic Competition: A Chamberlin-Heckscher-Ohlin Approach." *Journal of International Economics* 11 (1981): 305–340.

Helpman, Elhanan, and Razin, Assaf. "Increasing Returns, Monopolistic Competition, and Factor Movements: A Welfare Analysis." *Journal of International Economics* 14 (1983): 263–276.

Jones, Ronald W. "The Structure of Simple General Equilibrium Models." *Journal of Political Economy* 73 (1965): 557–572.

Lancaster, Kelvin. *Variety, Equity, and Efficiency.* New York: Columbia University Press, 1979.

Lancaster, Kelvin. "Intra-Industry Trade under Perfect Monopolistic Competition." *Journal of International Economics* 10 (1980): 151–175.

Varian, Hall R. *Microeconomic Analysis.* New York: Norton, 1978.

8 Trade Volume and Composition

We showed in chapter 7 that when countries do not differ by too much in their composition of factor endowments, the intersectoral patterns of trade can be explained by traditional factor proportions theory despite the existence of intraindustry trade. In the current chapter we probe deeper into trade structure in order to achieve two objectives.

The first is to develop an understanding of the determinants of the volume of trade. In the postwar period the volume of trade has grown faster than income, with the industrial countries experiencing a rate of trade growth about twice the rate of their GNP growth (e.g., Balassa 1978). We want to examine whether our theory can contribute to the explanation of this fact. In general, we wish to shed light on the separate roles played by cross-country differences in relative factor endowments and relative country size in the determination of the volume of trade.

Second, since the existence of differentiated products produces two types of trade, intersectoral and intraindustry, we would like to know how the composition of trade in terms of these components depends on the structure of the world economy. In particular, we will relate the share of intraindustry trade to cross-country differences in relative factor endowments and relative country size. We will discuss some empirical hypotheses that result from this analysis and relate them to existing evidence.

8.1 Trade Volumes in the Simple Model

In order to identify the special features of trade volume behavior for economies with differentiated products, we begin by briefly reproducing the results from chapter 1 about trade volumes in a standard two-country, two-sector, two-factor, Heckscher-Ohlin-type world economy. This is followed by a discussion of trade volumes in a two-country, two-sector, two-factor economy in which one sector produces differentiated products. The results of

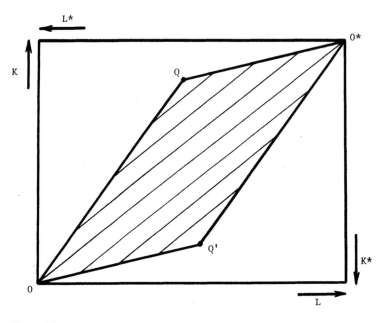

L*

K

Q

0*

Q'

K*

0

L

Figure 8.1

this analysis are compared with the corresponding results in the standard Heckscher-Ohlin model. An analysis of trade volumes in a multisector, multifactor, many-country world is presented in the next section.

Let us begin with the standard 2 × 2 × 2 trade model. Factor allocations (labor and capital) in an integrated equilibrium are presented in figure 8.1. The vector OQ represents employment in the manufactures sector and OQ' represents employment in the food sector (both with constant return to scale). Food production is relatively labor intensive. The parallelogram OQO^*Q' represents the factor price equalization set. Without loss of generality, consider only factor allocations that make the home country relatively capital rich, that is, above the diagonal OO^*. At these allocations the home country exports manufactures and imports food. The volume of trade, defined as the sum of exports across countries, is

$$VT = p(X - s\bar{X}) + (Y^* - s^*\bar{Y}), \qquad (8.1)$$

where food is taken to be the numeraire, p is the price of manufactures, $X(X^*)$ is the output of manufactures in the home (foreign) country, $Y(Y^*)$ is the output of food in the home (foreign) country, $\bar{X}$ is the output of manufactures in the world economy ($\bar{X} = X + X^*$), $\bar{Y}$ is the output of food in the world

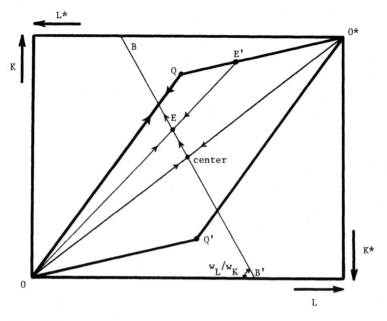

Figure 8.2

economy $(\overline{Y} = Y + Y^*)$, and $s\,(s^*)$ is the share of the home (foreign) country in world income and spending $[s = (Y + pX)/(\overline{Y} + p\overline{X})$ and $s + s^* = 1]$. Implicit in (8.1) is the assumption that tastes are homothetic and identical across countries.

We showed in chapter 1 that in this case the volume of trade is constant along straight lines parallel to the diagonal and the volume of trade is larger the further away a line is from the diagonal. Thus the heavy lines in figure 8.1 describe equal trade volume lines.

Now change the model: suppose that the manufacturing sector produces differentiated products with increasing returns to scale. The precise model is described in detail in chapter 7. Figure 8.2 reproduces the allocation box for this world economy following the construction of figure 7.1. The vector OQ describes aggregate employment in the manufacturing sector, the vector OQ' describes aggregate employment in the food industry, and OQO^*Q' is the factor price equalization set. We consider allocations above the diagonal OO^* so that the home country is relatively capital rich.

We showed in chapter 7 that for every allocation point in OQO^* the foreign country exports food, both countries export varieties of the manufactured product, but the home country is a net exporter of manufactures. The volume of trade is therefore equal to

$$VT = s^*pX + spX^* + (Y^* - s^*\bar{Y}),\tag{8.2}$$

where the first component represents exports of manufactures by the home country (it produces $n = X/x$ varieties, and a share s^* of the output of every variety is exported to the foreign country); the second component represents exports of manufactures by the foreign country (it produces $n^* = X^*/x$ varieties, and a proportion s of the output of every variety is exported to the home country); and the last component represents exports of food by the foreign country.

Because trade is balanced, the volume of trade also equals twice the exports of the home country as well as twice the exports of the foreign country:

$$VT = 2s^*pX,\tag{8.3}$$

$$VT = 2(spX^* + Y^* - s^*\bar{Y}).\tag{8.4}$$

These expressions can be used to study the dependence of the volume of trade on the cross-country distribution of world resources.

Start with the allocation point E in figure 8.2. A special characteristic of this point is that it is located on the income line BB' (with slope w_L/w_K) that passes through the center of the box, which means that at E (as well as at all other points of BB' in the factor price equalization set) the home and foreign country are of equal size. Now draw from E a ray through origin O in order to obtain OE'. By reallocating resources from E toward E' on this ray, we increase proportionately the endowment of labor and capital in the home country, resulting in the same proportional increases in the output of food and manufactures (the output of manufactures rises via an increase in the number of firms in the industry) as well as in income. How do these reallocations affect the volume of trade? It is apparent from (8.3) that they generate two opposing effects: the increase in production of manufactures in the home country tends to increase the volume of trade, whereas the decline in the relative size of the foreign country tends to decrease the volume of trade. Using "hats" to denote proportional rates of change (e.g., $\hat{X} = dX/X$), we have

$$\hat{V}T = \hat{s}^* + \hat{X}.\tag{8.5}$$

However, $\hat{s}^* = dGDP^*/GDP^* = -dGDP/GDP^* = -\hat{GDP}s/s^*$, and for movements on rays through O the following holds: $\hat{GDP} = \hat{X}$. Therefore

$$\hat{V}T = \hat{X}\left(1 - \frac{s}{s^*}\right)\tag{8.6}$$

for rays in OQO^* through O.

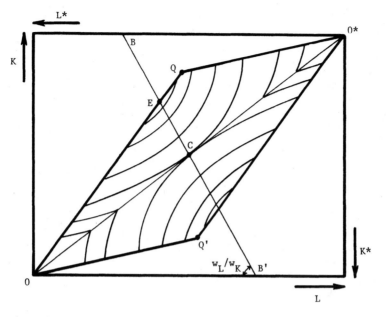

Figure 8.3

It is clear from (8.6) that for reallocations on rays through O the volume of trade rises as the reallocation brings about more equality in relative country size. Thus for such rays the volume of trade increases with reallocations toward BB', as indicated by the arrows in figure 8.2. In particular, since point E represents equal country size, any reallocation on OE' away from E reduces the volume of trade.

It is clear from this discussion that there exists a fundamental difference between the world economy with differentiated products and the standard Heckscher-Ohlin world economy as far as the volume of trade is concerned. Whereas in the economy with homogeneous products relative country size had no independent effect on the volume of trade (but only through its effect on the difference in factor composition), the existence of trade in differentiated products introduces a major link between the volume of trade and relative country size. It is also clear from (8.5) that reallocations that maintain constant relative country size, but bring about higher output in the manufacturing sector of the relatively capital-rich country, increase the volume of trade. Thus for a given relative country size the volume of trade is larger the larger the difference in relative factor endowments, just as in the homogeneous product case; here, however, it is also larger the more similar in size countries are.

This is seen most clearly in figures 8.3 and 8.4, in which curves indicate

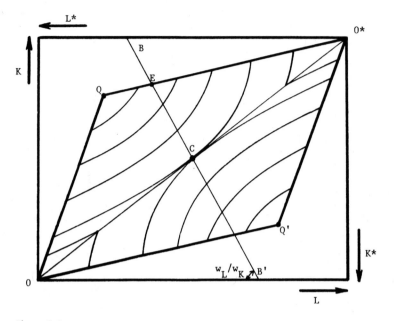

Figure 8.4

where the volume of trade is constant. In figure 8.3 the equal income line BB' is below Q, and in 8.4 it is above Q. In the former case the volume of trade is maximized at E, whereas in the latter it is maximized at Q. The convexity properties of the volume of trade isocurves are proved in the appendix. A comparison of figure 8.1 with figures 8.3 and 8.4 shows clearly how the existence of a sector with differentiated products introduces an important link between the volume of trade and relative country size.

It is also instructive to consider a world in which both products are differentiated. In this case every country imports from its trading partner a fixed share of the output of every commodity type that the partner produces, and the volume of trade is

$$VT = s(X_1^* + pX_2^*) + s^*(X_1 + pX_2),$$

where outputs of differentiated food are denoted by X_1 and X_1^*. Hence

$$VT = sGDP^* + s^*GDP = ss^*\overline{GDP}, \tag{8.7}$$

where $\overline{GDP}$ is gross domestic product in the world economy. It is readily seen from (8.8) that within the bounds of factor price equalization, which implies a constant $\overline{GDP}$, the volume of trade depends *only* on relative country size, and it is larger, the more equal the size of countries is. The volume of trade is largest

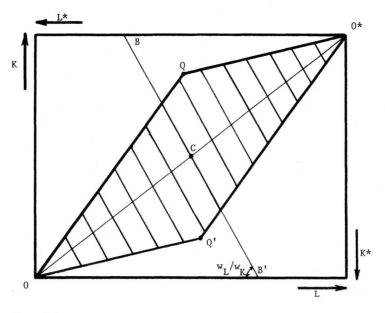

Figure 8.5

when both countries are of equal size *independently* of the composition of factor endowments. This is represented by the heavy volume of trade isocurves in figure 8.5, whose slope is $-w_L/w_K$. The volume of trade is largest on the line that passes through C, and it declines the farther away the endowment allocation is from this line. By comparing figure 8.5 to 8.3 and 8.1, we observe how the importance of relative country size in trade volume determination increases as we increase the number of differentiated products.

8.2 Trade Volume: Generalizations

We saw in the previous section that in the presence of differentiated products produced with economies of scale, the volume of trade depends in an important way on relative country size. In this section we extend the analysis to a multisector, multifactor, many-country world economy.

Consider the general model of a world economy developed in section 7.5. Let us divide the industries into two subsets: the subset I_H consists of sectors that produce homogeneous products with constant returns to scale or with increasing returns to scale and contestible markets, while its complement I_D produces differentiated products with increasing returns to scale. In a symmetrical factor price equalization equilibrium the volume of trade, defined to equal aggregate world exports, is

$$VT = \sum_{j \in J} \sum_{i \in I_H} \max\left(p_i X_i^j - s^j p_i \bar{X}_i, 0\right) + \sum_{j \in J} \sum_{i \in I_D} (1 - s^j) p_i X_i^j.$$

The first component describes the contribution of homogeneous products to the volume of trade, and the second component describes the contribution of differentiated products to the volume of trade.

Due to the existence of homogeneous products it is hard to provide links between this trade volume and some major cross-country differences, just as it is difficult to do so in the standard factor proportions trade world. However, if there is specialization in the production of homogeneous products—or if all industries produce differentiated product—we can describe interesting links. For in this case $i \in I_H$ implies either $X_i^j = 0$ or $X_i^j = \bar{X}_i$. Therefore

$$\max\left(p_i X_i^j - s^j p_i \bar{X}_i, 0\right) = \max\left(p_i X_i^j - s^j p_i X_i^j, 0\right) = (1 - s^j) p_i X_i^j,$$

and (8.9) reduces to

$$VT = \sum_{j \in J} \sum_{i \in I} (1 - s^j) p_i X_i^j = \sum_{j \in J} (1 - s^j) GDP^j = \sum_{j \in J} (1 - s^j) s^j \overline{GDP},$$

where $\overline{GDP} = \sum_{j \in J} GDP^j$. Since $\sum_{j \in J} s^j = 1$, this implies

$$VT = \left[1 - \sum_{j \in J} (s^j)^2\right] \overline{GDP}. \tag{8.8}$$

Hence the volume of trade is a fraction of the world's gross domestic product with the fraction $[1 - \sum_{j \in J} (s^j)^2]$ being a measure of dispersion in relative country size. The more equal the size of countries, the larger the $VT/\overline{GDP}$ ratio, and it is largest when countries are of equal size. Indeed, this provides a partial explanation of the fact that in the postwar period the volume of trade has grown faster than income because, as shown in Helpman (1948b), this relative country size dispersion measure has increased for the industrial countries, which have dominated world trade.

It should be observed that formula (8.8) for the volume of trade applies to circumstances that are more general than those for which it was derived. All it requires is complete specialization in production (which is assured in the case of differentiated products and which we have imposed on homogeneous products) and identical homothetic preferences. It does not require factor price equalization or equalization of prices for varieties of the same product, and it does not require equalization of output levels for firms in a differentiated product industry.

Whenever there is complete specialization in production (either intraindustry specialization or intersectoral specialization), then identical homothetic preferences and access to the same prices by all consumers imply that, on the one hand, country j consumes a fraction s^j of every good that is produced in the world economy and, on the other, it exports a fraction $(1 - s^j)$ of every good that it produces, with a fraction s^k of its output being exported to country k. Hence under these circumstances exports of j to k are

$$EX^{jk} = s^k \text{GDP}^j = s^k s^j \overline{\text{GDP}}, \tag{8.9}$$

which is a version of the gravity equation (e.g., see Anderson 1979 and Krugman 1980). It implies that the volume of trade within a subset of countries A is:

$$VT^A = \sum_{j \in A} \sum_{k \in A} EX^{jk} = \sum_{j \in A} \sum_{\substack{k \in A \\ k \neq j}} s_A^k s_A^j \frac{(\text{GDP}^A)^2}{\text{GDP}},$$

where $\text{GDP}^A = \sum_{j \in A} \text{GDP}^j$ is the group's gross domestic product and $s_A^j = \text{GDP}^j/\text{GDP}^A$ is the within group share of country j in gross domestic product. Since

$$\sum_{\substack{k \in A \\ k \neq j}} s_A^k = 1 - s_A^j, \qquad\qquad \text{(e.g., Balassa 1978)}.$$

this implies

$$VT^A = s^A \left[1 - \sum_{j \in A} (s_A^j)^2 \right] \text{GDP}^A, \tag{8.10}$$

where s^A is the share of the group in world gross domestic product.

Formula (8.8) is a special case of (8.10) because in the former the group is the entire world economy. The latter has also been derived under more general circumstances. Thus, if, say, the industrial countries maintain an approximately fixed relative size in the world economy, then the within group volume of trade will grow faster than the group's income if and only if the relative size of the industrial countries is equalized over time. Evidence on the links depicted by (8.10) is described in Helpman (1984b). Clearly these formulas provide better approximations the more specialization there is, and this means that the approximation is better, the larger the relative size of differentiated product industries. Generally, economies of scale lead to more specialization than would occur in a constant returns world; thus gravity equations will tend to fit the trade pattern better, the more important are increasing returns. A minor modification is required if there are nontradable goods and the share of income spent on these goods is constant and the same in every country. If such is not the case, developments in the nontradable sector introduce additional effects to the link between trade growth, output growth, and changes in relative country size.

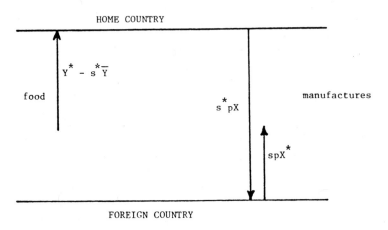

Figure 8.6

8.3 Trade Composition in the Simple Model

We now turn to the determinants of the decomposition of trade flows into an intraindustry and an intersectoral component. In this section attention is focused on the factor price equalization set in the $2 \times 2 \times 2$ model. We take the food industry to produce a homogeneous product and manufactures to be differentiated. Considering only factor allocations in the subset OQO^* of figure 8.2, we assume that the home country is relatively capital abundant, implying that it is a net exporter of manufactures and an importer of food. Figure 8.6 portrays these trade flows. The length of every arrow describes the value of exports in an industry. The volume of trade is equal to the sum of the length of these arrows.

We want to decompose these trade flows into intraindustry and intersectoral trade. There are some simple indexes that have been used for this purpose in various empirical studies (e.g., Grubel and Lloyd 1975, chapter 2), and we will reproduce them shortly. It is clear from figure 8.6 that the *net* flows within every industry describe what one would normally call intersectoral trade. Thus for the case described in the figure it seems appropriate to define the volume of intersectoral trade as exports of food by the foreign country plus *net* exports of manufactures by the home country. In this case the volume of intraindustry trade VT_{i-i}, which equals the total trade volume minus the volume of intersectoral trade, is equal to twice exports of manufactures by the foreign country (which is a *net importer* of manufactures); namely

$$VT_{i-i} = 2spX^*. \tag{8.11}$$

More generally, intraindustry trade in sector i products between two countries can be defined as twice the bilateral exports of the industry's products. Thus total intraindustry trade equals the sum of those components across industries and countries, or

$$VT_{i-i} = \sum_{j \in J} \sum_{\substack{k \in J \\ k \neq j}} \sum_{l \in I} \min(EX_l^{jk}, EX_l^{kj}), \tag{8.12}$$

where EX_l^{jk} is the value of exports of l goods from country j to country k. Equation (8.13) represents a special case of (8.14), in which intraindustry trade takes place in only one sector.

Now, using (8.11) and (8.3), the share of intraindustry trade in the total volume of trade is

$$S_{i-i} = \frac{VT_{i-i}}{VT} = \frac{sX^*}{s^*X}. \tag{8.13}$$

What (8.13) says is that for a given world distribution of income (s and s^* constant) the share of intraindustry trade is higher, the lower the relative output of the capital-intensive good in the capital-abundant country. This means that a redistribution of resources that leaves the world distribution of income unchanged but makes the countries more similar in relative factor endowments will raise the share of intraindustry trade. In particular, that share becomes one for points on the diagonal OO^* in figure 8.2, and it becomes zero if only one country produces manufactured goods (points on OQ' or O^*Q).

In between these extremes the intraindustry share is increasing in similarity of relative factor endowments, and it depends on country size. This is illustrated in figure 8.7. The curves in the figure describe combinations of factor endowments at which the share of intraindustry trade is constant. The farther away a curve is from the diagonal OO^*, the smaller is the share of intraindustry trade that it describes. The demonstration that this is in fact the shape of these curves is given in the appendix. It is apparent from the figure that the smaller the difference in factor composition and the smaller the size of the capital-rich country, the larger is the share of intraindustry trade.

8.4 Trade Composition: Generalizations and Empirical Hypothesis

We have now seen that in the $2 \times 2 \times 2$ model the share of intraindustry trade is related in a simple way to the cross-country differences in relative factor endowments; the more countries differ in the composition of factor endowments, the larger the share of intersectoral trade and the smaller the share of intraindustry trade. The question to be addressed in this section is whether

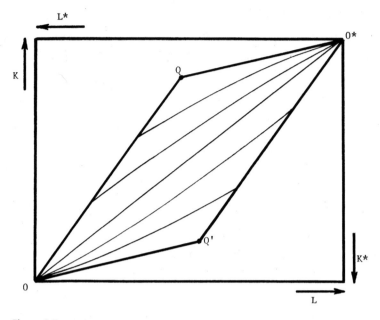

Figure 8.7

this strong result generalizes to more complex economic structures so that one could form, with a certain degree of confidence, a working hypothesis that relates differences in the composition of factor endowments to differences in the composition of the trade volume.

Consider a world that consists of J countries that produce and trade in I goods. We treat every sector as a producer of differentiated products, with homogeneous products considered to be a special case as explained in chapter 7. Assume, however, that goods are produced only with labor and capital and that the production functions are homothetic. In such a case the pricing equation (7.22) can be written as

$$p_i = \frac{\tilde{c}_i(w_L, w_K)}{\bar{c}_i(x_i)}, \quad i \in I, \tag{8.14}$$

where $\tilde{c}(\cdot)$ has all the properties of a unit cost function and $\bar{c}(\cdot)$ is increasing in x_i in the presence of economies of scale. This holds for a country that produces i products, though p_i might be smaller than the right-hand side of (8.16) for a country that does not produce them. Also under these conditions the measure of the degree of economies of scale $\theta_i(\cdot)$ does not depend on factor prices but only on the output level x_i. Hence (7.23) obtains the form

$$R_i(p, \bar{n}) = \theta_i(x_i), \quad i \in I. \tag{8.15}$$

It is particularly important to observe at this stage that if a comparison of country j with country k reveals that

$$\tilde{c}_i(w_L^j, w_K^j) < \tilde{c}_i(w_K^k, w_L^k),$$

then, due to homotheticity in production, average costs of producing a variety of product i are lower in country j than in k for every output level x_i. Hence in this case varieties of product i are not produced in country k. This means that for the purpose of a cross-country comparison of specialization patterns, the output levels x_i that are derived from (8.15) can be applied to all countries, because every country that produces product i has the same cost structure (even if it pays different factor rewards) and finds x_i to be the output level consistent with its firm's profit maximization.

Let therefore $\tilde{p}_i \equiv p_i \bar{c}_i(x_i)$, and rewrite (8.14) as

$$\tilde{p}_i \le \tilde{c}_i(w_L^j, w_K^j), \quad i \in I, j \in J, \tag{8.16}$$

with strict inequality implying that good i is not produced. Now since

$$a_{li}(w_L, w_K, x_i) = \frac{\tilde{a}_{li}(w_L, w_K)}{\bar{c}_i(x_i)},$$

where $\tilde{a}_{li}(w) = \partial \tilde{c}_i(w)/\partial w_l$, then by defining

$$\tilde{X}_i^j = \frac{X_i^j}{\bar{c}_i(x_i)} = \frac{n_i^j x_i}{\bar{c}_i(x_i)},$$

we can write the factor market-clearing conditions as

$$\sum_{i \in I} \tilde{a}_{Li}(w_L^j, w_K^j)\tilde{X}_i^j = L^j, \quad j \in J, \tag{8.17}$$

$$\sum_{i \in J} \tilde{a}_{Ki}(w_L^j, w_K^j)\tilde{X}_i^j = K^j, \quad j \in J. \tag{8.18}$$

The combination of (8.16)–(8.18) implies that gross domestic product of country j can be represented by

$$\text{GDP}^j = \tilde{\Pi}(\tilde{p}, L^j, K^j), \quad j \in J, \tag{8.19}$$

where $\tilde{p} = (\tilde{p}_1, \tilde{p}_2, \dots, \tilde{p}_I)$ and $\tilde{\Pi}(\cdot)$ is the usual restricted profit function derived from production functions that are the duals to the unit cost functions $\tilde{c}_i(w_L, w_K)$. In particular, since $\tilde{p}$ is the same in every country, it implies—due to the concavity of $\tilde{\Pi}(\cdot)$ in factor endowments—that countries with a high capital/labor ratio have a higher wage rate and a lower rental rate on capital than countries with a low capital/labor ratio.

The resulting specialization pattern can be described by means of a Lerner diagram as in figure 8.8 (see chapter 1). The capital/labor ratio of country j is

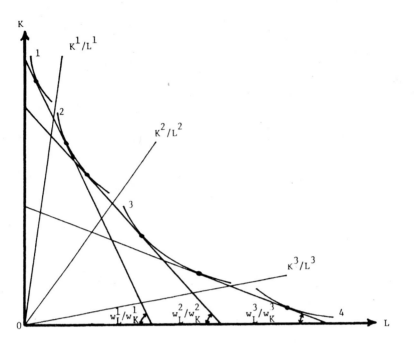

Figure 8.8

represented by the ray (K^j/L^j), its unit cost line by the downward-sloping straight line with slope (w_L^j/w_K^j), and every isoquant i describes the combination of factor inputs that produce an output level $1/\tilde{p}_i$ with the production function that is dual to the unit cost function $\tilde{c}_i(\cdot)$. Hence country 1, which is the relatively most capital-rich country, produces products of industries 1 and 2; country 2, which has the intermediate value of capital per worker, produces products of industries 2 and 3; and country 3, which is the relatively labor-rich country, produces products 3 and 4. It is clear from this figure that given that commodities 2 and 3 are differentiated products, there is intraindustry trade between countries 1 and 2 and between countries 2 and 3, but there is no intraindustry trade between countries 1 and 3 (even if sectors 1 and 4 produce differentiated products). More generally, in the absence of factor-intensity intervals, this analysis suggests that we should expect relatively more intra-industry trade between a pair of countries with a similar factor composition than between a pair of countries with a dissimilar factor composition.

In particular, since (8.19) implies

$$\frac{GDP^j}{L^j} = \tilde{\Pi}\left(\tilde{p}, 1, \frac{K^j}{L^j}\right)$$

(i.e., the more capital per worker a country has, the higher its GDP per capita), we suggest the empirical hypothesis that on average the more similar countries are in per capita income, the larger the share of intraindustry trade in their bilateral trade volume. This hypothesis finds support in Loertscher and Wolter (1980) for the year 1978 and in Helpman (1984b) for all the seventies. In addition it is clear from this discussion that in a time series of data for a group of countries we should expect the share of intraindustry trade in the within group volume of trade to be larger in time periods when the distribution of income per capita within the group is less dispersed than when it is more dispersed. Since these calculations require large amounts of data, time series analysis for long periods is not available. However, evidence reported in Helpman (1984b) supports this hypothesis for the seventies.

Although the formal analysis rested on the assumption that there is no factor-intensity reversal, our hypothesis remains valid in its presence, if there are not in some sense too many factor-intensity reversals. This can be seen in figure 8.8 by observing that isoquant 1 can be extended in a way that will make its lower part tangent to the unit cost line of country 3. In this case there is factor-intensity reversal and intraindustry trade between country 1 and 3 when sector 1 produces differentiated products. However, if this type of phenomenon is not very important, then our hypothesis remains valid.

A third hypothesis can be derived from our analysis, this time concerning the share of intraindustry trade for individual countries. Suppose that within groups of more capital-intensive industries there is relatively more production of differentiated products than within groups of less capital-intensive industries (we do not have evidence to support this assumption). Then countries with more capital per worker experience more intraindustry specialization than countries with less capital per worker. Hence we expect larger shares of intraindustry trade to be observed in countries with higher endowments of capital per worker or, alternatively, in countries with higher income per capita. Indeed, this positive correlation is reported in Havrylyshyn and Civan (1984) for a cross-sectional comparison of a large group of countries (see, in particular, their figure 1).

Finally, it is clear from figure 8.8 that because zero profits prevail on all product lines, a Krona worth of output of every product line in country 1 embodies more capital and less labor than a Krona worth of output on every product line of country 2 or 3, and a Krona worth of output of every product line in country 2 embodies more capital and less labor than a Krona worth of output on every product line in country 3. Hence the bilateral trade patterns of the factor content of net trade flows correspond to the factor proportions theory when the exporter's techniques of production are used to calculate factor content (see chapter 1). In particular, in every bilateral trade pattern, exports of the relatively capital-rich country embody a larger ratio of capital to labor services than the exports of the relatively labor-rich country. If the bilateral trade flows are balanced, then the relatively capital-rich country is a net exporter of capital services and the relatively labor-rich country is a net exporter of labor services.

Moreover, using a multifactor equivalent of (8.16)–(8.18), one can apply the restrictions on the factor content of bilateral trade flows that were derived in Helpman (1984a), which represent a generalization of our discussion of the two-factor case. To see this, generalize (8.16)–(8.18) to

$$\tilde{p}_i \leq \tilde{c}_i(w^j), \quad i \in I, j \in J, \tag{8.16}$$

with a strict inequality implying $\tilde{X}_i^j = 0$;

$$\sum_{i \in I} \tilde{a}_{li}(w^j)\tilde{X}_i^j = V_l^j, \quad l \in N, j \in J, \tag{8.17}$$

where w^j is the vector of factor rewards in country j and V_l^j is the quantity of factor l available in country j. The corresponding GDP function is $\Pi(\tilde{p}, \tilde{V}^j)$. Applying the analysis from chapter 1 [see (1.15)] to this $\tilde{\Pi}(\cdot)$ function, we obtain

$$(w^j - w^k) \cdot T_V^{jk} \geq 0, \quad k, j \in J, \tag{8.20}$$

where T_V^{jk} is the vector of gross imports of factor content by country j from country k, where the factor content is calculated by means of the exporter's techniques of production. By symmetry

$$(w^k - w^j) \cdot T_V^{kj} \geq 0, \quad k, j \in J. \tag{8.21}$$

Hence j's imports from k contain more factor content of those factors of production that are more expensive in j than in k, and j's exports to k contain more factor content of those factors of production that are cheaper in j than in k.

Appendix 8A: Geometrical Properties of Volume and Share Isocurves

We prove in this appendix that the volume of trade isocurves have the shapes depicted in figures 8.3 and 8.4 and that the share of intraindustry trade isocurves have the shapes depicted in figure 8.7. Both proofs rely on the observation that within the factor price equalization set, output and income levels are linear functions of factor endowments.

In the factor price equalization set the home country's output levels are linear functions of its factor endowment, and these functions are implicitly defined by

$$a_{LY}Y + a_{LX}X = L, \tag{8.A1}$$

$$a_{KY}Y + a_{KX}X = K, \tag{8.A2}$$

where a_{li} are taken from the integrated equilibrium.

Since

$$s^* = 1 - s = 1 - \frac{w_L L + w_k K}{\text{GDP}}$$

is also a linear function of (L, K) in FPE, then the volume of trade for endowment points above the diagonal OO^* in figure 8.3 and 8.4 [see (8.3)] is

$$VT = v(L, K) \equiv 2ps^*(L, K)X(L, K), \tag{8.A3}$$

and it is given by a product of two linear functions of (L, K).

Now consider two points, (L_1, K_1) and (L_2, K_2), such that

$$v(L_1, K_1) = v(L_2, K_2) = VT. \tag{8.A4}$$

Then, using $[s^*(i), X(i)]$ to denote the values of (s^*, X) that correspond to (L_i, K_i), the linearity of s^* and X in (L, K) implies that for $0 \le \lambda \le 1$,

$$v[\lambda L^1 + (1 - \lambda)L_2, \lambda K_1 + (1 - \lambda)K_2]$$

$$= 2p[\lambda s^*(1) + (1 - \lambda)s^*(2)][\lambda X(1) + (1 - \lambda)X(2)]$$

$$= VT\left\{\lambda^2 + (1 - \lambda)^2 + \lambda(1 - \lambda)\left[\frac{s^*(2)}{s^*(1)} + \frac{s^*(1)}{s^*(2)}\right]\right\},$$

where the last equality is obtained with the help of (8.A3) and (8.A4). However, since the function

$$y + \frac{1}{y}$$

obtains a minimum at $y = 1$, and this minimum equals 2, taking $y = s^*(2)/s^*(1)$ yields

$$v[\lambda L_1 + (1 - \lambda)L_2, \lambda K_1 + (1 - \lambda)K_2] > VT = v(L_1, K_1) = v(L_2, K_2)$$

for $s^*(1) \ne s^*(2)$.

A similar analysis can be applied to endowments below the diagonal. This means that a convex combination of two equal volume of trade endowment points on the same side of the diagonal yields an endowment point that has a larger trade volume, provided that the two endowment points are not on the same income line. Two points on the same income line and on the same side of the diagonal do not have the same volume of trade because the volume of trade is larger at the point farther away from the diagonal. The analysis of figure 8.2 shows also that the volume of trade isocurves are tangent to rays through the origin of the relatively capital-rich country. Hence the volume of trade iso-curves are shaped as in figure 8.3 and 8.4.

In figure 8.4 the volume of trade is largest at Q because it can be shown to always increase when moving on O^*Q from O^* to Q. And since Q is below the equal income line BB', the volume of trade increases on OQ when moving from O to Q. By similar reasoning, in figure 8.3 the volume of trade is largest at E. Since Q is above the equal income lines BB', then on OQ the volume of trade is largest at E.

It remains to prove the shape of the equal intraindustry trade share curves in figure 8.7. Using (8.15), we obtain for points above the diagonal

$$S_{i-i} = S(L, K) = \frac{s(L, K)}{s^*(L, K)} \cdot \frac{X^*(L, K)}{X(L, K)}, \tag{8.A5}$$

where all the functions on the right-hand side of (8.A5) are linear in (L, K).

Choose two endowment points above the diagonal, such that

$$S(L_1, K_1) = S(L_2, K_2) = S. \tag{8.A6}$$

Let (L_1, K_1) be described by E_1 in figure 8.A1. Then (L_2, K_2) cannot be on the income line BB', because the farther away from the diagonal a point is on BB', the smaller the share of intraindustry trade; this is evident from (8.A5). Suppose therefore that E_2 is to the right of BB'. It cannot be above OZ because points above this may represent a higher X/s ratio and a lower X^*/s^* ratio. It cannot be below O^*Z^* for similar reasons. Hence E_2 is in O^*E_1Z as drawn. By comparing E_2 with E_1, we find

$$\frac{X(1)}{X(2)} > \frac{s(1)}{s(2)}, \tag{8.A7}$$

$$\frac{s^*(1)}{s(1)} > \frac{s^*(2)}{s(2)}. \tag{8.A8}$$

Now, using (8.A5), (8.A6) and the linearity of the functions on the right-hand side of (8.A5), we obtain

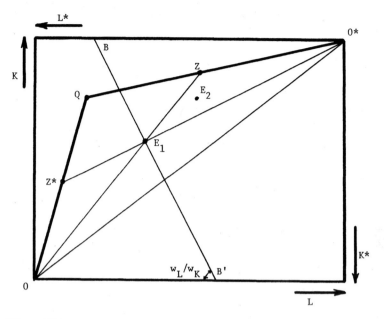

Figure 8A.1

$$S[\lambda L_1 + (1 - \lambda)L_2, \lambda K_1 + (1 - \lambda)K_2]$$

$$= \frac{\lambda s(1) + (1 - \lambda)s(2)}{\lambda s^*(1) + (1 - \lambda)s^*(2)} \cdot \frac{\lambda X^*(1) + (1 - \lambda)X^*(2)}{\lambda X(1) + (1 - \lambda)X(2)}$$

$$= S\frac{\beta_x s^*(1)/s(1) + (1 - \beta_x)s^*(2)/s(2)}{\beta_s s^*(1)/s(1) + (1 - \beta_s)s^*(2)/s(2)},$$

where

$$\beta_x = \frac{\lambda X(1)}{\lambda X(1) + (1 - \lambda)X(2)},$$

$$\beta_s = \frac{\lambda s(1)}{\lambda s(1) + (1 - \lambda)s(2)}.$$

From (8.A7) we have

$$\beta_x > \beta_s.$$

When combined with (8.A8), it implies

$$S[\lambda L_1 + (1 - \lambda)L_2, \lambda K_1 + (1 - \lambda)K_2] > S.$$

Hence, we have shown that convex combinations above the diagonal of endowment points that have equal intraindustry trade shares result in endowment points with a larger share of intraindustry trade.

Now on OQ the home country produces only manufactures and $Y^* = \bar{Y}$. Hence, using (8.4), the volume of trade is $2s(px^* + y)$. Combining it with (8.13), we obtain

$$S_{i-i} = \frac{pX^*}{pX^* + Y}.$$

Therefore on OQ the share of intraindustry trade is larger, the closer the endowment point is to the origin. At all points of the diagonal OO^* (except for the origins) the share of intraindustry trade is one, and it is zero on QO^*, because at the latter endowments the foreign country does not produce manufactures. Finally, since points on constant income lines that are closer to the diagonal represent a larger share of intraindustry trade, the curves that describe constant shares of intraindustry trade are shaped as in figure 8.7, and they represent larger shares of intraindustry trade, the closer they are to the diagonal.

References

Anderson, James E. "A Theoretical Foundation of the Gravity Equation." *American Economic Review* 69 (1979): 106–116.

Balassa, Bela. "The New Protectionism and the International Economy." *Journal of International Trade Law* (1978).

Grubel, Harry G., and Lloyd, Peter J. *Intra-Industry Trade: The Theory and Measurement of International Trade in Differentiated Products.* London: Macmillan, 1975.

Havrylyshyn, Oli, and Civan, E. "Intra-Industry Trade and the State of Development." In *The Economics of Intra-Industry Trade.* Tharakan, P. K. M. (ed.). Amsterdam: North Holland, 1984.

Helpman, Elhanan. "The Factor Content of Foreign Trade." *Economic Journal* 94 (1984a): 84–94.

Helpman, Elhanan. "Imperfect Competition and International Trade: Evidence from Fourteen Industrial Countries." Mimeo, 1984b.

Krugman, Paul R. "Differentiated Products and Multilateral Trade." Mimeo, 1980.

Loertscher, R., and Wolter, F. "Determinants of Intra-Industry Trade: Among Countries and Across Industries." *Weltwirtschafliches Archiv.* 8 (1980): 280–293.

9 Welfare

In the presence of increasing returns, trade always offers the opportunity for a simultaneous increase in the diversity of products available and in the scale at which each product is produced. If the world in fact takes advantage of this opportunity, there will be gains from trade over and above those from conventional comparative advantage. It also seems plausible that these gains could soften or reverse the adverse income distribution affects of trade on some factors of production.

Unfortunately imperfect competition, even if it takes as sanitized a form as monopolistic competition, does not lead the economy to an optimum. As a result there is no guarantee that expanding the economy's opportunities, through trade or anything else, necessarily leads to a gain. We cannot prove in general that countries gain from trade in the differentiated products model.

Nevertheless, we have shown in part II that for some market structures there is a presumption that trade is beneficial in the presence of economies of scale—indeed, that there are extra gains not captured by our usual notions of comparative advantage.

In this chapter we attempt to investigate this presumption for the model of chapter 7. Once we have done this, we turn to a consideration of the role of the "extra" gains from trade in modifying the implications of trade for income distribution.

9.1 Basic Considerations

As a first step toward an analysis of trade and welfare, we need to know precisely how changes in scale and diversity affect equilibrium utility levels. Our approach decomposes the comparison of autarky and free trade welfare into two steps. In the first step we ask whether free trade income and prices enable the economy to purchase autarky aggregate consumption quantities, provisionally disregarding the number of varieties available for consumption;

this is, disregarding the composition of these aggregates. The second step consists of deriving a welfare change that results from switching from autarky diversity levels to the free trade diversity levels. We deal in this section only with symmetrical equilibria in which firms break even.

A sufficient condition for the ability of an economy to purchase its autarky consumption levels in the free trade equilibrium is

$$\sum_{i \in I} c_i(w, x_i) X_i^A \leq \sum_{i \in I} c_i(w, x_i^A) X_i^A, \tag{9.1}$$

where $c_i(\cdot)$ are its average cost functions and w, x_i, $i \in I$, are the free trade equilibrium values of factor rewards and output levels per firm. Industry output levels X_i^A are equal to $n_i^A x_i^A$. This condition has also been used in chapter 4 in discussing gains from trade in the presence of contestable markets and in chapter 5 in discussing gains from trade in the presence of oligopolistic competition with free entry. It states that average output levels of firms are larger under free trade than in autarky.

The proof of our assertion concerning the sufficiency of (9.1) follows step by step the proofs in chapters 4 and 5. Free trade commodity prices cannot exceed average costs of production in the country under consideration, implying

$$p_i \leq c_i(w, x_i), \quad \text{for all } i.$$

Also, using the fact that autarky techniques of production are not necessarily the most efficient given free trade factor rewards, we have

$$c_i(w, x_i^A) \leq w \cdot a_i(w^A, x_i^A), \quad \text{for all } i.$$

Combining these inequalities with (9.1) and with factor market-clearing conditions, yields

$$p \cdot X^A \leq \sum_{i \in I} w \cdot a_i(w^A, x_i^A) X_i^A = w \cdot V = p \cdot X.$$

Hence the autarky consumption levels X_i^A are affordable under free trade when (9.1) is satisfied.

Indeed, condition (9.1) was shown to be sufficient for gains from trade in the cases of homogeneous products. It does not ensure, however, gains from trade in the presence of differentiated products, since, as we have seen in chapter 6, variety is valued per se. Therefore a country that can afford to purchase in the trading equilibrium the autarky consumption quantities but has to choose from a smaller diversity of products might in fact lose from trade. The second step is designed to exclude this possibility. In view of our discussion in chapter 6, it is clear that the diversity effect depends on the structure of preferences. It is therefore necessary to study separately each specification of preference, although it is clear that we are looking for an appropriate definition of average increase in diversity.

9.2 S-D-S Preferences

First, consider S-D-S preferences (in which each consumer loves variety). The consumer maximization problem is described in (6.4). By a transformation of variables, this problem can be represented as follows:

$$\max_{(\tilde{D}_1, \tilde{D}_2, \dots, \tilde{D}_I)} U(\tilde{D}_1, \tilde{D}_2, \dots, \tilde{D}_I) \tag{9.2}$$

subject to $\sum_{i \in I} \tilde{p}_i \tilde{D}_i \leq E$, where

$$\tilde{D}_i = n_i^{\sigma_i/(\sigma_i - 1)} D_i$$

is an index of consumption services derived from sector i varieties and

$$\tilde{p}_i = p_i n_i^{-1/(\sigma_i - 1)}$$

is the effective price of these services. The indirect utility function that arises from this problem is

$$U = U^*(\tilde{p}, E),$$

and we are interested in comparing $U^*(\tilde{p}^A, \tilde{p}^A \cdot \tilde{D}^A)$ with $U^*(\tilde{p}, \tilde{p} \cdot \tilde{D})$, where the superscript A stands for autarky values. Clearly the available number of varieties influences the effective prices that consumers pay for the consumption services, $\tilde{D}$ and, from the definition of $\tilde{p}$ this influence is represented by

$$n_i^{-1}/(\sigma_i - 1)_.$$

Consider therefore the following condition:

$$\sum_{i \in I} \alpha_i^* \left(\frac{n_i^A}{\bar{n}_i} \right)^{\frac{1}{\sigma_i - 1}} \leq 1, \tag{9.3}$$

where

$$\alpha_i^* = \frac{p_i X_i^A}{p \cdot X^A}.$$

This condition is certainly satisfied when there is more variety of every product in the trading equilibrium. But it can be interpreted as stating that on average there is more variety in the trading equilibrium than in autarky.

Now we state: *If average productivity and average variety do not decline as a result of trade, as measured by (9.1) and (9.3), then there are gains from trade.*

Proof:

By direct calculation,

$$\tilde{p} \cdot \tilde{D}^A = \sum_{i \in I}^{I} p_i \left(\frac{n_i^A}{\bar{n}_i}\right)^{\frac{1}{\sigma i - 1}} n_i^A D_i^A$$

$$= \sum_{i \in I} p_i X_i^A \left(\frac{n_i^A}{\bar{n}_i}\right)^{\frac{1}{\sigma i - 1}} \leq p \cdot X^A,$$

where the last inequality stems from (9.3). Hence

$$\tilde{p}^A \cdot \tilde{D}^A \leq p \cdot X^A.$$

However, (9.1) implies $p \cdot X^A \leq p \cdot X$ with $p \cdot X = \tilde{p} \cdot \tilde{D}$, which yields, on substitution,

$$\tilde{p} \cdot \tilde{D}^A \leq \tilde{p} \cdot \tilde{D}.$$

The last inequality implies

$$U^*(\tilde{p}, \tilde{p} \cdot \tilde{D}) \geq U^*(\tilde{p}, \tilde{p} \cdot \tilde{D}^A),$$

and the standard gains from trade argument implies

$$U^*(\tilde{p}, \tilde{p} \cdot \tilde{D}^A) \geq U^*(\tilde{p}^A, \tilde{p}^A \cdot \tilde{D}^A).$$

Combining the last two inequalities, we obtain

$$U^*(\tilde{p}, \tilde{p} \cdot \tilde{D}) \geq U^*(\tilde{p}^A, \tilde{p}^A \cdot \tilde{D}^A),$$

which proves the existence of gains from trade.

Thus we have seen that when average productivity and variety do not decline as a result of trade—using (9.1) and (9.3) to measure these changes—then a country gains from trade. It is useful to observe at this point that with S-D-S preferences condition (9.1) is necessarily satisfied when production functions are homothetic, because in this case the degree of monopoly power R_i is constant and the degree of economies of scale θ_i depends only on output, so that the condition $R_i = \theta_i(x_i)$ [see (7.23)] implies a unique equilibrium value of x_i when the degree of economies of scale declines with output. In this case $x_i = x_i^A$, and (9.1) holds with equality.

Our proof of the sufficiency of (9.1) and (9.3) for gains from trade suggests that the productivity condition and the diversity condition can in fact be combined into a single condition that allows for an explicit trade-off between productivity and diversity. This condition can be stated as

$$\sum_{i \in I} \alpha^{**} \frac{c_i(w, x_i)}{c_i(w, x_i^A)} \left(\frac{n_i^A}{\bar{n}_i}\right)^{\frac{1}{\sigma i - 1}} \leq 1, \tag{9.4}$$

where

$$\alpha_i^{**} = \frac{c_i(w, x_i^A) X_i^A}{\sum_{j \in I} c_j(w, x_j^A) X_j^A}.$$

We prove now that (9.4) is sufficient for gains from trade.

Proof:
From direct calculation,

$$\tilde{p} \cdot \tilde{D}^A = \sum_{i \in I} p_i X_i^A \left(\frac{n_i^A}{\bar{n}_i}\right)^{\frac{1}{\sigma i - 1}}.$$

However,

$$p_i \le c_i(w, x_i), \quad \text{for all } i.$$

Using these inequalities in conjunction with (9.4) implies

$$\tilde{p} \cdot \tilde{D}^A \le \sum_{i \in I} c_i(w, x_i) X_i^A \left(\frac{n_i^A}{\bar{n}_i}\right)^{\frac{1}{\sigma i - 1}} \le \sum_{i \in I} c_i(w, x_i^A) X_i^A.$$

However,

$$c_i(w, x_i^A) \le w \cdot a_i(w^A, x_i^A), \quad \text{for all } i.$$

Hence

$$\tilde{p} \cdot \tilde{D}^A \le w \cdot \sum_{i \in I} a_i(w^A, x_i^A) X_i^A = w \cdot V = \tilde{p} \cdot \tilde{D}.$$

Therefore $\tilde{D}^A$ is feasible in the trading equilibrium, implying $U(\tilde{D}) \ge U(\tilde{D}^A)$, namely gains from trade.

Condition (9.4) represents in a neat way the combined restrictions on productivity change and diversity change that are required for gains from trade. This restriction is more likely to be satisfied, the larger the output expansion in industries with *large* economies of scale (steep decline in average costs) and the larger the increase in variety in industries with *low* substitutability across varieties.

9.3 Lancaster Preferences

We consider only symmetrical equilibria in which varieties are evenly distributed on the circumference of a circle and all varieties of a product are equally priced. We also begin our analysis with the two-sector model in which one sector produces a homogeneous product and the other a differentiated product, with the former serving as numeraire.

In an equilibrium of this type of economy consumers end up having different utility levels. Therefore we need an index of aggregate welfare, and we choose average utility as the index. This can be interpreted in two ways. It can be thought of as a Bentham-type social welfare function which is quite popular in the public economics literature, or it can be interpreted as an expected utility level. The latter interpretation requires $U(\cdot)$ to be a von Neumann-Morgenstern utility function and the symmetrically located varieties to be drawn from a uniform distribution. It seems appropriate in the present context because the theory has nothing to say about the types of varieties that are available as opposed to their number. Hence our welfare indicator is

$$\tilde{U}(p, n, \text{GDP}) \equiv 2n \int_0^{1/2n} U^*\left[ph(\delta), \frac{\text{GDP}}{L} \right] d\delta, \tag{9.5}$$

where p is the price of every variety of the differented product and GDP/L is income per capita. Since $U^*(\cdot)$ is declining in the effective price $ph(\delta)$ and $h(\cdot)$ is an increasing function, we have:

$$\frac{\partial \tilde{U}(\cdot)}{\partial n} > 0.$$

Namely welfare increases with the number of available varieties.

Now we can establish: *If the upper tier utility function $U(\cdot)$ is Cobb-Douglas, and trade both brings about an increase in the output per firm of the differentiated product and makes more varieties available, then a country gains from trade.*

Proof:
By direct calculation (with a self-explanatory notation),

$$D_Y^A(\delta) + pD_X^A(\delta) = D_Y^A + pD_X^A = \frac{(Y^A + pX^A)}{L} \leq \frac{\text{GDP}}{L}, \quad \text{for } \delta \in (0, \frac{1}{2n^A}),$$

where the independence of the consumed quantities from δ stems from Cobb-Douglas preferences, and the inequality stems from $x \geq x^A$ via (9.1). Hence we have shown that *every* consumer (for all δ) can purchase his autarky consumption when faced with free trade income and prices, given the autarky varieties. This implies

$$\tilde{U}(p, n^A, \text{GDP}) \geq \tilde{U}(p^A, n^A, \text{GDP}^A).$$

However, since $n \geq n^A$ and $\tilde{U}(\cdot)$ is increasing in n,

$$\tilde{U}(p, n, \text{GDP}) \geq \tilde{U}(p, n^A, \text{GDP}) \geq \tilde{U}(p^A, n^A, \text{GDP}^A),$$

which proves the existence of gains from trade.

The two-sector result is easily generalized to a multisector economy in which the distribution of preferences for ideal varieties is uniform and independent across products. In this case the welfare indicator is

$$\tilde{U}(p, n, \text{GDP}) \equiv \left[\prod_{i=1}^{I} (2n_i) \right] \int_0^{1/2n_1} \cdots \int_0^{1/2n_I} U^* \left[ph(\delta), \frac{\text{GDP}}{L} \right] d\delta_1 \, d\delta_2 \ldots d\delta_I, \tag{9.6}$$

where p and n are vectors and $ph(\delta) \equiv [p_1 h_1(\delta_1), p_2 h_2(\delta_2), \ldots, p_I h_I(\delta_I)]$. Clearly $\tilde{U}(\cdot)$ is increasing in every component of n so that welfare rises with diversity. We will say that more diversity is available in the trading equilibrium if

$$\tilde{U}(p, n, \text{GDP}) \geq \tilde{U}(p, n^A, \text{GDP}). \tag{9.7}$$

This is clearly so when there are more varieties of *every* product. However, (9.7) is also satisfied in situations where fewer varieties of some products and more varieties of others are available in the trading equilibrium.

Now we establish: *If $U(\cdot)$ is Cobb-Douglas and (9.1) and (9.7) hold, then there are gains from trade.* The proof of this proposition follows step by step the proof of the gains from trade proposition for the two-sector case, and therefore it is not reproduced.

It is interesting to observe that with Cobb-Douglas preferences condition (9.7) does not depend on (p, GDP), which makes it more appealing—it never depends on GDP due to the homotheticity of $U(\cdot)$. In fact with C-D preferences, (9.7) is equivalent to

$$\gamma(n) \geq \gamma(n^A), \tag{9.7'}$$

where $\gamma(n)$ is an *exact index of diversity*, and it is defined by

$$\gamma(n) \equiv \sum_{i=1}^{I} \log \gamma_i(n_i), \tag{9.8}$$

with

$$\gamma_i(n_i) \equiv 2n_i \int_0^{1/2n_i} [h_i(\delta)]^{-\alpha_i} d\delta. \tag{9.9}$$

The functions $\log \gamma_i(n_i)$ can be interpreted as bringing to a common denominator the contribution of the number of product i varieties to total available diversity. A contribution of a product to total diversity is larger, the more rapidly its compensation function rises with distance from the ideal product; that is, the less substitution there is among varieties of a product (just as in the S-D-S case).

What happens when preferences are not of the Cobb-Douglas type? In this case consumption levels of goods depend on the distance of the consumer from his ideal product, and condition (9.1) does not ensure that for given autarky varieties every consumer can purchase his autarky consumption levels at post-trade prices and income. The point is that although the country can afford to buy in the trading equilibrium aggregate autarky consumption levels, *some* consumers may still experience a deterioration in their personal terms of trade when moving from autarky to free trade. This difficulty is well known from standard trade theory in situations without corrective income redistribution (e.g., see Caves and Jones 1981, chapter 2). It is usually resolved by allowing for costless income redistribution, and this approach can indeed also be applied to the present case. For this purpose define

$$\hat{U}(p, n, \text{GDP})$$

$$\equiv \max_{E(\delta)} \left[\prod_{i=1}^{I} (2n_i) \right] \int_0^{1/2n_1} \int_0^{1/2n_2} \cdots \int_0^{1/2_I} U^*[ph(\delta), E(\delta)] d\delta_1 d\delta_2 \ldots d\delta_I,$$

subject to $\left[\prod_{i=1}^{I} (2n_i) \right] \int_0^{1/2n_1} \int_0^{1/2n_2} \cdots \int_0^{1/2n_I} E(\delta) d\delta_1 d\delta_2 \ldots d\delta_I \leq \dfrac{\text{GDP}}{L},$

where $E(\delta) = E(\delta_1, \delta_2, \ldots, \delta_I)$ is the postdistribution income level of a consumer who uses a variety of product 1 which is a distance δ_1 from his or her ideal variety, a variety of product 2 which is a distance δ_2 from his or her ideal variety, and so on. Hence $\hat{U}(\cdot)$ is the maximum welfare attainable with an income redistribution scheme.

Using this function, replace (9.7) with the following definition of larger diversity in the trading equilibrium:

$$\hat{U}(p, n, \text{GDP}) \geq \hat{U}(p, n^A, \text{GDP}). \tag{9.7'}$$

Then we have this proposition: *If (9.1) and (9.7') hold, then there are gains from trade in the sense that*

$$\hat{U}(p, n, \text{GDP}) \geq \hat{U}(p^A, n^A, \text{GDP}^A) \geq \tilde{U}(p^A, n^A, \text{GDP}^A);$$

that is, larger average productivity and diversity in the trading equilibrium ensure higher welfare when income is optimally distributed.

The proof of this proposition also follows step by step the proof of the two-sector case, except that for current purposes one should use (9.1) to argue that aggregate autarky consumption is affordable in the trading equilibrium.

Therefore there exists an income distribution $E(\delta)$ that is feasible in the trading equilibrium, such that

$$p \cdot D^A(\delta) \leq E(\delta), \quad \text{for all autarky } \delta,$$

and it implies

$$U(p, n^A, \text{GDP}) \geq U(p^A, n^A, \text{GDP}^A).$$

Combining this formula with (9.7′) proves the proposition.

It is known from the example presented in Lawrence and Spiller (1983) that losses from trade are possible in the presence of differentiated products. We have, however, shown that there exist reasonable conditions that when satisfied, make trade gainful. These conditions are likely to be satisfied for countries that are small relative to the world economy.

9.4 Equilibrium Scale and Diversity

Our next step is to relate the sufficient conditions for gains from trade to "primitives"—to taste, technology, and resources. To do this it will be necessary to place some further restrictions on the model.

Our first restriction, used in the previous sections, is the assumption of *constant expenditure shares*. The assumption of Cobb-Douglas utility has been a useful simplification in many parts of this book. Here it ensures that the elasticity of demand facing an individual firm depends only on the number of varieties available in that industry, not on commodity prices and diversity in other industries. Consider a symmetric equilibrium in which the n_i firms in industry i all charge a price p_i. Each consumer spends a fixed share of income α_i on product i. It was shown in chapter 6 that in this case the elasticity of demand faced by a firm in industry i depends only on the number of varieties available in the industry. Hence

$$R_i(n_i) \equiv \left[1 - \frac{1}{\sigma_i(n_i)} \right]^{-1}. \tag{9.10}$$

It seems natural to expect that the elasticity of demand for individual varieties increases as variety increases, and thus that $R_i(n_i)$ is decreasing in n_i. Unfortunately this is not necessarily the case. As we will see shortly, it is much simpler to assure ourselves of gains from trade if it is true.

We now introduce another restriction: the production technology for differentiated products is *homothetic*. This has the implication that local economies of scale depend only on output. But in equilibrium we know that the degree of economies of scale must equal the degree of monopoly power:

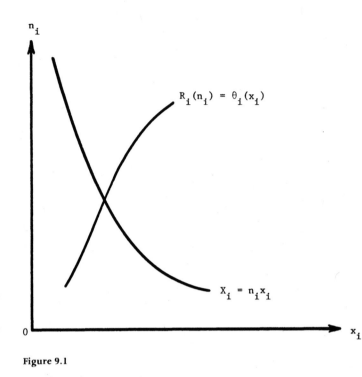

n_i

$R_i(n_i) = \theta_i(x_i)$

$X_i = n_i x_i$

0 x_i

Figure 9.1

$$R_i(n_i) = \theta_i(x_i).\tag{9.11}$$

This establishes a relationship between the scale of production and diversity, and between both and gross output $X_i = n_i x_i$.

Figures 9.1 and 9.2 summarize these relationships. They represent the thought experiment of choosing a level of gross output and finding the corresponding scale and diversity. Thus in each there is a rectangular hyperbola defined by $X_i = n_i x_i$ and another schedule defined by (9.11). It is at this point that the critical role of the relationship between diversity and the elasticity of demand emerges (we assume that economies of scale decline with output). If $R_i(n_i)$ is decreasing, we have the "normal" case illustrated in figure 9.1, where the locus $R_i(n_i) = \theta_i(x_i)$ is upward sloping. In this case an increase in gross output will be associated with an increase in both scale and diversity.

If, by contrast, $R_i(n_i)$ is decreasing in n_i, that locus will be downward sloping and might look as in figure 9.2. In this case an increase in gross output will be associated with an increase in diversity so large that average scale actually falls. We regard this as a perverse case and will assume that it does not occur.

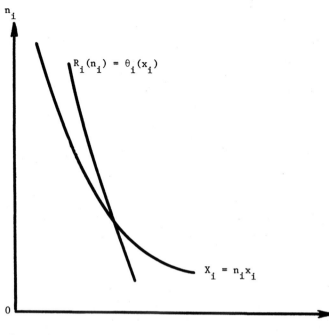

Figure 9.2

We are now able to restate our gains from trade criterion. We saw in previous sections that a country gains from trade if in general the scale of production and the diversity of products available to consumers after trade are larger than before trade. But we have just seen that under current assumptions larger scale and diversity are associated with larger industry gross output. Before trade it is the *country's* gross output that is relevent; after trade it is the *world's* output. Thus given the assumptions employed in this section, we have as a sufficient condition for gains from trade: *a country gains from trade if world output in differentiated industries is larger than the country's output in those industries would have been in autarky.* This condition can be weakened using the techniques developed in the earlier sections of this chapter, but we do not find it worthwhile to repeat the technical arguments.

This condition is very similar to the condition for gains from trade developed for the contestable markets approch in chapter 4. Like that criterion, it seems very mild. It does not require that our own country's increasing-returns sectors expand, nor indeed that any country's do so. It simply requires that results of trade not be so perverse as to lead the whole world to produce less of differentiated products than our individual country would have in the absence of trade. This seems to justify a presumption of gains from trade, and indeed of gains over and above those from conventional comparative advantage.

We have not yet, however, gone all the way to "primitives," defining the conditions for gains from trade in terms of tastes, technology, and factor endowments. This turns out to be difficult. We have only useful benchmark case. Gross output of every industry must rise if (1) industries receive constant expenditure shares, (2) technology is homothetic, and (3) all countries have the same relative factor endowments. We have already discussed this case in section 7.7. These assumptions assure that the proportional distribution of resources between industries is the same for the *world* economy after trade as for individual countries before trade and thus ensure that world output of every industry is larger than countries' autarky outputs.

9.5 Trade and Income Distribution

Increasing returns offer a potential source of gains from trade over and above that from comparative advantage, and we have just argued for a presumption that at least some of these gains will be realized in a differentiated products model. An immediate implication is that some of the standard results from comparative advantage models about trade and income distribution—results that since the analysis of Stolper and Samuelson have been known to be fairly pessimistic—may be reversed.

The basic result from constant-returns models is that owners of factors of production which are scarcer in a particular country than they are in the world as a whole are likely to lose as result of trade. In particular, the real rentals of some factors necessarily decline in terms of all goods as a result of trade. Unless there is a redistributional mechanism at work, owners of these factors will find small comfort in theorems that prove potential gains from trade; they will be made worse off.

Suppose, however, that there are increasing returns that provide additional gains. Then, if the changes in relative factor rewards are not too large, and the extra gains from larger scale are large enough, everyone might gain from trade. This will presumably happen if countries are sufficiently similar in relative factor endowments and if economies of scale are sufficiently important.

But what do we mean by the "similarity" of factor endowments and "importance" of scale economics? We know roughly what is meant here but do not have any general index of either concept. To solidify our intuition, we need to move to more structured examples.

Example 9.1 (Krugman 1981)

Consider a world of two countries, two factors, and two industries. Tastes for variety are assumed to be of the S-D-S form, and the upper tier utility function is Cobb-Douglas. Expenditure shares are assumed to be equal for the two industries, and the elasticity of demand for individual products, σ_i, is assumed to be the same in both industries; that is, $\sigma_i = \sigma$, $i = 1, 2$.

Technology also takes a special form. The two factors are assumed to be entirely sector specific, with input i used only in industry i. The production functions thus have only one argument, and they are assumed to be the same in both countries and both industries:

$$x_1 = f(l_1),$$

$$x_2 = f(l_2).$$

The degree of returns to scale in each sector is given as $\theta(x_i)$ and assumed to be decreasing with scale.

The final specializing assumption is on the distribution of world endowments. These are assumed to be such that after trade the two countries have equal GDP. Figure 9.3 illustrates the distributions of world endowments that produce the result. Given the symmetry of the setup, total income received by each factor is the same after trade; thus the locus of equal GDP is the diagonal from northwest to southeast. We can parameterize this locus as follows: choose units so the *world* endowment of each factor is 2; then country endowments are

$$L_1 = 2 - z, \quad L_1^* = z,$$

$$L_2 = z, \quad\quad L_2^* = 2 - z, \quad 0 < z < 1.$$

It is easy to see that as z ranges between 0 and 2, all allocations with equal GDP are traced out. We will only examine the range $0 < z < 1$; the other corner of the box is a mirror image and need not be separately considered. We can obviously interpret z as an index of the similarity of the two countries.

Let us begin with the closed economies. In each country firms will enter until profits are zero; this will give us our usual conditions:

$$p_i^A = \frac{w_i^A f^{-1}(x_i)}{x_i}, \quad p_i^{A*} = \frac{w_i^{A*} f^{-1}(x_i^*)}{x_i^*}, \quad i = 1, 2, \tag{9.12}$$

$$R = \theta(x_i), \quad R = \theta(x_i^*), \quad i = 1, 2, \tag{9.13}$$

where

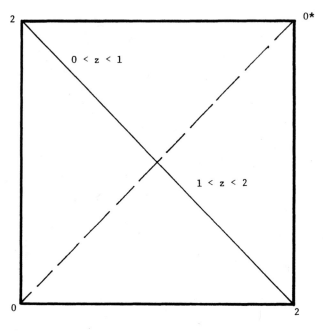

Figure 9.3

$$R = \left(1 - \frac{1}{\sigma}\right)^{-1}.$$

Since R is independent of the diversity of products available, (9.13) fixes outputs per firm at

$$x = x_i = x_i^*, \quad i = 1, 2. \tag{9.14}$$

The diversity of products is determined by full-employment conditions. Defining

$$l = f^{-1}(x)$$

as the input level per firm, which is in this equilibrium the same in both countries and industries, we have $n_i = L_i/l$ and $n_i^* = L_i^*/l$, or

$$n_1 = \frac{2 - z}{l}, \quad n_1^* = \frac{z}{l}, \tag{9.15a}$$

$$n_2 = \frac{z}{l}, \quad n_2^* = \frac{2 - z}{l}. \tag{9.15b}$$

Finally, clearing of commodity markets requires the value of output to be the same in every industry, because half of total spending is allocated to each industry. Hence

$$p_1^A n_1 x = p_2^A n_2 x, \quad p_1^{A*} n_1^* x = p_2^{A*} n_2^* x. \tag{9.16}$$

These are the equilibrium conditions. It is clear from them that the equilibrium of the home country is a mirror image of the equilibrium of the foreign country, with industry i in the home country looking like industry $j \neq i$ in the foreign country. It is also clear that output levels per firm and the number of firms in every industry are the same in autarky as in a free trade equilibrium, and we have indeed not used superscript A for these variables. This means, in particular, that trade does not affect productivity, so its welfare implications can be traced through changes in commodity prices, factor rewards, and available diversity. Using (9.12), (9.14), (9.15), and (9.16), and choosing good 1 to be the numeraire, autarky prices and factor rewards are calculated to be

$$p_1^A = 1, \qquad p_1^{A*} = 1,$$

$$p_2^A = \frac{(2-z)}{z}, \qquad p_2^{A*} = \frac{z}{(2-z)},$$

$$w_1^A = xl, \qquad w_1^{A*} = \frac{x}{l},$$

$$w_2^A = \frac{(2-z)x}{zl}, \qquad w_2^{A*} = \frac{zx}{(2-z)l}.$$

Now consider the trading equilibrium. Output levels per firm are the same as before and so is the number of firms in every country and industry. However, (9.12) and (9.16) are replaced by

$$p_i = \frac{w_i l}{x}, \quad p_i = \frac{w_i^* l}{x}, \quad i = 1, 2, \tag{9.12'}$$

$$p_1(n_1 + n_1^*)x = p_2(n_2 + n_2^*)x. \tag{9.16'}$$

Combing these conditions with (9.15) and using good 1 as numeraire, we obtain

$$p_1 = p_2 = 1,$$

$$w_1 = w_2 = w_1^* = w_2^* = \frac{x}{l}.$$

Hence trade brings about equalization of factor prices.

What about gains from trade? Since in the trading equilibrium output per firm is the same as in autarky and the number of varieties available in the trading equilibrium is $\bar{n}_i = n_i + n_i^*$, which is larger than in autarky, then condition (9.4) is satisfied, implying gains from trade for both countries. However, if ownership of factors of production is not evenly distributed in the population, then these gains are not equally shared. Indeed, by comparing equilibrium factor reward structures, one observes that as a result of moving from autarky to free trade there is a decline in relative rewards for the scarce factor in each country; factor 2 in country 1, and the symmetrically placed factor 1 in country 2. Since the assumed functional forms make the equilibrium values derived earlier independent of the distribution of the ownership of factors of production, it is relatively simple to calculate the welfare effect on owners of factors that result from trade.

It is clear intuitively that when $z = 1$, every factor gains from trade. However, as z becomes smaller, the Stolper-Samuelson effect reduces the welfare of factor 2 in the home country and factor 1 in the foreign country. The question we ask is how small can z be without causing losses from trade to either one of these factors.

Taking a logarithmic transformation of the Cobb-Douglas utility function, we calculate the equilibrium utility level of a person with income E to be

$$U = \frac{1}{\sigma - 1} \sum_{i=1}^{2} \log n_i + \sum_{i=1}^{2} \log \left(\frac{E}{p_i} \right).$$

This means that the welfare gain from trade for factor 2 in country 1 is

$$U_2 - U_2^A = \frac{1}{\sigma - 1} \sum_{i=1}^{2} [\log (n_i + n_i^*) - \log n_i]$$

$$+ \sum_{i=1}^{2} \left[\log \left(\frac{w_2}{p_i} \right) - \log \left(\frac{w_2^A}{p_i^A} \right) \right].$$

Substituting the equilibrium values into this expression, we obtain

$$U_2 - U_2^A = \frac{1}{\sigma - 1} [2 \log 2 - \sigma \log (2 - z) - (2 - \sigma) \log z]. \tag{9.17}$$

The same expression applies to the scarce factor of the foreign country.

It is clear from the right-hand side of (9.17) that as long as the elasticity of substitution is smaller than or equal to two (i.e., $1 < \sigma \leq 2$), then the scarce factors gain from trade (remember that $0 < z \leq 1$). Hence, if there is not "too much" substitutability across varieties, *everyone* gains from trade, independent of the distribution of factor ownership. If, however, $\sigma > 2$, then the right-hand side of (9.17) is an increasing function of z, and it is negative for z

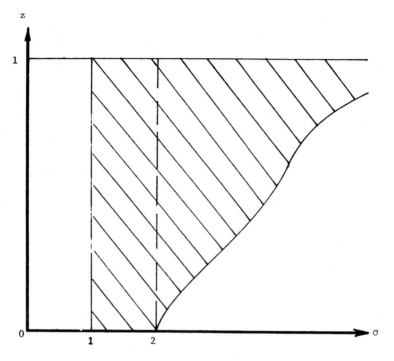

Figure 9.4

close to zero. Hence for every $\sigma > 2$, there exists a unique $\underline{z}$ such that for

$$\underline{z} \leq z < 1$$

the scarce factors do not lose from trade. The shaded area in figure 9.4 describes combinations of (σ, z) for which the scarce factors gain from trade.

This example thus illustrates the general point that we made earlier: if countries are sufficiently similar and there are important increasing returns— a state giving rise to the prevalence of intraindustry trade—scarce as well as abundant factors gain from trade.

References

Caves, Richard E., and Jones, Ronald W. *World Trade and Payments.* Boston: Little Brown, 1981.

Krugman, Paul R. "Intraindustry Specialization and the Gains from Trade." *Journal of Political Economy* 89 (1981): 959–973.

Lawrence, Colins, and Spiller, Pablo T. "Product Diversity, Economies of Scale and International Trade." *Quarterly Journal of Economics* 98 (1983): 63–83.

10   Transport Costs and
        Nontraded Goods

Up to this point our entire analysis—with the exception of our brief discussion of market segmentation in chapter 5—has been based on the assumption that goods can be transported internationally without cost. Yet it is clear that transport costs can have important consequences in the presence of economies of scale. By partially or wholly segmenting markets, transport costs give the size of the *domestic* market an important role. Defining that role is the main purpose of this chapter.

In this chapter we approach the effects of transport costs in two ways. The first is to adopt the common simplification of assuming that transport costs are either negligble or prohibitive; that is, that industries can be partitioned into fixed sets of costlessly tradable and completely nontradable goods. In the first section we further assume that all nontradable goods are produced with *constant* returns and show that this leaves our basic analysis essentially intact. In the second section we allow some goods produced with increasing returns to be nontradable. This introduces further complications: only with strong additional assumptions can we still say anything useful about trade patterns.

Nontraded goods produced with increasing returns create an incentive for factor movements, even when factor prices are equalized internationally. This incentive needs to be analyzed carefully; we offer some insights in the third section.

Finally, in the fourth section we take the other approach, that of explicit modeling of transport costs that are less than prohibitive. This is a difficult problem even in traditional models and more so here. We are able to explore it only through a special example. Yet the example is useful for it illustrates what we believe to be an important principle, the effect of *market size*; that is, the tendency of increasing-returns industries, other things equal, to concentrate production near their larger markets and export to smaller markets.

10.1 The Model with Nontraded Goods

As a first step toward an analysis of transport costs, we modify the basic model of chapter 7 by adding some constant-returns sectors producing nontradable goods. This modification essentially does not change the analysis of trade patterns.

As we have repeatedly found, the $2 \times 2 \times 3$ case is a good starting point. Let there be two countries, two factors of production, and three industries. Let industry 2 consist of many differentiated varieties, assumed costlessly tradable; industry 3 be a tradable constant-returns sector; and industry 1 be a *nontradable* constant-returns sector.

As usual we can derive a region of factor price equalization. First, we derive the integrated world equilibrium and find the input vectors $\bar{V}(1)$, $\bar{V}(2)$, and $\bar{V}(3)$ in that equilibrium. We then allocate these vectors between our two countries. There is only one new restriction. Since good 1 cannot be traded, its production must be allocated in proportion to countries' consumption (see chapter 1). In the case of identical homothetic tastes this means that if country j has a share s^j of world income, it must allocate resources $s^j \bar{V}(1)$ to the nontradable industry. Of course s^j is not independent of the country's endowment: $s^j = w \cdot V^j / w \cdot \bar{V}$, where w is the factor price vector in the integrated equilibrium.

To analyze the model, we proceed in two stages. First, we derive the set of endowments consistent with equal factor prices for a *given* distribution of world income and determine the pattern of production and trade given the endowment point. Then, we sketch out how the entire factor price equalization set can be derived (this is identical to the procedure in chapter 1).

Consider figure 10.1 in which we examine only endowments where the share of the domestic country in world income is $s = \overline{OC}/\overline{OO^*}$. If factor prices are equalized, the locus of endowments preserving the division of world income will be a downward-sloping line passing through point C, with slope $- w_L/w_K$; this line is shown as BB' in the figure. Also shown are the input vectors from the integrated equilibrium:

$$\bar{V}(1) = OQ_1 = O^*Q_1',$$

$$\bar{V}(2) = Q_1 Q_2 = Q_1' Q_2',$$

$$\bar{V}(3) = Q_2 O^* = Q_2' O.$$

Production of the nontraded good must be allocated between countries in proportion to their shares of world income. The resource allocation can be obtained as follows. First, draw through point C a line parallel to the *sum* of the

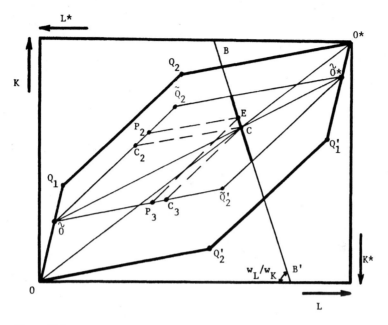

Figure 10.1

tradable input vectors $Q_1 Q_2$ and $Q_2 O^*$. This is shown as $\tilde{O}\tilde{O}^*$. It is immediately apparent from the geometry that $\overline{O\tilde{O}}/\overline{OQ_1} = \overline{OC}/\overline{OO^*}$ and similarly that $\overline{O^*\tilde{O}^*}/\overline{O^*Q_1'} = \overline{O^*C}/\overline{OO^*}$. Thus $O\tilde{O}$ is the home country's allocation of resource to the nontradable industry, and $O^*\tilde{O}^*$ is the foreign country's allocation to that industry.

The points $\tilde{O}$ and $\tilde{O}^*$ can now serve in effect as new origins for the allocation of resources to tradables. Factor price equalization requires that we be able to employ fully the remaining resources, using the integrated economy techniques; this means that the endowment point must lie in the parallelogram $\tilde{O}\tilde{Q}_2\tilde{O}^*\tilde{Q}_2'$. But we constructed the parallelogram on the assumption that the endowment lies on BB'. So the relevant set is that part of BB' lying inside the parallelogram, that is, the heavy part of BB'.

Suppose the endowment point is E; then we can follow the same procedure as in chapter 7 to obtain the pattern of production and trade. We require full employment of the supply of factor services represented by the endowment point; this implies home country allocations of resources to the industries $\tilde{O}P_2$ and $\tilde{O}P_3$. We also know that with identical homothetic tastes each country's consumption of factor services must lie on the diagonal, at point C. Thus factors devoted to the home country's consumption are $O\tilde{O}$, $\tilde{O}C_2$, and $\tilde{O}C_3$.

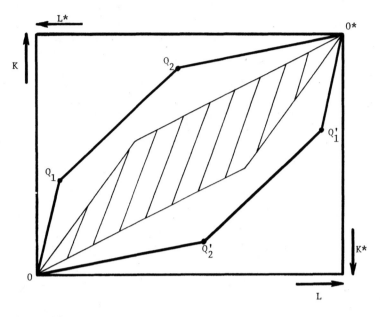

Figure 10.2

The home country is a net exporter of industry 2's products, and a net importer of industry 3's products, and net trade in factor services is measured by EC.

These results have been derived for a given world distribution of income, but it is now straightforward to proceed with the general analysis. We can sweep out the entire factor price equalization set by moving BB' from O to O^*. Clearly any point on OO^* lies in the set; the whole set is as shown by the shaded area in figure 10.2, a parallelogram running from O to O^*. As the figure shows, the factor price equalization set is smaller than the hexagon which would define that set if good 1 were tradable.

These results have been derived for a $2 \times 2 \times 3$ model, but they are as usual generalizable to more factors, goods, and countries. The integrated equilibrium is identical to that in chapter 7. The factor price equalization set is now, however, more constrained. Let I_N be the set of nontradable goods; then we have

$$\text{FPE} = \left\{ (V^1, V^2, \ldots, V^J) \mid \lambda_{ij} \geq 0, \sum_{j \in J} \lambda_{ij} = 1 \text{ for all } i \in I \right.$$

$$\text{and } \lambda_{ij} = w \cdot V^j / w \cdot \bar{V} \text{ for } i \in I_N \text{ such that } V^j = \sum_{i \in I} \lambda_{ij} \bar{V}(i)$$

$$\left. \text{for all } j \in J \right\}.$$

Obviously this set has full dimensionality only if the number of *tradable* sectors is at least as large as the number of factors; and it is also obvious that the factor price equalization set is smaller because some goods are nontradable. Nevertheless, the basic result of this section is that nontradables can be added to the model without much difficulty if they are all produced with constant returns.

10.2 Nontraded Goods Produced with Increasing Returns

Suppose that we retain the approach laid out in the previous section and continue to assume that factor prices are equalized through trade, but now allow some increasing-returns sectors to produce nontradable outputs. How does this modify the analysis?

The crucial point in this case is that *it is no longer possible to reproduce the integrated equilibrium through trade.* There may still be factor price equalization, but this does not have the usual interpretation that the location of productive factors does not matter; in general, both the scale of production and the diversity of products available to consumers in any one country will be less than in the integrated world economy.

The failure to reproduce the integrated economy poses difficulties in predicting the trade pattern. In the last section, as in previous chapters, we were able to go from identical homothetic preferences and factor price equalization directly to a statement of net trade in embodied factor services. Once some increasing-returns sectors become nontraded, the analysis breaks down in two ways. First, because relative prices and the diversity of products available are different in each country—both from one another and from those in the integrated world economy—*the shares of expenditure falling on industries will not be the same in different countries,* even with identical homothetic preferences.

Second, because the scale of production will vary across countries, *the factor intensity of the same industry will vary among countries.*

These two problems in combination make any general propositions about the trade pattern difficult. It is possible, however, to continue to apply our usual analysis in one special but useful case. This is the case of *constant expenditure shares* and *homothetic production functions.* In this case, resources devoted to each nontraded industry in a country will simply be proportional to that country's income.

To see this, note that with homothetic technology the price of good i in country j, will be

$$p_i^j = \frac{\tilde{c}_i(w)}{\bar{c}_i(x_i^j)},$$ (10.1)

where x_i^j is the output per firm in that country. Also the unit input of factor l into that industry will be

$$a_{li}(w, x_i^j) = \frac{\tilde{a}_{li}(w)}{\bar{c}_i(x_i^j)}, \quad \text{for all } l \in N.$$ (10.2)

The total allocation of l to sector i is therefore

$$V_l^j(i) = a_{li}(w, x_i^j) X_i^j$$
$$= \frac{x_{li}(w) X_i^j}{\bar{c}_i(x_i^j)}.$$ (10.3)

Finally, the constant expenditure share implies the equilibrium condition for nontradables

$$p_i^j X_i^j = \alpha_i \text{GNP}^j,$$ (10.4)

where α_i is the industry's share of expenditures and GNP is the country's income.

Conditions (10.1)–(10.4) imply the following condition for allocation of factor l to nontradable section i

$$V_l^j(i) = \frac{\alpha_i \text{GNP}^j \tilde{a}_{li}(w)}{\tilde{c}_i(w)}, \quad \text{for } i \in I_N.$$ (10.5)

Thus if factor prices are equalized, each country devotes resources to nontradables in proportion to its share of world income.

Although the allocation of factors is the same as in the integrated equalibrium, the results are not. In particular, both diversity and the scale of production of differentiated products will be less than in the integrated economy —the difference being greater, the smaller the country's share of world income.

Formally the diversity and scale of production in a particular nontraded industry i in a country, are determined by two relationships. First, profit maximization plus free entry require that returns to scale equal the ratio of price to marginal revenue:

$$R_i(n_i^j) = \theta_i(x_i^j),$$ (10.6)

where n_i^j is the number of differentiated products produced by industry i in country j. As in chapter 7, we assume that $\theta_i(x_i)$ is decreasing in output and that

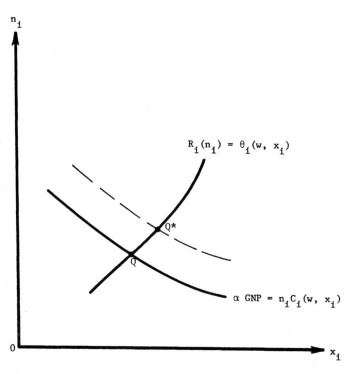

Figure 10.3

$R_i(n_i)$ is decreasing in diversity. This implies that (10.6) can be drawn as an upward-sloping line in (n_i^j, x_i^j) space, as in figure 10.3.

The other relationship is market clearing. Since there are no profits in equilibrium, total expenditure on an industry's output must equal the total cost of production:

$$\alpha_i \text{GNP}^j = n_i^j C_i(w, x_i^j), \tag{10.7}$$

This can be represented as a downward-sloping curve in (n_i^j, x_i^j) space, as in figure 10.3.

Now in comparing countries with each other, the only difference is in income. In the trading economy the relationship (10.6) will be unaffected by country size, but (10.7) will be shifted outward for countries with large income. As the figure shows, larger countries will have both larger scale and greater diversity than smaller countries in every nontraded increasing-returns sector.

10.3 Factor Mobility

We have just seen that larger countries will produce more nontraded differentiated products at a larger scale (and thus lower price) than smaller. This means that even if factor prices are equalized across countries, the *real* earnings of factors are not. For this section let us assume S-D-S preferences, so that all households have the same tastes. Then we can say unambiguously that a household owning a given bundle of factors will be better off if it resides in country 1 than in country 2 if country 1 has a larger GNP (*not* GDP), as we will see in a moment. This appears to create an incentive for factor movement toward larger countries. Such movement will only increase these countries' scale advantage, possibly leading to a cumulative process (see Helpman and Razin 1980).

In analyzing this possibility, it is crucial to ask whether the owners of factors of production move with their factors. In principle there can be three forms of migration: (1) owners and factors move together, (2) factors move but owners do not, and (3) owners move but factors do not. There have been important real-world examples of all three. The first may be illustrated by traditional migration, the immigrants bringing their labor and human capital with them. The second may be illustrated by international capital movements, with individuals who invest abroad spending part of their income on domestic nontraded goods. The third case can be illustrated for the nineteenth century by absentee Irish landlords living in London, for the twentieth by oil sheiks taking up residence in Beverly Hills. It is useful to consider each case in turn.

Suppose then that factors and their owners always move together. If factor prices are equalized, any household will be unambiguously better off if it moves to a country with a larger share of world income and expenditure. Such movement will make large countries larger and small countries smaller. In the limiting case where all factors are perfectly mobile, there will be a number of possible equilibria. Some equilibria involve two or more countries having exactly the same share of world income; this looks unstable, though we have not specified a dynamic adjustment process. The other equilibria are with all factors of production concentrated in one country, thus achieving the integrated world economy. Which country gets the honor is arbitrary.

Next suppose alternatively that factors of production can be moved without their owners. This case is fundamentally different in two ways. First, if factor prices are equalized, there is no incentive for factor movement. A household that rents some of the factors of production it owns to firms in another country does not thereby reap the advantages of lower prices and greater diversity of nontraded goods in that country. Second, there is no cumulative process tending to magnify inequality of size. The scale of nontraded goods industries depends on the size of the demand from domestic residents. If factors of production are imported, but the earnings of these factors are expatriated abroad—that is, if GDP increases but GNP does not—then scale does not increase and no benefits are gained.

Finally, consider the third case where owners of factors move but factors do not. This is more like the first case than the second. There is a clear incentive to move to larger countries. When owners move, they enlarge the nontradable sectors of their new homes and thereby reinforce their advantage. In the limiting case of perfect mobility one country—it is arbitrary which— becomes the world's *rentier*.

These polar cases are obviously too extreme to be very realistic. A reasonable model would distinguish between mobile and immobile factors of production and between mobile and immobile owners, with some relationship between factor ownership and the characteristics of the owners. For example, one might have immobile land owned by mobile landlords, mobile capital owned by immobile capitalists, and mobile laborers who take their labor with them.

There is a general point that emerges from this analysis, however; this is that the crucial effect of factor movements is their effect on the size of the market, not on the volume of production. These will sometimes move together, but not always.

10.4 Transport Costs and Market Size Effects

So far we have dealt with transport costs only by the extreme device of making them either zero or prohibitive of trade. What we would like to do now is to analyze the more general case where transport costs limit trade without necessarily eliminating it. Unfortunately this is a quite complex subject. All that we can do here is develop a special example. The example is nevertheless useful because it illustrates what is surely an important principle: the tendency of increasing-returns industries, other things equal, to locate where their markets are largest and export to other markets (see Krugman 1980).

Our example depends on a number of simplifying assumptions. First, we assume that there are only two industries, one producing a differentiated product and the other a homogeneous product. We assume constant expenditure shares, and let the subutility in the differentiated sector take the S-D-S form.

We assume that there are two countries, but only one factor of production, and that the homogeneous product is costlessly tradable and both countries produce it after trade. This ensures that the wage rate will be the same in both countries. In other words, we arrange matters so that the relative size of markets for the differentiated product is the only determinant of the trade pattern.

If market size is to matter, it must be costly to ship the differentiated product. We assume that these costs take a special form, the "iceberg" transport technology: for every unit shipped, only $1/\tau$ units arrive, where $\tau > 1$.

The strong structure we have put on our example allows us easily to derive prices and output per firm. Suppose provisionally that all firms charge a price p and that there are n domestic firms, n^* foreign firms. The price to consumers of an imported variety will be $p\tau$. Solving the consumer's maximization problem, it is clear that the demand of *domestic* residents for a *domestic* product is

$$D = \frac{p^{-\sigma}}{np^{1-\sigma} + n^*(p\tau)^{1-\sigma}} \alpha wL, \tag{10.8}$$

where α is the share of spending falling on the differentiated product and wL is the home country's income. Similarly the demand of *foreign* residents for a *domestic* product is

$$D^* = \frac{(p\tau)^{-\sigma}}{np^{1-\sigma} + n^*(p\tau)^{1-\sigma}} \alpha wL^*. \tag{10.9}$$

The overall demand for the product is $D + D^*$. If firms regard themselves as too small to affect the denominators, they will see themselves as facing a combined export and domestic demand curve with constant elasticity σ. This immediately tells us that output per firm will obey the equilibrium condition

$$R = \theta(x), \tag{10.10}$$

where as usual $R = (1 - 1/\sigma)^{-1}$.

Since the situation of firms in the foreign country is the same, this fixes output per firm in both countries. But since we have equal wage rates and average cost pricing, the prices charged per firm in each country will also be the same,

$$p = w\bar{c}(x). \tag{10.11}$$

Next we turn to market clearing. The gross output of the differentiated industry in each country [from (10.8) and (10.9)] is given by

$$X = nx$$

$$= \frac{np^{-\sigma}}{np^{1-\sigma} + n^*(p\tau)^{1-\sigma}} \alpha wL + \frac{n(p\tau)^{-\sigma}}{n(p\tau)^{1-\sigma} + n^*p^{1-\sigma}} \alpha wL^*\tau, \tag{10.12}$$

$$X^* = n^*x$$

$$= \frac{n^*(p\tau)^{-\sigma}}{np^{1-\sigma} + n^*(p\tau)^{1-\sigma}} \alpha w L\tau + \frac{n^* p^{-\sigma}}{n(p\tau)^{1-\sigma} + n^* p^{1-\sigma}} \alpha w L^*. \tag{10.13}$$

Note that we have to multiply foreign demand by τ to take account of indirect demand for goods used up in transit.

We can simplify the notation by choosing units so that $w = p = 1$ and by defining $\rho = \tau^{1-\sigma} < 1$. The equations then become

$$\frac{x}{\alpha} = \frac{1}{n + n^*\rho} L + \frac{\rho}{np + n^*} L^*, \tag{10.14}$$

$$\frac{x}{\alpha} = \frac{\rho}{n + n^*\rho} L + \frac{1}{np + n^*} L^*. \tag{10.15}$$

These are two equations in n and n^*. They may not have nonzero solutions for both n and n^*; if they do not, the solution will be either

$$n = 0, \quad n^* = \frac{\alpha(L + L^*)}{x},$$

or

$$n = \frac{\alpha(L + L^*)}{x}, \quad n^* = 0.$$

If both n and n^* are positive, we can solve (10.14) and (10.15) to get

$$n = \frac{\alpha}{(1 - \rho)x}(L - \rho L^*), \tag{10.16}$$

$$n^* = \frac{\alpha}{(1 - \rho)x}(L^* - \rho L). \tag{10.17}$$

One more definition will allow a final simplification. Let $s_n = n/(n + n^*)$, $s_L = L/(L + L^*)$; that is s_n and s_L are the shares of the home country in output of the increasing-returns industry and in labor, respectively. Then taking account of the possibility of zero output, we have

$$s_n = \begin{cases} 0, & \text{for } s_L \leq \dfrac{\rho}{1 + \rho}, \\[2ex] (1 - \rho)^{-1}[(1 + \rho)s_L - \rho], & \text{for } \dfrac{\rho}{1 + \rho} < s_L < \dfrac{1}{1 + \rho}, \\[2ex] 1, & \text{for } s_L \geq \dfrac{1}{1 + \rho}. \end{cases} \tag{10.18}$$

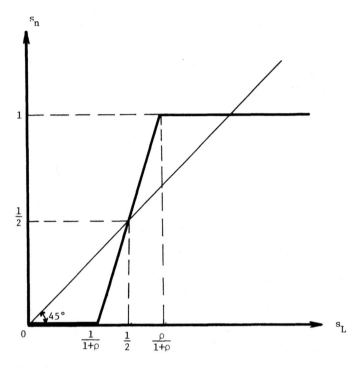

Figure 10.4

Figure 10.4 illustrates the implications of (10.18). First, it is immediately apparent that both countries will produce the differentiated product only if s_L lies in the range

$$\frac{\rho}{1 + \rho} < s_L < \frac{1}{1 + \rho}.$$

If $s_L > 1/(1 + \rho)$, we will be driven to a solution in which only the home country produces the product; if $s_L < \rho/(1 + \rho)$, only the foreign country produces it. This means that if countries are sufficiently unequal in size, whichever country is larger will produce all the increasing-returns products. Note that the width of the band of nonspecialization depends on ρ, which in turn depends on our index of transport costs τ. If transport costs are low, $t \cong 1$, then $\tilde{p} = 1$, and even small differences in country size will lead the differentiated product industry to concentrate in the larger country.

Within the band of incomplete specialization the relationship between s_L and s_n is steeper than a 45° line; thus whichever country is larger will have a more than proportional share of varieties and will therefore run a trade surplus in differentiated products.

We have shown for this example then that in the presence of transport costs the differentiated industry tends to concentrate in the larger market. In effect a large domestic market serves as a base for exports—a proposition that has always seemed plausible to practical people but is hard to capture in formal models. We have been able to work only with a highly specialized example; it is probable, however, that "home market effects" of the kind we have illustrated here are actually quite pervasive.

References

Helpman, Elhanan, and Razin, Assaf. "Monopolistic Competition and Factor Movements." Seminar Paper No. 155. Institute for International Economic Studies, University of Stockholm, 1980.

Krugman, Paul. "Scale Economies, Product Differentiation, and the Pattern of Trade." *American Economic Review* 70 (1980): 950–959.

11   Intermediate Inputs

Our analysis of trade in differentiated products so far has assumed that all goods are final goods. In reality, however, a large proportion of trade is in intermediate inputs. And some authors, particularly Ethier (1979, 1982), have argued that it is in intermediate rather than final goods production that product differentiation is most important. In other worlds, the taste for variety implicit in the demand for ever more-specialized machine tools, motors, control mechanisms, and so forth, is a more powerful source of trade and gains from trade than the desire for variety by ultimate consumers. This is a plausible suggestion, and trade in differentiated intermediate goods is certainly important enough for us to ask whether introducing it changes our basic results.

We will show in this chapter that the pattern of trade in a world with product differentiation in intermediate goods depends crucially on whether or not these goods are tradable. If they are, the analysis is similar to that with differentiated final goods. If, however, intermediate goods are not tradable, the results change considerably.

11.1 Integrated Equilibrium

Suppose that there are three goods produced in the world economy: two homogeneous final goods, X and Y, and a differentiated intermediate product Z. X and Y are produced at constant returns to scale and in perfectly competitive markets. Z is produced with variety-specific increasing returns to scale, and the Z market is characterized by monopolistic competition. Good Y, which we choose as numeraire, is produced using only the primary inputs K and L; thus we can write a unit cost function for Y:

$$c_Y(w_L, w_K).$$

Good X, however, is produced with constant returns to scale, using not only K and L but also a number of varieties of the intermediate input Z. We will assume that if all varieties available are sold at the same price p_Z, we can write an average cost function for X of the form

$$c_X(w_L, w_K, p_Z, n),$$

where n is the number of available varieties of Z. Diversity will be assumed to be "productive" in the sense that $c_X(\cdot)$ is decreasing in n.

A number of special production models can give rise to a cost function of this form. For example, Ethier (1982) has suggested a formulation in which individual varieties of the intermediate enter symmetrically into a constant elasticity of substitution production function, in a fashion analogous to Spence-Dixit-Stiglitz consumption preferences. In Ethier's formulation no capital and labor are used in producing the final good. We can easily introduce these factors by writing a two-level production function of the form

$$X = f[L, K; \Phi(Z_1, Z_2, \ldots)], \tag{11.1}$$

where $f(\cdot)$ exhibits constant returns to scale, Z_ω, $\omega = 1, 2, \ldots$, is the input of variety ω of Z, and

$$\Phi(Z_1, Z_2, \ldots) = \left[\sum_\omega Z_\omega^\beta \right]^{1/\beta},$$

where $\beta = 1 - 1/\sigma$.

It is straightforward to show that (11.1) implies an average cost function of the form

$$c(w_L, w_K, p_Z n^{-1/\sigma}),$$

where $c(\cdot)$ is the unit cost function associated with $f(\cdot)$. Thus the larger is n, the lower the effective price of *intermediate* inputs.

In the appendix to this chapter we show a Lancaster-type formulation of differentiated intermediate products, which leads to similar results.

We assume that each variety of the intermediate input is produced with the same decreasing average cost function:

$$c_Z(w_L, w_K, z),$$

where z is the production of each variety. The degree of economies of scale in the production of intermediate inputs is

$$\theta_Z(w_L, w_K, z).$$

On the demand side we assume as usual that everyone has the same homothetic preferences. Thus a share $\alpha_X(p)$ of expenditure falls on X, $\alpha_Y(p)$ on Y, where $p = (p_X, p_Y)$. This determines demand for final goods.

Demand for the intermediate good Z reflects the input choices of firms producing X. We will assume that the producer of each individual variety takes as given the output of X, the factor prices w_L and w_K, and the prices of other firms producing varieties of Z. The perceived elasticity of demand facing producers of Z will thus generally depend on the factor prices, the prices of varieties of Z, and the number of available varieties; then the elasticity of demand will take the form

$$\sigma(w_L, w_K, p_Z, n).$$

In particular cases this formulation can be simpler. If the production function takes the form (11.1), and the number of available varieties is large, each producer will simply face a fixed elasticity of demand σ.

Corresponding to the elasticity of demand is a degree of monopoly power,

$$R(w_L, w_K, p_Z, n) = \left[1 - \frac{1}{\sigma(\cdot)} \right]^{-1}.$$

We can now describe the equilibrium of an integrated world economy. First, we need pricing conditions for our three sectors. Good Y is the numeraire and is produced competitively and sold at marginal cost. Thus we must have

$$1 = c_Y(w_L, w_K). \tag{11.2}$$

Good X is also produced by competitive firms, so the pricing equation is

$$p = c_X(w_L, w_K, p_Z, \bar{n}). \tag{11.3}$$

The Z industry is monopolistically competitive. Then with monopolistic competition and free entry which drives profits to zero, we can describe the simultaneous determination of the price of Z and of output per firm by the two equations (see chapter 7):

$$p_Z = c_Z(w_L, w_K, z), \tag{11.4}$$

$$R(w_L, w_K, p_Z, \bar{n}) = \theta_Z(w_L, w_K, z). \tag{11.5}$$

Factor market-clearing conditions can be described using the cost functions. In each sector per unit factor demands are the derivative of the cost function:

$$a_{lY}(w_L, w_K) = \frac{\partial c_Y(w_L, w_K)}{\partial w_l}, \qquad l = L, K,$$

$$a_{lX}(w_L, w_K, p_Z, \bar{n}) = \frac{\partial c_X(w_L, w_K, p_Z, \bar{n})}{\partial w_l}, \qquad l = L, K,$$

$$a_{lZ}(w_L, w_K, z) = \frac{\partial c_Z(w_L, w_K, z)}{\partial w_l}, \qquad l = L, K.$$

Thus factor market-clearing conditions take the form

$$a_{LY}(w_L, w_K)\bar{Y} + a_{LX}(w_L, w_K, p_Z, \bar{n})\bar{X} + a_{LZ}(w_L, w_K, z)\bar{Z} = \bar{L}, \qquad (11.6)$$

$$a_{KZ}(w_L, w_K)\bar{Y} + a_{KX}(w_L, w_K, p_Z, \bar{n})\bar{X} + a_{KZ}(w_L, w_K, z)\bar{Z} = \bar{K}, \qquad (11.7)$$

where $Z = \bar{n}z$.

Finally, we turn to goods market clearing. The essential point here is that inputs of Z are like a productive factor in the X industry, so we can derive per unit use of Z by differentiating the average cost function:

$$a_{ZX}(w_L, w_K, p_Z, \bar{n}) = \frac{\partial c_X(w_L, w_K, p_Z, \bar{n})}{\partial p_Z}.$$

Thus the output of Z in the integrated economy is

$$\bar{Z} = a_{ZX}(w_L, w_K, p_Z, \bar{n})\bar{X}. \qquad (11.8)$$

The market-clearing condition for X (we can omit Y because of the budget constraint) is

$$\alpha_X(p) = \frac{p\bar{X}}{p\bar{X} + \bar{Y}}, \qquad (11.9)$$

and

$$\bar{Z} = \bar{n}z. \qquad (11.10)$$

The nine conditions (11.2)–(11.10) determine nine variables: w_L, w_K, p, p_Z, X, Y, z, $\bar{n}$, and $\bar{Z}$. It is also useful to define industry input vectors: $\bar{V}(X)$, $\bar{V}(Y)$, and $\bar{V}(Z)$ as vectors of capital and labor employed in each industry. For expositional purposes we will assume that in the integrated equilibrium X production is most capital intensive and Y production most labor intensive.

11.2 Trading Equilibrium: Tradable Differentiated Products

Suppose that there are two countries, with the primary factors of production K and L immobile. As usual we begin by asking whether the trading world economy can reproduce the integrated equilibrium and what patterns of international specialization are required to accomplish this. The answer will turn out to depend crucially on whether intermediate inputs are tradable. In this section we assume that they are; in the next we assume that they are not.

Figure 11.1 illustrates the factor price equalization set when all goods are

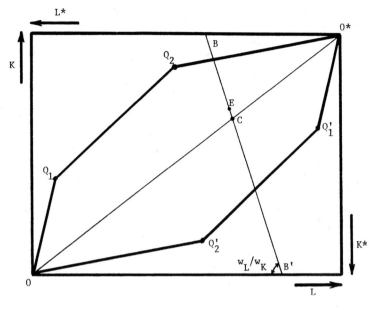

Figure 11.1

tradable. In the figure OQ_1 and O^*Q_1' represent $\overline{V}(X)$, $Q_1'Q_2'$ and Q_1Q_2 represent $\overline{V}(Z)$, and Q_2O^* and $Q_2'O$ represent $\overline{V}(Y)$. Any point in the hexagon enclosed by these vectors is consistent with factor price equalization. Although trade in factor services is determinate, the pattern of trade in goods is indeterminate when the endowment point lies within the factor price equalization set. Intraindustry trade is, however, certainly possible. For example, if the countries have the same composition of factors, so that the endowment lies on OO^*, a feasible allocation of world production is to have each country produce the three goods in the same proportion. Since each country will produce different varieties of Z, there will be intraindustry trade in intermediate products, and this will in fact be the only trade.

When all goods are tradable, then introducing differentiated intermediate goods does not appreciably alter our view of trade. We should note that although our model assumes that final products are homogeneous and produced with constant returns, as long as all goods are tradable, this makes little difference. A model where both middle and final products are differentiated has similar implications (see Helpman 1981). We will in fact use such models in our analysis of multinational firms in chapters 12 and 13.

One way to look at this model is the way suggested by Ethier (1979, 1982): this can be viewed as an example of international economies of scale. For the

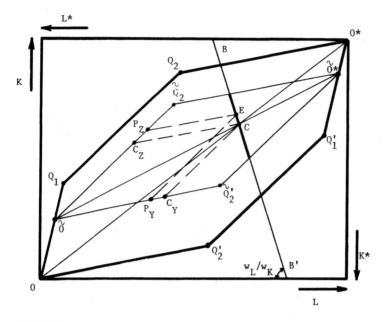

Figure 11.2

world economy there are effectively increasing returns to the production of X, because the larger the output of X, the larger can be both the number of varieties and scale of production of Z. It is not necessary, however, for the X industry to be concentrated in any one country to realize these economies of scale. In a world where differentiated inputs are costlessly tradable, it is the world scale of production, not the level of production in any one country, that matters.

The key to this result is the tradability of intermediate goods. Making the final good nontradable restricts the factor price equalization set but has little effect on the character of the outcome. Indeed, if X is nontradable, the model of this section becomes isomorphic to the model with nontraded goods presented in the first section of chapter 10. We conclude this section by demonstrating this equivalence.

Figure 11.2 illustrates the determination of the trade pattern for a given endowment point E under the assumption that X is nontradable. The vectors OQ_1, Q_1Q_2, Q_2O^*, O^*Q_1', $Q_1'Q_2'$, and $Q_2'O$ are as defined for figure 11.1; we add the factor price line BB', with slope $-w_L/w_K$. $\overline{OC}/\overline{OO^*}$ is the home country's share of world income, s.

Because countries have identical homothetic preferences, home country consumption of each final good will be the same fraction s of world production. Choose units so that $\overline{OQ}_1$ is world consumption of X; then home country consumption is found by drawing a line through C parallel to Q_1O^*, yielding consumption of X equal to $\overline{O\tilde{O}}$. But we have assumed X nontradable, so $O\tilde{O}$ also represents resources devoted to X production by the home country.

Since production of X is proportional to income, so is use of intermediate inputs Z. Choose units so that $\overline{Q_1Q_2}$ is world production of Z and $\overline{Q_2O^*}$ is world production of Y. We use $\tilde{O}$ and $\tilde{O}^*$ as new origins, with $\tilde{O}\tilde{Q}_2$ and $\check{Q}_2\tilde{O}^*$ parallel to Q_1Q_2 and Q_2O^*, respectively. Then $\overline{\tilde{O}C_Z}$ is domestic use of Z, and $\overline{\tilde{O}C_Y}$ is domestic consumption of Y. $\overline{\tilde{O}P_Z}$ is domestic production of Z, and $\overline{\tilde{O}P_Y}$ is domestic production of Y. Net trade in factor services is measured by EC.

It is apparent that the pattern of production and trade in the case of tradable differentiated intermediate inputs looks very much like trade when final products are differentiated. As long as both countries produce Z, they will specialize in the production of different varieties, and there will be intraindustry trade in intermediate goods. The region of factor price equalization and intraindustry trade is an elongated parallelogram around the diagonal, and it can be constructed analogously to figure 10.2.

11.3 Trading Equilibrium: Nontraded Intermediates

In the last section we saw that a world with differentiated intermediate products looks very much like a world with differentiated final products if the intermediates are tradable. Suppose, however, that we reverse the tradability assumptions, so that differentiated intermediates are not tradable but final goods are. This produces a major change in implications, as we will now show.

It will be important, for reasons that will immediately become clear, to allow for the existence of *three* final goods, 1, 2, and 3, together with the differentiated intermediate Z. We assume that Z is an input only into the production of good 1. Also for expositional convenience we assume that the capital intensity ranking is 1, Z, 2, 3 in the integrated equilibrium. The conditions of integrated equilibrium are identical to those stated in (11.2)–(11.10) with the addition of a third constant-returns, homogeneous sector.

Under what conditions will a trading world reproduce the integrated equilibrium? The point here is that in order to be in the same situation as in the integrated economy, producers of X must be able to use all varieties of Z as inputs. But Z is nontradable. This means that we can reproduce the integrated economy only if *all 1 and all Z production are located in the same country*. In effect we must have an "industrial complex" combining the 1 and Z sectors concentrated in one country.

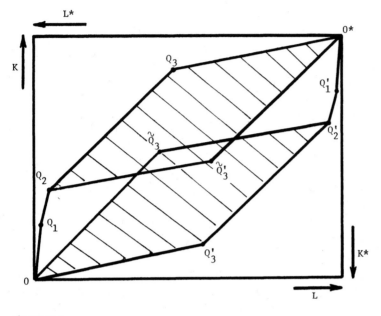

Figure 11.3

The implications are shown in figure 11.3. OQ_1 and O^*Q_1' represent $\bar{V}(1)$, the allocation of resources to good 1 in the integrated equilibrium; Q_1Q_2 and $Q_1'Q_2'$ represent $\bar{V}(Z)$; Q_2Q_3 and $Q_2'Q_3'$ represent $\bar{V}(2)$; and Q_3O^* and $Q_3'O$ represent $\bar{V}(3)$. To reproduce the integrated equilibrium, the industrial complex consisting of 1 and Z together must be concentrated in one country. The resources devoted to that complex are $\bar{V}(1, Z) = V(1) + \bar{V}(Z)$ and are represented in the figure by OQ_2 and O^*Q_2'.

The derivation of the factor price equalization set now proceeds in a way parallel to our analysis (in chapters 3 and 4) of models with three homogeneous products, one of which is produced with increasing returns. The set FPE is the same as if there were country- and industry-specific external economies in the production of good 1. If factor prices are equalized, the $(1, Z)$ industrial complex must be located either in the home or the foreign country. If it is located in the home country, the home country devotes resources OQ_2 to $(1, Z)$ and can fully employ its resources with integrated economy techniques as long as the endowment point lies in $Q_2Q_3O^*\tilde{Q}_3'$. If $(1, Z)$ is concentrated in the foreign country, the foreigners devote resources O^*Q_2' to the complex, and the integrated economy can be reproduced for points in $O\tilde{Q}_3Q_2'Q_3'$. The set of factor price equalization thus consists of the union of these parallelograms, represented by the shaded area.

There are four points to make about this analysis of factor price equalization. The first is that for the factor price equalization set to have full dimensionality, and thus for a factor price equalization equilibrium to be at all interesting, we must have at least as many sectors that are *not* part of industrial complexes as there are factors of production. This was the reason for introducing the extra sector. [We have not completely defined what is meant by an industrial complex. Obviously $(1, Z)$ is one; a more general view is given in the next section.]

Second, the existence of nontraded differentiated inputs may give rise to interindustry specialization and trade even if countries do not differ in relative factor endowments. Even if the endowment point in figure 11.3 lies on the diagonal OO^*, production of X will be concentrated in only one country, and there will therefore be interindustry trade—in contrast to the result where differentiated goods are traded and interindustry trade reflects differences in factor endowments.

Third, there may be more than one equilibrium pattern of interindustry specialization and trade. Referring again to figure 11.3, if the endowment point lies in the *intersection* of $Q_2 Q_3 O^* \tilde{Q}_3'$ and $O\tilde{Q}_3 Q_2 Q_3'$, then the $(1, Z)$ complex may be located in either country. Where it is located is of course of no welfare significance if factor prices are equalized.

Fourth, we should be cautious in assuming that factor prices are equalized. Without going into a full analysis, in a world with nontraded inputs produced with increasing returns, having a factor endowment in the factor price equalization set does not guarantee factor price equalization. As in chapter 3, other equilibria might be sustainable.

It is instructive at this point to return to the issue of national versus international economies of scale. Clearly, when there are nontraded intermediate inputs produced with increasing returns, the implicit economies of scale in producing final goods become national rather than international in character. Then the scale of the domestic rather than the world industry matters.

Saying that economies of scale are national in this case is, however, a statement about the trade pattern, *not* about welfare. Although there are in effect national increasing returns to the production of good 1, this does not mean that producing this good is especially desirable. In fact as long as we have factor price equalization and average cost pricing, who produces what is of no welfare significance. What matters for welfare here, as in earlier chapters, is the scale of the world industry, for though nontraded intermediates may create national returns to scale from the point of view of predicting the trade pattern, in welfare terms returns to scale remain international in scope.

11.4 A Generalization: Forward and Backward Linkages

In the simple model just developed, there was an obvious and clear-cut "industrial complex" in the form of the $(1, Z)$ sector. Z was the only intermediate input into sector 1; sector 1 was the only consumer of Z. What we will do in this final section is develop a more general concept of industrial complexes. By an *industrial complex* we will mean a set of sectors that must be concentrated in the same country to reproduce the integrated equilibrium. As we will see, an industrial complex may contain more than two sectors, and the linkages among sectors may be fairly subtle.

Consider a world with a number of sectors, some of which produce differentiated products. We assume that the set of sectors I can be partitioned into two subsets: a set of nontradable differentiated intermediate inputs I_N and a set of tradables I_T (nontraded final goods are omitted for simplicity). In an integrated economy each sector would produce with resources

$$\overline{V}(i), \quad i \in I.$$

We want to determine which allocations of world resources across countries will allow us to reproduce the integrated equilibrium. To do this, we need to ask what the linkages are between nontraded and traded goods. Consider the set of all *pairs* of sectors (i, i'), where $i \in I_N$ and $i' \in I_T$. We can partition *this* set into two subsets, a subset of linked pairs, where i is an input into i', and a subset of nonlinked pairs. Let us denote the set of linked pairs as Λ.

We can now define the set of allocations FPE that allows us to reproduce the integrated equilibrium:

$$\text{FPE} = \left\{ (V^1, \dots, V^J) \middle| \exists \lambda_{ij} \geq 0, \sum_{j \in J} \lambda_{ij} = 1 \text{ for } i \in I, \lambda_{ij} \in \{0, 1\} \right.$$
$$\text{for } i \in I_N, \text{ and } \lambda_{i'j} = \lambda_{ij} \text{ for } (i, i') \in \Lambda,$$
$$\left. \text{such that } V^j = \sum_{i \in I} \lambda_{ij} \overline{V}(i) \text{ for } j \in J \right\}.$$

In words, the allocation of sectors across countries must involve concentration of production for each nontraded input, and any industry that uses that input must be concentrated in the same place.

If there is a simple one-to-one relationship between inputs and final goods, as in the example presented in the previous section, then all that this implies is that an intermediate input and its user must be concentrated in the same country. The more interesting implication, however, is that when a final goods producer uses more than one nontraded input, or an input is used by more than one producer, industrial complexes may combine a number of sectors.

Figure 11.4 illustrates schematically the main possibilities. First, in part a of the figure we show a situation where a final goods sector uses two nontraded inputs. The requirement that the final goods sector be concentrated in the same place as each nontraded input means that all three form an industrial complex that must be located in the same country. This case, where the final sector's demand for several inputs ties them together, can be called a case of *backward linkage*.

Part b of the figure illustrates the opposite case, where a single input is used in more than one sector. Again this requires concentration of all three sectors in the same country to reproduce the integrated equilibrium. Thus here an industrial complex is created by *forward linkage*.

Finally, part c illustrates what can happen if both forward and backward linkage are present. Here there are six sectors that must be concentrated together to reproduce the integrated equilibrium. The linkages between these sectors are fairly subtle. Final sectors 1 and 3 do not share the use of any intermediate inputs; intermediate sectors 1 and 3 do not have any common customers.

The implication of our analysis is that the linkage effects of nontraded intermediate inputs produced with economies of scale can be a source of differences in industrial structure between countries even when the countries have similar factor endowments. We should keep in mind, however, that as long as factor prices are equalized there is no sense in which one industrial structure is more desirable than another. And net trade in factor services will continue to be determined by differences in factor endowments.

It is interesting to compare the concept of linkages developed here with the possibilities of linkage in the external effects model of chapter 3. In that chapter we allowed for the possibility of interindustry external effects. It is clearly possible to explain industrial complexes in an external effects approach by postulating positive, country-specific external effects across a group of industries. As in this chapter the implication will be that to reproduce the integrated equilibrium will require concentration of the whole group of industries. However, in an external effects approach the nature of interindustry linkages is obscure because it is hidden inside a black box. It is not clear what one ought to look for as a source of linkage effects.

By contrast, in the model laid out here it is very clear what gives rise to linkages. This does not mean that there may not also be more subtle external effects, but we have shown that these are not *necessary* to explain industrial complexes.

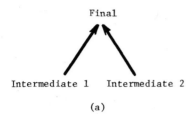

Final

Intermediate 1   Intermediate 2

(a)

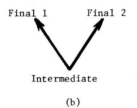

Final 1   Final 2

Intermediate

(b)

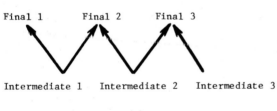

Final 1   Final 2   Final 3

Intermediate 1   Intermediate 2   Intermediate 3

(c)

Figure 11.4

Appendix 11A: A Model of Differentiation in Intermediate Goods

We provide in this appendix an illustrative example of technology and market structure with a differentiated intermediate good that is an alternative to the example given in the text. The analysis in the chapter is not dependent on the special assumptions we make either here or in the text, but the two examples may help give some further insight into the justification for the general formulation.

Suppose then that to produce good X requires carrying out of a large number of activities: each activity uses capital, labor, and an intermediate input. Formally, let there be a continuum of these activities, indexed by ω, which we view as being located around a unit circle. These activities are required in fixed proportions.

The intermediate input we view as being produced in a limited number of distinct varieties. Each of these varieties has a location on the unit circle corresponding to the activity to which it is most suited. When a variety is used in another activity, it is less effective. We represent the production function for X as

$$X = \min_{\omega} F\left\{ K(\omega), L(\omega), \frac{Z(\omega, \omega')}{h[\tilde{\delta}(\omega, \omega')]} \right\}, \tag{11.A1}$$

where $K(\omega)$ and $L(\omega)$ are the inputs of capital and labor into activity ω. $Z(\omega, \omega')$ is the input of Z into activity ω; its effectiveness depends on the distance between ω and the location ω' of the variety of Z used. The function $h(\cdot)$ is analogous to the compensation function defined in chapter 6 and has the same properties.

Analogously to the analysis in chapter 6, then, the producer of a variety ω' of Z will capture a range of demand, serving activities from some lower bound $\underline{\omega}$ to an upper bound $\overline{\omega}$, with the range depending on the price of the variety and the prices of neighboring varieties. For a given output of X, a reduction in the price of an individual variety will lead to increased demand because of substitution between other inputs and Z within the initial market range and a widening of its range of sales.

The average cost of producing X can be written as the integral of the average cost of each of the activities required for production. Suppose there are n symmetrically located varieties of Z and that each one is sold at a price p_Z. Then it is straightforward to show that the average cost of X takes the form

$$c_x(w_K, w_L, p_Z, n) = 2n \int_0^{1/2n} c_\omega[w_K, w_L, p_Z h(\delta)] d\delta, \tag{11.A2}$$

where $c(\cdot)$ is the average cost of an activity. This average cost is decreasing in n.

References

Ethier, Wilfred J. "Internationally Decreasing Costs and World Trade." *Journal of International Economica* 9 (1979): 1–24.

Ethier, Wilfred J. "National and International Return to Scale in the Modern Theory of International Trade." *American Economic Reviews* 72 (1982): 389–405.

Helpman, Elhanan. "International Trade in Differential Middle Products." Working Paper No. 81-4, Foerder Institute for Economic Research, Tel Aviv University, 1981. To appear in *Structural Adjustment in Developed Open Economics*. Hague, D., and Jungenfelt, K. G. (eds.). London: Macmillan.

IV   Multinational Corporations

In this concluding part of the book we take the basic approach of part III and extend it to develop a theory of multinational enterprise. There are two strands to this theory. First, we draw on the industrial organization literature for an explanation of the incentives to integrate two or more economic activities within a single firm. Second, we use our basic trade approach to explain the incentives to disperse economic activities geographically. The combination of these two kinds of incentives leads to multinational firms.

Chapter 12 begins with a minimal model of multinationals, where firms may be headquartered in one country and produce in another. Chapter 13 presents a more complex analysis in which vertically integrated firms may also engage in intrafirm trade.

Three main themes have emerged so far from our attempts to explain trade patterns. First, under a large variety of industrial structures the predictive power of the factor proportions trade theory remains valid for the intersectoral pattern of trade and, in particular, for the factor content of trade flows. Second, in the presence of economies of scale large volumes of trade are consistent with small differences across countries in the composition of factor endowments. Third, the decomposition of trade volumes into an intraindustry and an intersectoral component can be related to fundamental characteristics of the countries whose trade flows are examined. In this and in the following chapter we extend the theory in order to describe an additional component of international trade. This is intrafirm trade, that is, trade among affiliates of the same multinational enterprise.

The introduction of multinational firms into the study of trade flows is desirable even if one is not interested in intrafirm trade per se, because the behavior of other major trade variables, like the volume of trade and the share of intraindustry trade, is influenced by the existence of multinational corporations, which have grown in importance in the conduct of world trade. In the United States, for example, at the all-manufacturing level multinational corporations accounted in 1970 for 62 percent of exports and 34 percent of imports (see U.S. Tariff Commission 1973, p. 322). Hence a full explanation of existing trade structures cannot be provided without taking account of the role of multinationals.

Our theory builds on two main premises: that there is product differentiation and economies of scale in some industries, and that there are inputs—such as management, marketing, and product-specific R & D—that are highly specialized and that can be located in one country and serve product lines in another country. These premises have emerged from the large descriptive literature on multinational corporations and from empirical studies of the incidence of multinationality (see Caves 1982).

In this chapter the theory deals with single-product firms; we deal with vertically integrated firms in the next chapter. Firms maximize profits and therefore make cost-minimizing location choices of product lines. This feature brings about the emergence of multinational corporations as a response to tendencies of factor rewards to differ across countries. Here the emphasis is on one source of pressure on relative factor rewards—differences in relative factor endowments. Transport costs and tariffs are assumed away, so production facilities are not established in order to save transport costs or in order to produce behind tariff walls. Other reasons for multinationality, like tax advantages of various forms, are also not considered.

Apart from describing in a general equilibrium system conditions that cause firms to choose multinationality, the theory provides an explanation of trade patterns in which the multinational corporations play a central role. There is intersectoral, intraindustry, and intrafirm trade. However, since in this chapter we deal only with single-product firms, the intrafirm trade component consists only of trade in invisibles, that is, in "headquarter services"; we deal with intrafirm trade in intermediate inputs in the next chapter.

12.1 The Basic Model

In this chapter we employ a modified version of the $2 \times 2 \times 2$ model from chapter 7 in which one sector produces differentiated products. It is assumed that there are two factors of production; labor, L, and capital, K. Food is produced by means of a standard linear homogeneous production function with the associated unit cost function $c_Y(w_L, w_K)$, where w_l is the reward to factor l. A producer of food has to employ all inputs in the same location. In a competitive equilibrium the price of food, taken to be the numeraire, equals unit costs:

$$1 = c_Y(w_L, w_K). \tag{12.1}$$

The structure of production of manufactured products is more complicated. Manufacturers require inputs of labor, capital, and headquarter service H. Headquarter services is a differentiated product, and a firm has to adapt it in order to make it suitable for the production of its variety of the finished good. Once adapted, this input becomes a firm-specific asset in the sense used by Williamson (1981), and it is *tied* to the entrepreneurial unit. However, it can serve many plants, and it need not be located within a plant in order to serve its product lines. In particular, it can serve plants that are located in other countries (see Hirsch 1976, Helpman 1984, and Markusen 1984). Inputs that fit this description are management, distribution, and product specific R & D. The importance of such assets in the operation of multinational corporations is described in Caves (1982, chapter 1).

Let $C^P(w_L, w_K, h, x)$ be the costs required to produce x units of a variety of the differentiated product in a single plant when h units of H have been adapted for its particular use. A possible form of this function is $C^P = f(w_L, w_K) + g(w_L, w_K, h, x)$, where $f(\cdot) > 0$ and $g(\cdot)$ is positively linear homogeneous in (h, x). Here $f(\cdot)$ generates a plant-specific fixed cost and the variable cost component exhibits constant returns to scale. In general, we assume that $C^P(\cdot)$ is associated with an increasing returns to scale production function in which h is essential for production. Also we let $C^H(w_L, w_K, h)$ be the minimum costs required in order to produce h in the desired variety, where $C^H(\cdot)$ is associated with a nondecreasing returns to scale production function. Then the firm's single-plant cost function is

$$C(w_L, w_H, x) = \min_h \left[C^P(w_L, w_K, h, x) + C^H(w_L, w_K, h) \right].$$

This function has obviously the standard properties of cost functions associated with increasing returns to scale production functions. One can also define cost functions for larger numbers of plants, but we do not need it for what follows. The point worth noting, however, is that the firm or corporation has fixed costs that are corporation specific but not plant specific (the cost of producing h and adapting it); it has plant-specific fixed costs and plant-specific variable costs.

The assumption that $C^P(\cdot)$ is associated with an increasing returns to scale production function implies that it pays to concentrate production in a single plant, unless there are transportation costs or differences across locations in product prices. Since impediments to trade are not considered, the previously described single-plant cost function is what is relevant for what follows. All varieties will be assumed to have the same cost structure.

It is assumed that there is Chamberlinian-type monopolistic competition in the differentiated product sector with unrestricted entry. Hence firms equate marginal revenue to marginal cost, and free entry brings about zero profits in every firm. In a symmetrical equilibrium these two conditions can be written as

$$p = c(w_L, w_K, x), \tag{12.2}$$

$$R(p, \bar{n}) = \theta(w_L, w_K, x), \tag{12.3}$$

where p is the price of every variety of the differentiated product; $c(w_L, w_K, x) \equiv C(w_L, w_K, x)/x$ is average cost, $R(\cdot)$ is our measure of the degree of monopoly power, $\bar{n}$ is the number of varieties available to consumers, and

$\theta(\cdot)$ is our measure [using $C(\cdot)$] of the degree of returns to scale in the production of manufacturers. The formal conditions of industry equilibrium (12.1)–(12.3) are identical to conditions (7.12)–(7.14) from chapter 7. The important difference lies in the interpretation of the technology available to corporations in the differentiated product industry.

As in most trade theory we will assume that factors of production do not move across national borders. However, due to the technology available in the manufacturing sector, the firm-specific asset h can serve product lines in plants located in countries other than the country where the headquarters are located. The specificity of h also implies that arm's-length trade in headquarter services is an inferior organizational form to a multinationally integrated firm (see Klein, Crawford, and Alchian 1978). We will call the country where the headquarters are located the parent country of the corporation and the country where the subsidiary is located the host country.

12.2 Equilibrium in an Integrated Economy

As a first step toward the study of international trade between economies of the type described earlier we discuss in this section the equilibrium of an integrated economy. The features of the integrated economy will then be used to derive the relationship between patterns of cross-country distributions of the world's endowment of labor and capital, on one side, and trade patterns and volumes of trade, on the other.

In an integrated economy factor prices are the same everywhere, and all the firms operating in the sector that produces differentiated products have the same structure. Every firm produces one variety, and there is no overlap in varieties produced by different firms. All firms employ the same quantity of capital and labor, charge the same price for every variety, and produce the same final output and the same quantity of appropriate headquarter services. Free entry into the industry brings profits down to zero. The number of corporations $\bar{n}$ is treated as a continuous variable.

Apart from (12.1)–(12.3) the equilibrium conditions consist of equilibrium conditions in factor and commodity markets. Following the procedure discussed in chapter 7, we arrive at the equilibrium conditions in factor markets:

$$a_{LY}(w_L, w_K)\bar{Y} + a_{LX}(w_L, w_K, x)\bar{X} = \bar{L}, \tag{12.4}$$

$$a_{KY}(w_L, w_K)\bar{Y} + a_{KX}(w_L, w_K, x)\bar{X} = \bar{K}, \tag{12.5}$$

where $a_{lY}(w_L, w_K) = \partial c_Y(w_L, w_K)/\partial w_l$, $l = L, K$, is the cost-minimizing input of factor i per unit output of food; $a_{lX}(w_L, w_K, x) = \partial c(w_L, w_K, x)/\partial w_l$, $l = L, K$, is the cost-minimizing input of factor l per unit output of manufactures, $\overline{L}$ and $\overline{K}$ are the quantities of labor and capital available in the world economy, $\overline{Y}$ is the output of food and $\overline{X}$ is the output of manufactures, defined as

$$\overline{X} = \overline{n}x. \tag{12.6}$$

Finally, the commodity market-clearing condition [see (7.17)] is

$$\alpha_Y(p, \overline{n}) = \frac{\overline{Y}}{(\overline{Y} + p\overline{X})}, \tag{12.7}$$

where $\alpha_Y(\cdot)$ is the share of spending allocated to food. Conditions (12.1)–(12.7) represent the equilibrium conditions of the integrated economy. They implicitly define equilibrium values for factor rewards (w_L, w_K), pricing and output of manufacturing varieties (p, x), industry output levels $(\overline{Y}, \overline{X})$, and the numbers of varieties available to consumers $(\overline{n})$.

In what follows, we assume that the food industry is relatively labor intensive; namely

$$\frac{a_{KX}}{a_{LX}} > \frac{a_{KY}}{a_{LY}}.$$

Under this assumption the allocation of resources in the integrated equilibrium can be described by means of the box diagram in figure 12.1, which is analogous to figure 7.1. The vector OQ describes employment in the manufacturing sector, and the vector OQ' describes employment in the production of food.

12.3 The Pattern of Trade

In the standard $2 \times 2 \times 2$ Heckscher-Ohlin model, in which there are no factor-intensity reversals and preferences are homothetic and identical across countries, the set of endowment allocations can be divided into two subsets. In one subset there is factor price equalization and no specialization in production. In the other subset every country pays a lower reward to the factor of production with which it is relatively well endowed and a higher reward to the other factor of production, and at least one country specializes in the production of the good which is a relatively heavy user of its cheaper factor of production. If figure 12.1 were to describe feasible allocations across countries for a standard Heckscher-Ohlin-type economy, then the set of factor price equalization would be represented by OQO^*Q' and the other set by its complement.

The results that emerge in the present model are richer. It is useful to

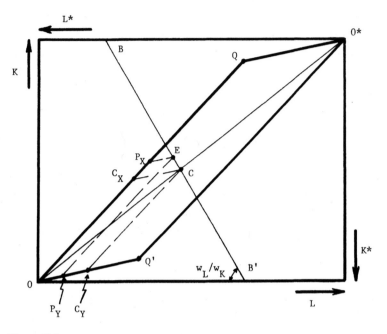

Figure 12.1

describe them by starting with intercountry factor allocations in the set OQO^*Q' of figure 12.1. Due to the symmetry in structure it is sufficient to analyze endowment points above the diagonal OQ^* where the home country is relatively capital rich. Allocations in this set were discussed in chapter 7, and we can therefore be brief.

Take, for example, the factor endowment point E. It is straightforward to see that with this world structure there is an equilibrium with factor price equalization. In this equilibrium firms based in one country have no incentive to open subsidiaries in the other country in order to locate product lines there. Assuming that under these circumstances all operations of a firm will be concentrated in the parent country, the output levels of food and manufactures in the home country are described by $\overline{OP_Y}$ and $\overline{OP_X}$, given a choice of units such that $\overline{Y} = \overline{OQ'}$ and $\overline{X} = \overline{OQ}$. The output levels in the foreign country are given by $\overline{P_YQ'}$ and $\overline{P_XQ}$.

Now, due to the fact that profits are zero, all income is factor income. Hence, by drawing through E a line BB' whose slope is $-w_L/w_K$, this line represents the cross-country income distribution. The relative income of the home country is $\overline{OC}$ divided by $\overline{CO^*}$. Since both countries have the same spending pattern, the home country consumes a proportion s of the world's output $\overline{Y}$, where s is its share in world income. Hence, by drawing a line through C parallel to OQ, its consumption of food can be represented by $\overline{OC_Y}$, where C_Y is the intersection point of this line with OQ'. Since production of food in the home country is represented by $\overline{OP_Y}$, the home country imports food. Finally, since trade is balanced, the home country is a net exporter of manufactures.

It is clear from this discussion that factor endowment points *above* OQO^* would lead to unequal factor prices if firms had to employ all factor inputs in the same country. Suppose that under these circumstances capital would be cheaper in the home country and labor would be cheaper in the foreign country (this is assured if production is homothetic). Now consider what would happen if firms did not have to employ all labor and capital at a single location; in particular, assume that they could locate headquarter activities in the parent country and production activities in the other country. Corporations would choose the home country as their parent country, and they would open subsidiaries in the foreign country. These moves would reduce the demand for labor in the home country and increase it in the foreign country, while increasing the demand for capital in the home country and reducing it in the foreign country. An equilibrium would be attained either when factor prices were equalized or the home country became the parent of all corporations (with unequal factor prices all headquarters are located in the capital-cheap country).

When factor price equalization obtains, there are many equilibrium configurations with various degrees of foreign involvement of the corporations in the differentiated product industry, just as there are many such configurations in the factor price equalization set OQO^*. In the latter case we adopted the convention that firms do not decentralize their activities unless this is necessary to achieve factor price equilization. In the current case such decentralization *is* necessary, but we maintain the spirit of the first convention by minimizing the extent of decentralization. The rule to be adopted is to consider equilibria with the smallest number of multinational corporations. This choice can be justified as the limit of a sequence of economies in which it is costly to locate plants abroad, but these costs tend to zero.

Our discussion of the decomposition of a firm's activities into headquarters and production can now be cast into a somewhat more formal framework in order to bring out as clearly as possible the analogy between previous derivations of trade patterns and the derivation of trade patterns with active multinational corporations.

Recall that h was chosen so as to minimize overall costs. The first-order condition of this cost minimization problem is

$$-C_h^P(w_L, w_K, h, x) = C_h^H(w_L, w_K, h).$$

The right-hand side represents the cost of a marginal expansion of headquarter activities, and the left-hand side represents cost savings from such an expansion. Given the values of factor rewards and output per firm in the integrated equilibrium, this condition determines the equilibrium level of headquarter activity h.

Now, using the equilibrium value of h, employment levels per unit output at headquarters and plants are given by

$$a_{lH}(w_L, w_K, h) = \frac{\partial}{\partial w_l} C^H(w_L, w_K, h)/h,$$

$$a_{lP}(w_L, w_K, h, x) = \frac{\partial}{\partial w_l} C^P(w_L, w_K, x)/x,$$

for $l = L, K$. The relationship between these input-output ratios and the a_{li}'s used in (12.4)–(12.5) is

$$a_{lX}(w_L, w_K, x) = a_{lP}(w_L, w_K, h, x) + a_{lH}(w_L, w_K, h)\frac{h}{x}, \quad l = L, K.$$

The headquarter and plant input-output ratios can be used to rewrite the factor market-clearing conditions in a form that underlines the different nature of a corporation's activities. Namely

$$a_{LY}(w_L, w_K)\bar{Y} + a_{KP}(w_L, w_K, h, x)\bar{X} + a_{KH}(w_L, w_K, h)\bar{H} = L, \tag{12.4'}$$

$$a_{KY}(w_L, w_K)\bar{Y} + a_{KP}(w_L, w_K, h, x)\bar{X} + a_{KH}(w_L, w_K, h)\bar{H} = K, \tag{12.5'}$$

where $\bar{H} = \bar{n}h$. Thus there are three outputs: food $\bar{Y}$, manufactures $\bar{X}$, and headquarter services $\bar{H}$.

In figure 12.2 the employment vector in the manufacturing sector OQ is decomposed into headquarter employment OD and plant employment DQ. The assumption is that headquarter activities are the most capital intensive, that plant activities in the manufacturing sector are of intermediate capital intensity, and that food production is the least capital intensive (in Helpman 1984, plant activities in the manufacturing sector are the least capital intensive). It is clear from our discussions in previous chapters that if arm's-length trade was possible in Y, X, and H, then $ODQO^*D'Q'$ would have been the factor price equalization set. However, since H services are specialized and every firm supplies its own requirements, they are not traded at arm's length. Hence points in the shaded areas of figure 12.2 are consistent with factor price equalization only when firms go multinational. In OQO^*Q' there is factor price equalization with national firms.

We have therefore identified the conditions that lead to the formation of

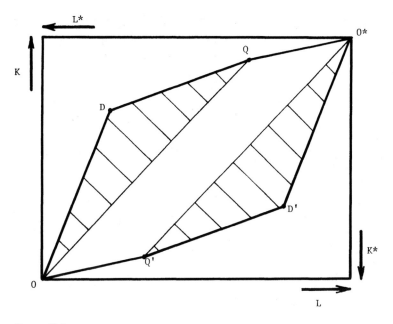

Figure 12.2

multinational corporations. Multinational corporations develop whenever the endowment allocation lies outside the parallelogram OQO^*Q', and they bring about factor price equalization in the shaded areas of figure 12.2.

Now consider what happens at endowment points in the shaded areas of figure 12.2. In particular, consider points E in ODQ of figure 12.3, which reproduce the relevant features from figure 12.2. If all the resources of the home country are employed in the production of manufactures, and if its corporations employ in the foreign country the vector EE_m in plant production (where E_m is the intersection point with OQ of a line drawn through E parallel to DQ), then the aggregate world equilibrium corresponds to the equilibrium of the integrated economy. The employment vector EE_m describes the smallest equilibrium foreign involvement of domestic multinationals consistent with full employment.

The structure of employment is as follows. In the home country the vector OE_H is employed in the production of headquarter services, and the vector $E_H E$ is employed in plant production of differentiated products. Home multinationals employ in the foreign country the vector $E_m E$ in plant production of differentiated products. Also foreign-based firms employ the vector QE_m in the manufacturing sector and the vector O^*Q in food production.

More precisely, since $Y = O$ and $Y^* = \bar{Y}$, the numbers of corporations n and

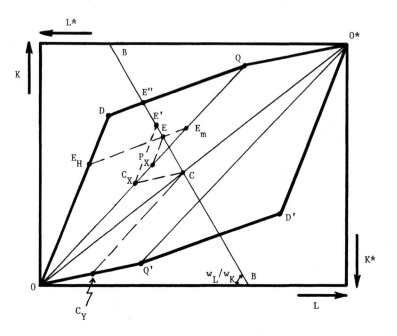

Figure 12.3

n^*, and the number of foreign subsidiaries μ located in the foreign country are obtained from the following factor market-clearing conditions:

$$a_{LP}(n - \mu)x + a_{LH}nh = L, \quad a_{LY}\bar{Y} + a_{LP}(n^* + \mu)x + a_{LH}n^*h = L^*,$$

$$a_{KP}(n - \mu)x + a_{KH}nh = K, \quad a_{KY}\bar{Y} + a_{KP}(n^* + \mu)x + a_{KH}n^*h = K^*.$$

Clearly the number of varieties produced in the home and foreign country does not equal n and n^*. The number of varieties produced in the home country is $M = n - \mu$, and the number of varieties produced in the foreign country is $M^* = n^* - \mu$.

To summarize, we have seen that endowment points in the set ODQ lead to an equilibrium with factor price equalization and the emergence of multinational corporations. Under our assumption about locational tendencies of corporations, in this set the home country (which is relatively capital rich) specializes in the production of manufactured products and in headquarter activities, and it serves as a base for the multinational corporations. It imports the homogeneous product, and there is intraindustry trade in differentiated products. Part of the intraindustry trade is carried out by multinationals.

At point E in figure 12.3 the home country is a net exporter of differentiated products. This can be seen as follows. Draw through E the line BB' whose slope

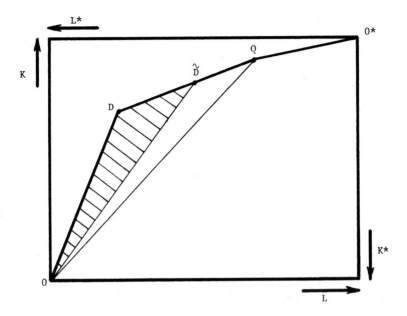

Figure 12.4

is $-w_L/w_K$, in order to obtain C. Now construct a parallelogram between O and C, using the slopes of OQ and OQ', to obtain C_X and C_Y. Home country consumption of food is represented by $\overline{OC}_Y$, and its consumption of manufactures is represented by $\overline{OC}_X$. By drawing through E a line which is parallel to OD, we obtain P_X, with $\overline{OP}_X$ representing home production of manufactures. Hence the home country's net exports of manufactures equals $\overline{C_XP_X}$. However, the home country need not be a net exporter of manufactures. Figure 12.4 describes a division of ODQ into two subsets by means of the line $O\tilde{D}$. At endowment points in the shaded area the home country is a *net importer* of manufactured products. The dividing line $O\tilde{D}$ is constructed as follows. Draw in figure 12.3 a line through C_X parallel to OD and denote its intersection point with BB' by E'. Then it is clear from the figure that at endowment points on $E'C$ the home country is a net exporter of manufactures and that at endowment points on $E''E'$ the home country is a net importer of manufactures. Now, by drawing a ray through O and E', we obtain $O\tilde{D}$ in figure 12.4. Algebraically the home country is a net importer of manufactured products if and only if $sM^* > s^*M$.

It is also clear from figure 12.3 that C represents the factor content of consumption. Therefore EC is the vector of the factor content of net imports (including invisibles). This vector is consistent with the prediction of the Heckscher-Ohlin theory; the relatively capital-rich country is a net exporter of capital services and a net importer of labor services.

Finally, observe that at E there is intrafirm trade in headquarter services. The existence of intrafirm trade is of course well documented in the empirical literature (e.g., see U.S. Tariff Commission 1973, chapter 2, and Buckley and Pearce 1979). This takes the form of imports of the parent firm from its subsidiaries as well as exports of the parent firm to its subsidiaries. Much of this trade stems from vertical integration, which we cover in the next chapter. However, there is one genuine component of intrafirm trade that is well represented by our model—the invisible exports of the parent to its subsidiaries of headquarter services.

Observe that due to the zero profit condition (12.2) plant costs are lower than the revenue obtained from sales. This means that a typical multinational corporation is making "profits" in its subsidiary, because the subsidiary hires in the host country only labor and capital for plant operation. This means that the "profits" of the subsidiary are just sufficient to cover the cost of headquarter services produced and located in the parent country. The difference between revenue and plant costs of all subsidiaries is $\mu(w_L a_{LH} + w_K a_{KH})h$. This can be considered to be either profits repatriated by the parent firms or payments by the subsidiaries for services rendered by the parent firms (a major issue in discussions of transfer pricing). From an economic point of view the second interpretation is the appropriate one. Hence μc_H, where $c_H = (w_L a_{LH} + w_K a_{KH})h$, represents intrafirm trade.

12.4 The Volume of Trade

We have seen how the trade pattern is related to the distribution of the world's endowment of factors of production. As is clear from the partition of the endowment set into the subsets in which different patterns of trade obtain, the pattern of trade depends on two factors: relative country size in terms of GNP, and the difference in relative factor endowments. For example, if the home country is relatively small and it has a relatively large endowment of capital, then the endowment point is in $OD\tilde{D}$ of figure 12.4. Then there are multinational firms based in the home country, the home country exports manufactures and invisible headquarter services to its subsidiaries, it imports food, and it is a net importer of manufactures.

Differences in relative factor endowments and the relative size of countries are observable economic variables of major interest. We therefore provide in this section a description of the effects that these two variables have on the volume of trade. Our findings are summarized by the equal volume of trade curves in figure 12.5.

Start by considering endowment points in the set OQO^*. In this region there

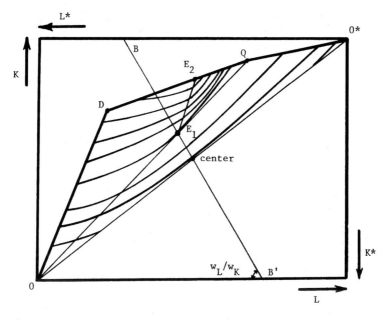

Figure 12.5

are no multinational firms. The volume of trade is defined in the usual way as the sum of exports, where the summation is over countries and sectors. Due to balanced trade this is equal in a two-country world to twice the exports of one of the countries. We showed in the first section of chapter 8 that in this set the volume of trade increases with differences in relative factor endowments and decreases with differences in relative country size (the latter applying when the manufacturing sector is sufficiently large). The equal volume of trade curves were shown there to have the shape exhibited in figure 12.5.

For endowment points in ODQ the foreign country exports the homogeneous good (because it is the only producer of it) and M^* varieties of the differentiated product. some of the varieties that it exports are produced by firms based in the foreign country, and μ of them are produced by subsidiaries of multinational corporations based in the home country. This means that a proportion s of its output of food and manufactures is exported and that the volume of trade can be represented as

$$VT = 2s(\bar{Y} + pxM^*), \quad \text{for } E \in ODQ, \tag{12.8}$$

where s is the share of the home country in spending, which is equal to its share in GNP. In this definition of the volume of trade we include the volume of trade in headquarter services. It is therefore the total volume of trade and not only the component of trade in goods.

Condition (12.8) implies that given the relative country size, the volume of trade increases with the number of varieties produced in the foreign country, and given the number of varieties produced in the foreign country, the volume of trade increases with the relative size of the home country.

It is useful to pause at this stage in order to observe that depending on accounting practices the foreign country may record a difference between its gross domestic product and its gross national product. The point is of course that headquarter services of multinational corporations are traded within the firms, so that the value of output of goods in the host country is larger than its GNP. If the value of output of goods is taken to be GDP, then a discrepancy between GNP and GDP arises. If, however, imports of headquarter services are treated as imports of intermediate inputs (which they should be from an economic point of view), then there will be no discrepancy between GNP and GDP. The problem that arises is not only due to the fact that these intermediate inputs are services but that they are also not traded at arm's length and are therefore not directly recorded in trade statistics.

Now, since in ODQ both s and M^* are linear functions of (L, K), the proof from the appendix to chapter 8 can be applied to (12.8) in order to show that equal trade volume curves in ODQ are quasi concave and have therefore the shape exhibited in figure 12.5.

Moreover, since

$$\bar{Y} + pxM^* = GNP^* + c_H\mu - s^*\overline{GDP} + \iota_H\mu$$

where $c_H = (w_L a_{LH} + w_K a_{KH})h$ is the value of headquarter services supplied by a typical parent firm to its foreign country subsidiary, μ is the number of subsidiaries located in the foreign country, and $\overline{GDP}$ is world GDP, then (12.8) can be rewritten as

$$VT = 2(ss^*\overline{GDP} + c_H s\mu), \quad \text{for } E \in ODQ. \tag{12.9}$$

This representation shows that for $\mu = 0$, the volume of trade is maximized when countries are of equal size (point E_1 in figure 12.5), as we have shown also in chapter 8, and that the larger μ is, the larger the relative size of the home country for trade volume maximization. Maximizing VT for a given μ yields

$$s = \frac{1}{2}\left(1 + \frac{c_H\mu}{\overline{GDP}}\right), \quad \text{for } E \in ODQ. \tag{12.10}$$

Points that satisfy (12.10) are represented by the line $E_1 E_2$ in figure 12.5. Since endowments that generate the same degree of multinationality μ are represented by lines parallel to OQ, as in figure 12.6, then the equal volume of trade

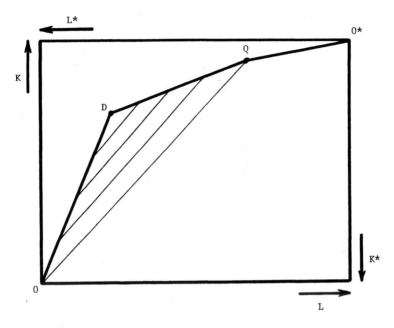

Figure 12.6

lines in figure 12.5 have a constant slope on $E_1 E_2$, and this slope equals the slope of OQ. The volume of trade is largest at E_2.

In summary, figure 12.5 represents a fairly detailed description of the relationship between factor endowments and the volume of trade. It shows that in some sense the larger the difference in relative factor endowments, the larger is the volume of trade. On the other hand, relative country size has an ambiguous effect on the volume of trade in the region that leads to the emergence of multinational corporations. Although a small upward bias in the relative size of the relatively capital-rich country increases the volume of trade, too much of this bias will reduce it. Thus the presence of multinational corporations weakens the link between the volume of trade and the degree of dispersion in relative country size. This suggests an empirical hypothesis: the larger the role of multinationals in the world economy, the weaker the effects of relative country size dispersion on the volume of trade.

12.5 Intraindustry and Intrafirm Trade

In this section we investigate the dependence of the shares of intraindustry and intrafirm trade on cross-country differences in relative factor endowments.

The volume of intraindustry trade is defined as the total volume of trade minus the sum over all sectors of the absolute value of the difference between imports and exports [see (8.14)]. In the current model this reduces to

$$\text{VT}_{i-i} = 2px \min (sM^*, s^*M). \tag{12.11}$$

The definition of the volume of intrafirm trade is more complicated. Exports of the parent firms of headquarter services are undoubtedly part of this volume of trade. The problem arises with the treatment of the final differentiated products. If parent firms serve as importers of the finished products that are manufactured by their subsidiaries, then this appears in the data as intrafirm trade, and similarly, if subsidiaries serve as importers of the differentiated products that are manufactured by parent firms. In some cases the treatment of these flows of goods as intrafirm trade has no economic justification because it is more the consequence of bookkeeping practices than true economic calculus. In the present model there is no natural choice—much depends on the implicit assumptions about the marketing technology. We choose therefore to define intrafirm trade as trade in headquarter services:

$$\text{VT}_{i-f} = c_H \mu, \tag{12.12}$$

where $c_H = (w_L a_{LH} + w_K a_{KH})h$.

We have shown in section 8.3 that for endowment points in OQO^* the share of intraindustry trade is a declining function of the difference in relative factor endowments and that relative country size has no particularly strong independent affect. The share of intrafirm trade is zero in OQO^*, because in this region there are no multinational corporations.

Using (12.8) and (12.11), we obtain

$$S_{i-i} = \frac{px \min (sM^*, s^*M)}{s(\overline{Y} + pxM^*)}, \quad \text{for } E \in ODQ.$$

We have shown, however, that ODQ can be divided into two subsets, described in figure 12.4, such that in $O\tilde{D}Q$ the home country is a net exporter of manufactured products ($s^*M > sM^*$), whereas in $ODD̃$ the foreign country is a net exporter of manufactured products ($sM^* > s^*M$). Hence

$$S_{i-i} = \frac{pxM^*}{\overline{Y} + pxM^*}, \quad \text{for } E \in O\tilde{D}Q,$$

$$S_{i-i} = \frac{s^*pxM}{s(\overline{Y} + pxM^*)}, \quad \text{for } E \in OD\tilde{D}.$$

It is immediately clear from the first formula that in $O\tilde{D}Q$ the share of

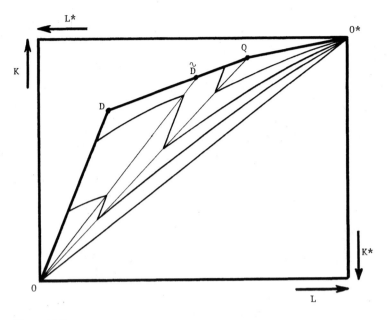

Figure 12.7

intraindustry trade is constant on lines parallel to OD, because on these lines M^* is constant. It can also be shown that the second formula implies constant S_{i-i} curves in $OD\tilde{D}$ that have the shape depicted in figure 12.7. Figure 12.7 describes constant S_{i-i} curves in the factor price equalization set. In OQO^* they are taken from figure 8.7 and are straight lines in $O\tilde{D}Q$.

It is clear from figure 12.7 that the emergence of multinational corporations changes in an important way the link between differences in relative factor endowments and the share of intraindustry trade. In OQO^* there is a negative association between them. However, when the difference in factor composition becomes large enough so as to bring about the emergence of multinational corporations, this association turns positive, as long as the capital-rich country is a net exporter of manufactures. When the difference in composition of factor endowments becomes large enough so that the capital-rich country begins to be a net importer of manufactures (concentrating a large part of its resources in producing headquarter services), the negative association between factor dispersion and the share of intraindustry trade is restored. It can also be seen from the figure that this pattern requires the capital-rich country to be sufficiently small, and this is the major way in which relative size affects these results.

Now consider the share of intrafirm trade. Using (12.8) and (12.12), this is calculated to be

$$S_{i-f} = \frac{VT_{i-f}}{VT} = \frac{c_H\mu}{2s(\bar{Y} + pxM^*)}.$$

However, due to balanced trade

$$s(\bar{Y} + pxM^*) = s^*pxM + c_H\mu,$$

where the right-hand side describes foreign country imports, which consist of differentiated products and headquarter services. Therefore

$$S_{i-f} = \frac{1}{2} \frac{c_H\mu}{s^*pxM + c_H\mu}.$$

It is easy to see from figures 12.3 and 12.6 that for constant relative country size an increase in the difference in factor composition increases the number of multinational corporations and reduces the number of varieties produced in the home country. Hence larger differences in factor composition are associated with larger shares of intrafirm trade.

The broad picture that emerges from this analysis is that for a given relative country size the share of intrafirm trade is larger, the larger the difference in relative factor endowments, but that in the presence of multinational corporations no clear-cut relationship exists between the share of intraindustry trade and differences in relative factor endowments. Hence we find that a link that is quite strong in the absence of multinational corporations is weaker in their presence. It suggests the hypothesis that the larger the involvement of multinational corporations in the world economy, the weaker the affect of changes in the degree of dispersion in income per capita on the share of intraindustry trade.

References

Buckley, P. J., and Pearce, R. D. "Overseas Production and Exporting by the World's Largest Enterprises: A Study in Sourcing Policy." *Journal of International Business Studies* 10 (1979): 9–20.

Caves, Richard E. "International Corporations: The Industrial Economics of Foreign Investment." *Economica* 38 (1971): 1–27.

Caves, Richard E. *Multinational Enterprise and Economic Analysis.* Cambridge, England: Cambridge University Press, 1982.

Dixit, Avinash, and Norman, Victor. *Theory of International Trade.* Cambridge, England: Cambridge University Press, 1980.

Helpman, Elhanan. "A Simple Theory of International Trade with Multinational Corporations." *Journal of Political Economy* 92 (1984):451–471.

Hirsch, Seev. "An International Trade and Investment Theory of the Firm." *Oxford Economic Papers* 28 (1976):258–270.

Klein, Benjamin, Crawford, Robert, and Alchian, Arman A. "Vertical Integration, Appropriable Rents, and the Competitive Contracting Process." *Journal of Law and Economics* 21 (1982):297–326.

Markusen, James R. "Multinational, Multi-Plant Economies, and the Gains from Trade." *Journal of International Economics* 16 (1984):205–226.

U.S. Tariff Commission. *Implications of Multinational Firms for World Trade and Investment and for U.S. Trade and Labor.* Washington, D.C.: Government Printing Office, 1973.

Williamson, Oliver E. "The Modern Corporation: Origins, Evolution, Attributes." *Journal of Economic Literature* 19 (1981):1537–1568.

13   Vertical Integration

In the last chapter we developed a simple model of multinational firms, building on the trade theory of chapter 7. In our first model of multinationals each firm produced only a single product. Thus multinational operation could only mean having headquarters in one country and a production facility in another. Since impediments trade were absent, this multinational operation was undertaken solely to exploit cross-country differences in factor rewards.

Although we believe such a model is useful and illuminating, it misses some important aspects of actual multinational enterprises. For one thing actual multinationals often produce in several countries. The model of chapter 12 also allowed for intra*firm* trade only in a very limited sence, which was trade in headquarters services. In reality there is sizable intrafirm trade in intermediate goods (see Buckley and Pearce 1979). Thus we turn to an analysis in which firms can both produce in more than one country and engage in intrafirm trade in intermediate goods.

In this chapter we incorporate a model of vertically integrated firms, based on Helpman (1983a), into our basic general equilibrium trade framework. The combination leads to a theory of international trade in which vertically integrated firms—firms with production facilities in more than one country—trade in finished goods, intermediate inputs, and invisibles. The existence of integrated firms somewhat modifies our analysis of the volume of trade and the share of intrafirm trade.

13.1 The Structure of Production

We assume that there are two factors of production: labor and capital. There are also two final products: homogeneous food, which is produced with L and K under constant returns to scale, and a differentiated manufactured product which is produced with L, K, a middle product Z, and headquarter services. All available technologies of production are common knowledge in the world economy.

The production function of food requires all inputs to be employed in the same location. Its unit cost function is $c_Y(w_L, w_K)$, where w_l is the reward to factor l. In a competitive equilibrium food is priced according to marginal cost. Thus, taking food to be the numeraire,

$$1 = c_Y(w_L, w_K). \tag{13.1}$$

The production of a variety of the manufactured product requires labor and capital, specialized headquarter services (as in the previous chapter), and a specialized intermediate input Z. Thus headquarter services and intermediate inputs are also differentiated, and every variety of the finished good requires a particular variety of this input in its production (see Helpman 1983b, for a more flexible formulation of the technology). Headquarter services are produced with labor and capital under increasing returns to scale by means of the technology discussed in the previous chapter. The resulting cost function is

$$C^H(w_L, w_K, h).$$

Intermediate inputs are produced using labor, capital, and headquarter services. The required variety of the headquarter services is the same as that required for the corresponding finished good, and a firm that produces finished products can use its headquarters to service also the production of middle products. This is a reasonable assumption for manufactured goods that require similar technologies in the production of components and final assembly of goods. The cost function of a variety of the middle product is

$$C^Z(w_L, w_K, h, z),$$

with $C^Z(\cdot)$ declining in h.

This feature of production generates an incentive for vertical integration; an incentive that is strengthened when intermediate inputs are produced under increasing returns to scale, as is assumed in what follows. For with increasing returns to scale in the production of middle products, it pays to concentrate the production of every variety. Hence, if the middle product is produced by a different firm, then a duopoly situation arises between the independent supplier and the user of the middle product, thereby reinforcing the rationale for vertical integration (see Williamson 1971, Porter and Spence 1977, and Klein et al. 1978).

This reasoning provides the basis for the formal model of the firm that we will use—a vertically integrated firm, which will also be referred to as a corporation. The important point to notice is that this particular structure of the corporation stems from an endogenous decision to maximize profits according to technology and market conditions.

We assume that the headquarter services of multinational corporations are tied to the entrepreneurial unit (the parent firm) and that entire product lines can be shifted to any desirable geographical location. We also assume for simplicity that the efficiency of services obtained from headquarters does not depend on the location of the product line and the output level of the middle product. We will consider the possibility of geographical reallocations of lines that produce varieties of the finished good as well as middle products. However, due to the fact that production of middle products requires know-how that is available mainly in the center, it is less efficient to separate the production of middle products from the base than to do so with regard to finished goods.

Now we are ready to derive the cost function of the integrated firm. We do it for the case where the same factor rewards have to be paid in all activities, because our analysis of trade structure will be restricted to endowment distributions that belong to the factor price equalization set.

Let

$$C^P(w_L, w_K, h, z, x)$$

be the cost function of a single plant. It is associated with an increasing-returns technology that produces x units of a variety of the finished manufactured product when z units of the appropriate middle product and h units of the appropriate headquarter services are available. The total costs of production of x are

$$C(w_L, w_K, x) = \min_{(h, z)} [C^P(w_L, w_K, h, z, x) + C^H(w_L, w_K, h)$$
$$+ C^Z(w_L, w_K, h, z)].$$
(13.2)

Given our assumptions about the cost functions $C^P(\cdot)$, $C^H(\cdot)$, and $C^Z(\cdot)$, the integrated cost function $C(\cdot)$ exhibits increasing returns to scale. We will use properties of this cost function in the formulation of the integrated equilibrium.

13.2 The Integrated Economy

To study the nature of trade in regions of factor endowments in which factor price equilization obtains, we begin with a description of the equilibrium of an integrated economy. We assume that production technologies are common knowledge and that preferences are homothetic and identical for all inhabitants of the world economy.

In an integrated equilibrium factor and commodity prices are the same everywhere. In the food sector, which is competitive, producers engage in marginal cost pricing. In the manufacturing sector producers engage in Chamberlinian monopolistic competition, and firms in this sector are vertically integrated for the reasons described in the previous section. There is free entry into industries, and as a result all producers make zero profits. The number of corporations in the differentiated product industry is large and treated as a continuous variable.

Adding to (13.1) the pricing and the zero profit condition in the manufacturing sector, as well as factor market and commodity market-clearing conditions, we obtain the following set of equilibrium conditions:

$$1 = c_Y(w_L, w_K), \tag{13.3}$$

$$R(p, \bar{n}) = \theta(w_L, w_K, x), \tag{13.4}$$

$$p = c(w_L, w_K, x), \tag{13.5}$$

$$a_{LY}(w_L, w_K)\bar{Y} + c_{LX}(w_L, w_K, x)\bar{X} = \bar{L}, \tag{13.6}$$

$$a_{KY}(w_L, w_K)\bar{Y} + c_{KX}(w_L, w_K, x)\bar{X} = \bar{K}, \tag{13.7}$$

$$\bar{X} = \bar{n}x, \tag{13.8}$$

$$\alpha_Y(p, \bar{n}) = \frac{\bar{Y}}{(\bar{Y} + p\bar{X})}, \tag{13.9}$$

where

$$a_{lY}(w_L, w_K) \equiv \partial c_Y(w_L, w_K)/\partial w_l, \ l = L, K;$$

$$a_{lX}(w_L, w_K, x) \equiv \partial c(w_L, w_K, x)/\partial w_l, \ l = L, K;$$

$\bar{Y}$ is the output level of food; $\bar{n}$ is the number of firms in the differentiated product industry; and $(\bar{L}, \bar{K})$ are the endowments of labor and capital.

The average cost function $c(w_L, w_K, x)$ is equal to $C(w_L, w_K, x)/x$, where $C(\cdot)$ is the integrated cost function from (13.2), and the index of economies of scale $\theta(\cdot)$ is associated with $C(\cdot)$. It is easily seen from a direct comparison that these equilibrium conditions are identical to the equilibrium conditions of the 2×2 economy discussed in chapter 7.

13.3 Trade Patterns

It is shown now how the pattern of trade of a two-country world is related to differences in factor endowments, holding constant the resources of the world

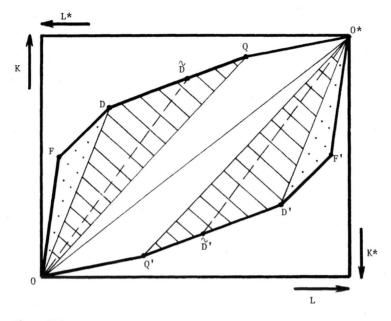

Figure 13.1

economy at the levels postulated in the previous section. This procedure identifies the dependence of trade patterns on relative country size and differences in relative factor endowments.

Consider the box diagram in figure 13.1, which describes the feasible allocations of factor endowments between a home country with the origin O and a foreign country with the origin O^*. In this figure the vector OQ and O^*Q' describe the total (direct plus indirect) employment of resources by the differentiated product industry in the equilibrium of the integrated economy. Similarly the vectors OQ' and O^*Q describe total integrated equilibrium employment of resources in the food industry.

We begin by considering allocations of factors of production that can be represented by points in the set OQO^*. Using the standard parallelogram construction, it is clear from figure 13.1 that in this case there exists an equilibrium with factor price equalization in which factor prices, commodity prices, output levels, and techniques of production are the same as in the equilibrium of the integrated economy, with every corporation employing its inputs in a single country. In these trading equilibria the home country imports food, and it is a *net* exporter of finished differentiated products. Every country produces varieties of the finished manufactured good and exports them to its trading partner. Hence there is intersectoral trade with the relatively capital-rich country importing the homogeneous product, and there is intraindustry trade in varieties of the differentiated product. At endowment points in the set OQO^* there is no incentive for the formation of multinationals, and there is therefore no intrafirm trade.

An important feature of OQO^* is that at its endowment points every country can fully employ its labor and capital using the techniques of production from the integrated equilibrium, and with every firm concentrating production activities in a single country. Clearly every endowment allocation above this set implies that at least one country cannot fully employ its resources with these techniques or production, which means that factor price equalization cannot obtain when every firm employs its inputs in a single country. In this case we would expect the wage rate to be higher in the home country and the reward to capital to be higher in the foreign country [this occurs when $C(\cdot)$ is associated with a homothetic production function]. In other words, at endowment points above OQO^* corporations have an incentive to reallocate activities across national borders in order to exploit differences in factor prices. These reallocations eliminate cross-country differences in factor prices or lead to specialization.

Following the procedure used in chapter 12, it is assumed that corporations establish subsidiaries abroad in a way that minimizes foreign involvement. Moreover, since in the current model corporations are integrated vertically, it is assumed that the first activities to be shifted to subsidiaries are product lines of finished goods and that product lines of intermediate inputs are the last ones to be separated from the entrepreneurial unit (the corporation's base). This last assumption can be justified by the observation that it is often more costly to separate the production of middle products from the center than finished product lines, because middle products require know-how that is more readily available at the center. Such costs are not explicitly considered in this study, but it is useful to interpret what follows as a description of the limit of a sequence of economies in which such differential costs exist, and these costs converge to zero. There is conceptually no difficulty in analyzing the consequences of alternative assumptions, although no alternative is explored in this book.

Using these assumptions, we can identify subsets of allocations in which factor price equalization obtains as a result of the formation of multinational corporations. These subsets are described by the dotted and the striped areas in figure 13.1. In that figure the employment vector OQ in the manufacturing sector is decomposed into three employment vectors: employment in the production of headquarters services OF, employment in the production of middle products FD, amd employment in the production of finished goods DQ. Clearly every variety of the finished good is produced with h units of specialized headquarter services and z units of a specialized middle product, in addition to its share of labor and capital in DQ. The vectors O^*F', $F'D'$, and $D'Q'$ are constructed symmetrically. It is assumed in this construction that headquarter services are the most capital intensive, that intermediate inputs are of intermediate capital intensity, and that finished goods are the most labor intensive (see Helpman 1983b for an alternative assumption).

Our assumption that product lines of finished goods are the first to be moved to subsidiaries implies that in the striped areas of figure 13.1 there is factor price equalization with subsidiaries of the relatively capital-rich country producing only finished manufactured products. As we showed in the previous chapter, in this region of factor endowments the capital-rich country imports food, and it is a net exporter of finished manufactured products if the difference in relative factor endowments is not too large (the endowment point is below $O\tilde{D}$ or above $O^*\tilde{D}'$) or a net importer of manufactured products if the differences in relative factor endowments is sufficiently large (above $O\tilde{D}$ or below $O^*\tilde{D}'$). There will be intraindustry and intrafirm trade in both regions.

As far as intrafirm trade is concerned, observe that it consists of two components; there is trade in headquarter services, just as in the model of chapter 12, but there is also an additional component of intrafirm trade in intermediate inputs. The point is that every multinational firm provides headquarter services to its subsidiaries, and since intermediate inputs are being produced by the parent company, they also have to be exported to the subsidary. Hence in the striped areas there is intrafirm trade in both goods and services.

As far as intraindustry trade is concerned, an interesting complication arises. As was made clear in the previous chapter, in the striped areas there is two-way trade in finished manufactured products so that there is undeniably intraindustry trade. Nevertheless, the volume of intraindustry trade will depend on how narrow one defines product categories, because there is also trade in intermediate inputs. Thus, if in the industrial classification finished products are classified to be different from middle products, then only two-way trade in finished products contributes to the volume of intraindustry trade. However, at existing levels of disaggregation of empirical data, finished goods and intermediate inputs that are used in their production often appear in the same category; electronics, chemicals, and wood products are examples of industries in which it occurs. Hence from a practical point of view trade in middle products might be included in the volume of intraindustry trade.

Now consider factor allocations in the dotted areas of figure 13.1. In these

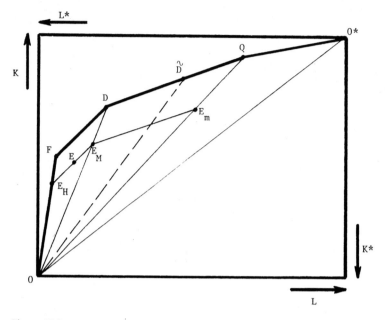

Figure 13.2

areas factor price equalization requires some multinational corporations to shift to subsidiaries production of intermediate inputs. For concreteness, consider point E in figure 13.2. Given that product lines of finished goods are the first to be shifted to subsidiaries, and that foreign involvement is minimized, the allocation of employment is as follows (line $E_H E_M$ is parallel to FD and $E_M E_m$ is parallel to DQ):

1. The home country allocates OE_H to the production of headquarter services.

2. It allocates $E_H E$ to the production of intermediate inputs.

This ensures full employment in the home country. Moreover home country multinationals employ resources in the foreign country in order to produce intermediate inputs and finished manufactured products:

3. The vector EE_M is employed by multinationals in order to produce intermediate inputs in subsidiaries.

4. The vector $E_M E_m$ is employed by multinationals in order to produce finished goods in subsidiaries.

Hence OE_m is the employment vector by home-based firms.

The foreign country allocates O^*Q to the food industry and QE to the manufacturing sector. Part of the latter is employed by home-country-based multinational corporations, as we explained before. Foreign-country-based firms employ QE_m in its manufacturing sector.

This allocation of resources implies the following pattern of trade:

1. The capital-rich country imports food and varieties of the finished manufactured product.

2. It exports intermediate inputs and headquarter services.

3. There is intrafirm trade (all of the capital-rich country's exports constitute intrafirm trade because they are traded within its multinational companies).

4. There is no intraindustry trade for narrowly defined product categories. However, if middle products and finished manufactured products are lumped together in the industrial classification, there will also be intraindustry trade.

The pattern of trade that we have described for factor allocations in the shaded areas of figure 13.1 is close to the observed trade pattern. Other interesting possibilities arise when the relative factor-intensity ranking of various activities is changed (see Helpman 1983b). It is, for example, conceivable that in some industries intermediate inputs require more labor-intensive techniques than finished products or that headquarter services are more labor intensive than intermediate inputs. A richer choice of inputs, and in particular differentiation across labor categories, might prove useful in shading additional light on observed trade structures.

13.4 Trade Volumes and Trade Shares

This section contains an analysis of the total volume of trade, the volume of intrafirm trade, the share of intraindustry trade, and the share of intrafirm trade, with an emphasis on novel features that arise from the existence of intermediate inputs. As far as the behavior of the total volume of trade is concerned, the detailed analysis in section 12.4 applies directly to the endowment allocation set in which middle products are produced only in parent firms (i.e., the set $ODQO^*$ in figure 13.2). Thus the main conclusion of the analysis that, controlling for relative country size, the volume of trade is larger, the larger the difference in relative factor endowments, applies to the set $ODQO^*$ in figure 13.2, whereas relative country size per se has an ambiguous effect on the volume of trade in ODQ. The interesting possibilities in the currrent context arise in the set OFD in which subsidiaries of home-country-based multinationals produce also middle products.

In OFD the relatively labor-rich country exports all varieties of the finished differentiated product as well as food, neither one being produced in the home country. Since the volume of trade is defined as aggregate exports, then

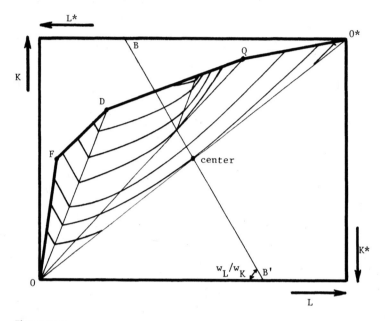

Figure 13.3

assuming balanced trade, the volume of trade equals twice the exports of the foreign country; namely

$$VT = 2s(\overline{Y} + px\overline{M}), \quad \text{for } E \in OFD, \tag{13.10}$$

where s is the share of the home country in world income and spending and $\overline{M} = \overline{n}$ is the number of varieties of the differentiated finished product that are produced in the world economy. It is therefore clear that in this set reallocations of factor endowments that do not change relative country size (as measured by relative GNP) do not change the volume of trade. The volume of trade is larger, the larger the relatively capital-rich country that serves as parent for the multinational corporation.

Figure 13.3 describes equal volume of trade curves, by reproducing the relevant part from figure 12.5. These curves are straight lines with slope $-w_L/w_K$ in region OFD.

The behavior of the share of intraindustry trade in OFD depends on whether in the industrial classification middle products belong to the same category as finished manufactured goods. If they do not, then the share of intraindustry trade is zero in this region. Using the results from chapter 12, we may then conclude that for fixed relative country size, and starting with identical factor compositions, the share of intraindustry trade declines with initial widenings of differences in factor composition; then it begins to rise when the differences increase to the point where multinational corporations start forming. It ends up falling when the capital-rich country becomes a net importer of finished manufactured goods, and it falls to zero (remaining at that level) when multinational corporations start shifting middle product lines to subsidiaries.

If middle products and finished goods are classified in the same category, then $O\tilde{D}$ in figure 13.2 (taken from figure 12.4) does not describe the dividing line between declines and increases in the share of intraindustry trade with widening differences in factor composition, and there exists intraindustry trade in OFD. We will not, however, discuss this case.

Now consider the behavior of the share of intrafirm trade. In the current model intrafirm trade consists of trade in headquarter services and in middle products. Without dealing explicitly with the problem of transfer pricing, it seems safe—due to the existence of zero profits—to calculate the volume of intrafirm trade as the difference between the subsidiaries' total revenue and their direct labor and capital costs. In the absence of zero profits this procedure is questionable, but it is accurate in the present context.[1] Hence the volume of intrafirm trade is

$$\text{VT}_{i-f} = px\mu - w_L L^f - w_K K^f,$$

where μ is the number of foreign subsidiaries and (L^f, K^f) is their labor and captial employment (the calculations are restricted to the factor prices equilization set).

The quantity of labor L^f is the sum of two components: labor employed directly in the production of finished goods and labor employed directly in the production of middle products. Similarly for capital K^f. Therefore

$$w_L L^f + w_K K^f = C^p \mu + C^z \eta,$$

where C^p is the equilibrium value of $C^p(w_L, w_K, h, z, x)$, C^z is the equilibrium value of $C^z(w_L, w_K, h, z)$, and η is the number of subsidiaries producing also middle products. Hence, using the zero profit condition (13.5) together with (13.2), we obtain

$$\text{VT}_{i-f} = (C^H + C^z)\mu - C^z \eta. \tag{13.11}$$

1. The problem of choosing a method for the allocation of shared costs has received some attention in recent years (e.g., see Mirman and Tauman 1982). However, there does not seem to exist a universally applicable rule.

It is apparent that the shifting of finished good product lines to subsidiaries increases the volume of intrafirm trade, whereas the shifting to subsidiaries of middle product lines reduces the volume of intrafirm trade.

The analysis of the relationship between the share of intrafirm trade and differences in relative factor endowments presented in chapter 12 also applies to the current model for endowment allocations in sets in which middle products are produced only in the centers, because in these cases the centers provide the subsidiaries with *all* inputs apart from direct labor and capital use in the production of finished goods. This means that in the set ODQ the share of intrafirm trade is larger, the larger the difference in relative factor endowments, provided relative country size does not change. In OQO^* there is no intrafirm trade.

In the set OFD all varieties of the finished differentiated product are produced by subsidiaries of home-country-based multinational corporations so that $\mu = \overline{M}(\equiv \overline{n})$, and it is constant, implying by (13.11) that the volume of intrafirm trade is larger, the fewer varieties of the middle product are produced by subsidiaries.

Using (13.10) and (13.11), we have

$$S_{i-f} = \frac{(C^H + C^Z)\overline{M} - C^Z\eta}{s(pxM + Y)}, \quad \text{for } E \in OFD. \tag{13.12}$$

Hence, since the number of multinational firms that produce middle products in subsidiaries increases with the difference in factor composition for a given relative country size (in figure 13.2 EE_M increases as E is shifted to the northwest), the share of intrafirm trade declines when the difference in relative factor endowments increases. This negative relationship stems from the fact that larger differences in relative factor endowments lead to a reallocation of activities within multinational corporations toward greater self-sufficiency of subsidiaries, thereby reducing intrafirm trade.

We conclude therefore that the existence of vertically integrated multinational corporations breaks the monotonic link between differences in relative factor endowments and the volume of trade, on one hand, and the share of intrafirm trade, on the other. The volume of trade and the share of intrafirm trade increase as the difference in relative factor endowments widens so long as this difference is not too large. But when the difference in relative factor endowments is sufficiently large, the shifting by multinational corporations of intermediate input product lines to subsidiaries reduces the share of intrafirm trade while maintaining a constant volume of trade.

References

Buckley, P. J., and Pearce, R. D. "Overseas Production and Exporting by the World's Largest Enterprises: A Study in Sourcing Policy." *Journal of International Business Studies* 10 (1979): 9–20.

Caves, Richard E. *Multinational Enterprise and Economic Activity.* Cambridge, England: Cambridge University Press, 1982.

Helpman, Elhanan. "A Simple Theory of International Trade with Multinational Corporations." *Journal of Political Economy* 92 (1984), in press.

Helpman, Elhanan. "The Multiproduct Firm: Horizontal and Vertical Integration." MIT Department of Economics. Working Paper No. 332, 1983a.

Helpman, Elhanan. "Multinational Corporations and Trade Structure." MIT. Mimeo, 1983b.

Klein, Benjamin, Crawford, Robert, and Alchian, Arman A. "Vertical Integration, Appropriable Rents, and the Competitive Contracting Process." *Journal of Law and Economics* 31 (1978): 297–326.

Mirman, Leonard J., and Tauman, Yair. "Demand Compatible Equitable Cost Sharing Prices." *Mathematics of Operations Research* 7 (1982): 40–56.

Porter, Michael E., and Spence, A. Michael. "Vertical Integration and Differentiated Inputs." Harvard Institute of Economic Research. Discussion Paper No. 576, 1977.

Williamson, Oliver E. "The Vertical Integration of Production: Market Failure Considerations." *American Economic Review* 61 (1971): 112–123.

We began this book with the intention of providing an integrated framework for the analysis of trade in a world where returns to scale are not always constant and where markets are not always perfectly competitive. The results of this effort are reported in chapters 3 through 13. We have not developed of course a general theory—the lack of any universally accepted model of imperfect competition makes such a claim impossible to make. But we have developed an approach that allows us to analyze trade under a variety of different market structures, and to do so in a way that stresses certain common themes. The purpose of this concluding chapter is to review what we have learned, and to suggest directions for future research.

14.1 The Pattern, Volume, and Composition of Trade

One of the basic messages of this book is that the theory of comparative advantage is alive and well—but it has lost some of its monopoly position. Even with economies of scale and imperfectly competitive markets, for a wide variety of market structures differences in the characteristics of countries are a major predictor of the pattern of trade. In a world where increasing returns are present, however, comparative advantage resulting from differences between countries is not the only reason for trade. Economies of scale provide an additional incentive and will give rise to trade even if countries are identical in tastes, technologies, and factor endowments.

Through most of this book we have assumed that the important difference between countries is in their endowments of productive factors. Trade in such a world is in part a way for countries to indirectly exchange factor services. In the constant returns world discussed in chapter 1, this is the whole story. We have shown that under certain conditions trade will continue to equalize factor prices even in a world where there are increasing returns in some sectors, and that when it does, the pattern of trade in embodied factor services still will be a reflection of differences in countries' factor endowments. If there are some goods produced with economies of scale, however, it would be wrong to say that trade is simply an indirect way of trading resources; even if countries have identical relative factor endowments, and thus have no net trade in factor services, they will still engage in specialization and trade because of increasing returns. Thus our general view, which is illustrated by the approaches of chapters 3, 4, and 7, is of a pattern of trade shaped by the underlying exchange of factors but with an overlay of additional specialization to realize economies of scale.

Several qualifications to this view should be noted. First, our statement that trade patterns will reflect factor endowments needs to be treated carefully in a world with multinational enterprises. In such a world, as shown in chapters 12 and 13, countries still will be net exporters of factors in which they are abundant, but only if our definition of trade includes the invisible trade involved in multinational operation. In principle this raises no difficulties, but it means that we must be cautious in interpreting empirical tests based on data on visible trade flows.

Second, transportation costs and other barriers to trade can introduce additional complications. One is the effect, demonstrated in chapter 10, of market size: increasing returns industries will tend to concentrate in countries with large domestic markets. A second, shown in chapter 11, is the arbitrariness introduced into the pattern of specialization when intermediate goods are both nontradable and produced under increasing returns.

A third complication is that if factor endowments do not lie in the set of factor price equalization, the pattern of trade becomes much harder to analyze. Under most market structures (though not the contestable markets case discussed in chapter 4) it is necessary to make the additional and implausible assumption of homotheticity of production functions in order to say something useful about trade patterns when factor prices are not equalized.

In general, however, the models developed in this book support a basic view in which trade patterns reflect comparative advantage plus additional specialization to realize scale economies. This view in turn suggests two further general conclusions, which are discussed in chapter 8: one about the volume of trade, the other about its composition.

In a constant-returns world the volume of trade would depend entirely on differences between countries; if all countries had identical relative factor endowments, technology, and tastes, there would be no trade at all. In a world where some goods are produced with increasing returns, however, some specialization and trade will persist even between identical countries. In the limit, if all countries are completely specialized, the share of trade in world income will depend only on how many countries there are and how equal they are in income. In general, if some goods are produced with constant returns and others with increasing returns, and there is incomplete specialization in some sectors, the volume of trade will tend to be larger, the more different countries are in factor endowments but also the more equal they are in income.

The more similar countries are in their factor endowments, the less net trading in factor services they will do. Yet trade will persist if there are goods produced with increasing returns. This suggests that as countries become more similar, their trade will increasingly become two-way exchanges of goods produced with similar factor proportions. In some circumstances, particularly where product differentiation is important, we can think of individual goods as being grouped into "industries" within which factor proportions are more or less the same. When this is true, we expect to see countries with very different factor proportions mostly engaging in *inter*industry trade and similar countries engaging mostly in *intra*industry trade.

Finally, our analysis has shed light on the determinants of intra*firm* trade. In chapters 12 and 13 we studies models in which there are integrated firms that need not have all their activities in the same country. The possibility of multinational operation enlarges the set of allocations consistent with factor price equalization. If we assume that purely national operation is preferred to multinationalism, we will see that multinational enterprises—and intrafirm trade—will emerge only when differences in factor endowments are too large for arm's-length trade to equalize factor prices. This intrafirm trade may involve both trade in invisibles, such as headquarters services (chapter 12), and in visible intermediate inputs (chapter 13). And the share of intrafirm trade will be larger, the larger the difference in the countries' composition of factor endowments.

14.2 Trade and Welfare

The relationship between the importance of economies of scale and imperfect competition, on one side, and the welfare effects of trade, on the other, is a somewhat paradoxical one. In a world that deviates from the perfect competition/constant-returns norm of traditional theory, there are increased potential gains from trade, in the sense that even identical countries can be made better off by opening trade. Unfortunately the imperfection of markets simultaneously creates the risk that a national economy will not only fail to take advantage potential gains from trade but may actually lose.

Our analysis suggests four sources of potential *extra* gains from trade in a world with imperfect competition and economies of scale. These four sources can provide gains over and above those from conventional comparative advantage or even gains from trade when there is no comparative advantage (e.g., when countries have identical relative factor endowments).

These source of additional potential gain are the following:

1. *Own production effects.* Trade will tend to produce gains over and above those that would occur in a constant-returns world if it leads on average to an expansion of a country's increasing-returns industries. As we showed in chapters 3, 4, 5, and 7, increases in scale can be viewed as a kind of technological progress that raises the efficiency of the economy. Less obviously, expansion of the output of firms with large monopoly power is similar in its welfare implications to expansion of increasing-returns sectors (chapter 5 shows that there is a formal equivalence). Thus to the extent that international competition has a procompetitive effect, inducing imperfectly competitive firms to lower their prices and produce more, this provides a source of gains.

2. *Concentration of production.* Under some circumstances international trade will lead to a concentration of each increasing-returns industry in a single country. We showed that this will happen when there are country- and industry-specific external economies if factor prices are equalized (chapter 3), or when markets are contestable (chapter 4). Such concentration creates a presumption of larger scale of production worldwide than any one country would have had in autarky. This in turn suggests that prices of increasing-returns goods will fall, benefiting even countries that cease their production as a result of trade (i.e., countries whose own production effects run the wrong way).

3. *Rationalization.* In imperfectly competitive industries trade will tend to increase competition and reduce profits. If there is free entry and exit, this will lead, other things equal, to a reduction in the number of firms and an increase in the output per firm, which will increase productivity under increasing returns. Thus both in industries producing homogeneous products (chapter 5) and those producing differentiated products (chapter 7) the tendency of international competition to reduce the number of firms is a force working toward additional gains from trade.

4. *Diversity.* Finally, a trading world economy can provide a greater variety of products than any one country. This can lead to gains either because consumers value variety (chapter 9) or because this allows production of more specialized intermediate inputs (chapter 11).

Our method of analysis in this book has been to derive sufficient conditions for gains from trade under alternative assumptions about market structure. In each case the sufficient condition ends up telling us that gains from trade are ensured if the "extra" effects (over and above comparative advantage) run the right way. The question then becomes one of presumption: How likely is it that these effects will increase the gains from trade rather than reduce or eliminate them?

For two of our effects there is a clear presumption of positive effects on welfare. If concentration of production occurs, it is hard to believe that cases where productivity of increasing-returns industries falls are more than a curiosum (although examples can be contrived). Similarly trade will almost certainly lead to an increase in the diversity of products available. Less certain is the rationalizing effect of trade, but it seems to be a reasonable presumption that the increased competition caused by trade will lead to fewer, larger firms.

The major source of uncertainty then is the own production effect. In contrast to the other effects, it is easy to imagine situations where trade leads to a contraction of those sectors of a country that either produce with increasing returns or are highly monopolized. This possibility lies at the core of Frank Graham's famous argument for protection.

Our analysis suggests that the importance of the own production effect, and therefore the importance of the possibility of losses from trade, might not be very great. Even if our own country's production in increasing returns or imperfectly competitive industries falls as a result of opening trade, the other effects will tend to work in our favor. And in some important cases *what happens to our own production of increasing-returns goods does not matter at all.* Whenever we have the combination of average cost pricing (so that there are no economic profits) and factor price equalization, the only scale variable that matters is the scale of output in the *world* economy. How much our own country produces is of no welfare significance. Or to put it another way, what matters is the world pattern of production, not how that production is distributed among countries.

Our analysis in this book then suggests an overall presumption that trade remains beneficial in a world characterized by economies of scale and imperfect competition. Indeed, the presumption is for extra gains, over and above the conventional gains from trade. This in turn suggests an important distributional point (formalized in chapter 9): in contrast to the conventional result, it is possible for all factors of production to gain from trade if countries are sufficiently similar in relative factor endowments (and the extra gains we have been discussing are large enough).

14.3 Future Directions

We hope the framework presented in this book will serve the purpose of making the analysis of economies of scale and imperfect markets part of the core of trade theory rather than a peripheral concern. There are, however, important issues in international economics that will require new tools, going beyond what we have developed here. What we would like to do in this concluding section is to point out two problems that we believe are in particular need of further work.

The first problem is the modeling of dynamics. It seems likely that in the real world much international specialization results not so much from static economies of scale as from dynamic forms of increasing returns, such as the learning curve. To some extent the analysis of static scale economies may proxy for these dynamic effects, but we are not satisfied that it does so adequately. The problem is that in imperfectly competitive markets competition in a dynamic setting may contain features that static models cannot capture. For example, firms may attempt to use irreversible investment in R & D or capital as a strategic move, designed to affect other firms' behavior. But if some inputs are being used for strategic purposes, it will no longer be true that firms minimize cost. Since much of our analytical apparatus relies on cost minimization, this will require revision of the theory.

In addition to requiring us to rethink the models of market structure we use, a dynamic version of our theory would require us to integrate imperfect competition, capital theory, and growth theory. Capital and growth in trade are not new ideas, but to integrate the combination with imperfectly competitive markets is (we can report from experience) not a simple task.

The other problem we see left unresolved is that of modeling trade policy. The analysis of welfare in this book has always contrasted trade with autarky, rather than compared trading positions, which is what must be done for a useful analysis of trade policy. To carry out policy analysis will require a further development of analytical tools. However, we believe that the methods of welfare analysis we use in this book can serve as the basis for the next stage.

So there is still much work to be done. Yet the message of this book is how *much* can be understood. Only a few years ago many people thought that nothing systematic could be said about trade in the presence of increasing returns and imperfect competition. We hope we have shown convincingly how wrong that was. The job is not completed, but there is every reason to believe that it is a job we can do.

Index

Aggregate demand function
  ideal variety model, 124, 127–129
  love of variety model, 119
Alchian, A. A., 230
Anderson, J. E., 167
Arm's-length trading, 234
Average cost pricing, 35–37
  contestable markets, 67
  Cournot model, 93
Average diversity increase measure, 181

Balassa, Bala, 159
Baumol, William J., 35, 68
Benthamite social welfare function, 184
Bertrand, behavior, 35
Bilateral monopoly, 40
Bilateral trade pattern, 173
  FP model, 25–27
Brander, James, 86, 107
Brand switching, 128
Brecher, R. E., 24, 27
Buckley, P. J., 238, 247

Caves, Richard, E., 227, 229
CES subutility function, 117
Chamberlian equilibrium, 36, 131, 138
  multinational single-product firms, 229
  multinational vertically integrated firms,
    250
Chamberlin-Hecksher-Ohlin model, 152
Chamberlin large group case, 35, 138, 146
Choudri, E. V., 24, 27
Circle model, 120
Civan, E., 173
Cobb-Douglas preferences (upper tier), ideal
  variety model, 129, 144, 152, 157, 184–
  186, 187, 191
Collusion, 34
Comparative advantage theory, 261
Compensation function, Lancaster model, 121
Competition effects of trade, 87
Composition of trade, 159–178
  differentiated products model, 168–169

multinational vertically integrated, 255–259
  summary of model results on, 261–263
Concentrated production, 75
Constant demand elasticity, approximation,
  119
Contestable markets, 35, 67–83, 262
  definition, 67
  integrated equilibrium, 71–72
  trading equilibrium, 72–75
  volume of trade, 165
Cooperative behavior, 34
Country size and trade volume, 159
  differentiated products model, 163
  Hechscher-Ohlin model, 163
  measure of relative country size dispersion,
    166
Cournot behavior, 35, 85
Cournot model
  direction of trade, 88
  general equilibrium, 88–96
  partial equilibrium, 86–88
  with segmented markets, 105
Crawford, Robert, 230
Cross-hauling, 86, 108

Decentralization multinationals, 233
Degree of monopoly power, definition, 33,
  187
Determinants of trade patterns, 151–157. See
  also Composition of trade
Differentiated products, 113, 115–129
  equilibrium conditions, 135–136
Dixit, Avinash, 11, 25, 117, 118
Dixit and Stiglitz, 118
Domestic market as export base, 209
Dumping, 107
Dynamic scale economies, 32, 38–39
Dynamic vs. static analysis, 39

Eaton, J., 85
Economies of scale, 31
  competitive equilibrium, 34
  definition, 33

Economies of scale (cont.)
degree of, 187
homotheticity, 34
internal to firm, 32
local index of, 33
market structure and, 31, 34–36
Elasticity of demand, intermediate goods
model, 213
Entry
differentiated products model, 136
intermediary input model, 213
multinational single-product firm, 229
multinational vertically integrated, 250
Entry assumption, 34
Entry deterrence, 35
Equal volume of trade curves. See Volume
isocurves
FP model, 23
Equilibrium conditions
differentiated product model, 136–138
differentiated products model with entry
$N \times M$ case, 144
differentiated products model without entry,
146
multinational multiproduct firms, 250
Ethier, Wilfred J., 37, 38, 54, 57, 64, 212, 215
Exact index of diversity, 185
Existence of equilibrium, contestable markets
model, 80–81
External economies, 36–38, 45–66
autarky equilibrium, 50
definition, 36
gains from trade, 51
industrial complexes, 221
marginal vs. average cost pricing, 47
production function, 45
resource allocation, 47
specialization in trading equilibrium, 61
trade intermediary goods, 38
trade pattern, 55–57
trading equilibrium, 50

Factor content of trade
bilateral, 174
contestable market model, 74, 78
Cournot model, 93
Cournot model with entry, 103
differentiated product model with entry,
142
differentiated products model with entry,
$N \times M$ case, 145
differentiated products model without entry,
147–148
external economies, 61
factor proportion model, 17
industrial complexes, 221
multinational single-product model, 237
Factor endowment and trade volume, 159
Heckscher-Ohlin model, 163

differentiated products model, 163–164
Factor intensity and nontraded goods, 201
Factor intensity reversals, 172, 173
Factor mobility, 197
market size effect, 205
nontraded increasing-returns model,
204–205
ownership of factors and migration, 204
perfect mobility, 204, 205
volume of production, 205
Factor price equalization, 13–16
external economies, 59–63
full dimensionality of the FPE set, 16, 146
intermediate nontradable goods, 219
likelihood, 16, 146
multinational single-product model,
232–233
multinationals, 251–252
nontradables, 198
volume of trade, 164, 166
Factor price equalization set
contestable markets, 73
Cournot with free entry, 102
definition, 13, 15
differentiated products model with entry,
141
differentiated products model with entry
$N \times M$ case, 145
differentiated products model without entry,
149
geometrical representation, 15
intermediate goods tradable, 214–215
intermediate goods nontradable, 218
industry- and country-specific external
economies, 60
linkages, 220
multinational multiproduct firm, 249
multinational single-product model, 233
nontradables constant returns, 200
nontraded goods, 20
seller concentration model, 92
volume and share isocurve, 174
Factor proportions theory, 11–29
False comparative advantage, 152
Firm-specific assets
headquarter services, 228
multinational single-product firms, 230
Firms' behavior, differentiated products
model, 132–134
Foreign involvement of multinationals, 252
FPE. See Factor price equalization
Free entry in Cournot model, 100–104
homothetic technology, 101
Free entry, Cournot with segmented markets,
109
Full dimensionality of FPE set, 16, 146

Gabszewicz, Jaskold, 119
Gains from possibility of trade, 86

Gains from trade
  concentration of product effects and, 264
  contestable markets model, 79, 81–83
  Cournot model, 96–100
  Cournot model with entry, 103
  Cournot with segmented markets, 107–111
  diversity effect and, 264
  external economies, 64–66
  FP model, 28–29
  own production effects and, 264
  rationalization effect and, 264
  summary of results on, 263–265
Gains from trade and differentiated products
    model, 179–195
  correctivity income distribution, 186
  decomposition, 179
  diversity and productivity conditions, 182
  general S-D-S sufficient conditions, 183
  income distribution 179, 190–195
  Lancaster preferences, 183–187
  Spence-Dixit-Stiglitz preference, 181–183
  sufficient conditions, primitives, 189
  sufficient conditions, variety-free, 180
Graham, Frank D., 51, 265
Graham effect, 51–53
  Kemp-Neghishi conditions, 52
  sufficient conditions, 53
Gravity equation, 167
Gross domestic product function, 25
Grossman, Gene M., 85
Grubel, Harry G., 168

Hanoch, Giora, 33
Havrylyshyn, Oli, 173
Headquarter services, 228, 234, 248
  multinational multiproduct firm, 249, 253
Heckscher-Ohlin model, 11, 131, 142, 151,
    156, 157, 159–161, 231
  factor proportions theory, 17
Heckscher-Ohlin theorem, 19
Helpman, Elhanan, 27, 49, 57, 89, 97, 128,
    139, 173, 174, 204, 215, 247, 248, 253, 255
Hierarchical classification of products, 115
Hirsch, Seev, 228
Home market effect. See Market size effect
Homothetic preferences, factor proportions
    model, 12
Horizontal differentiation, 119
Host country definition, 230

Iceberg transportation costs, 206
Ideal variety, approach to differentiated
    products, 120–129
Index of aggregate welfare, 184
Indivisibility of firms, 148–151
Industrial classification and trade volume,
    256
Industrial complex, 217
  definition, 220

Integrated equilibrium, 12–13
  Cournot with free entry, 102
  definition, 11
  differentiated product model, 134–139
  differentiated product model without entry,
    147
  ideal variety model, 135
  intermediary inputs, 211–214, 213
  multinational single-product firm, 230
  multinational vertically integrated, 249–250
  nontradables constant returns, 198
  nontradables increasing returns, 201
  nontradable intermediate inputs, 217
  seller concentration model, 91
  trade pattern in, 16–19
Integer problem. See Indivisibility of firms
Integrated world equilibrium, 12–13
Interindustry trade, 131, 142, 168–174
  nontradable intermediate inputs, 219
Intermediary inputs, 211–224
  Lancaster preferences, 223–224
  multinational multiproduct firms, 248, 253
  nontraded final goods and, 216
  nontradable, 217–219
  product category definitions and, 253
  tradable differentiated goods, 214–217
International economies of scale
  intermediate goods, 215–216
  nontradable intermediate goods, 192
Intrafirm trade, 227, 238
  intermediate products, 247
  measure of, 242
  multinational single-product model, 241–244
  multinational vertically integrated model,
    252–253
  share in trade, 257–258
  summary of results of models on, 263
  volume of, 255–259
Intraindustry trade, 131, 142, 159, 168,
    168–174
  country shares and capital abundance, 173
  index of, 168
  intermediate inputs, 215
  multinationals, 228, 236, 243, 253, 255–259
  relative country size, 243
  single-product multinationals, 241–244
Intrasectoral trade, 131
Invisible exports, 238
Invisible trade, 262

Jones, Ronald W., 139

Kemp, Murray C., 51
Klein, B., 230, 248
Komiya, Ryutaro, 20
Krugman, Paul R., 86, 107, 110, 167, 191, 205

Lancaster, Kelvin, 120, 134, 152
Lancaster model, 120

Lancaster preferences, 133–134, 138–139,
  144–152. *See also* Ideal variety
Leamer, Edward, 19, 129
Lerner diagram, 24, 171–172
Limit pricing monopoly, 85
Linkages, forward and backward, 220–224
  backward definition, 221
  forward definition, 221
Lloyd, P. J., 168
Loertscher, R., 173
Love of variety approach to differentiated
  products, 117–120
  demand function of, 118

Market segmentation, 86, 109–111
Market segmentation analysis, 110
Market size effect, 197, 209
  iceberg model, 206
  relative country size equilibrium, 208
  transport cost and, 205–209
Market width, 126
Markusen, J. R., 87, 208
Marshall, Alfred, 37
Matthews, R. C. O., 56
Melvin, J. R., 17
Migration, 204–205
Mirman, L. J., 257
Mirror image countries, 54, 193
Monopolistic competition, 35, 115
Monopoly power, degree of, 187
Monopoly rents, 67, 95
Multinational corporations, 227–259. *See
  also* Single-product multinational firms;
  Vertically integrated multinationals
  importance in world trade, 227
Multinational firms, 39
Multiplant operations and economies of scale,
  32

Negishi, Takashi, 39, 51
Noncooperative behavior, 34
Nontradable goods
  constant-returns model, 198–201
  in factor proportions model, 19–22
  increasing-returns model, 201–203
  transition t competitive, 128, 197–209
  volume of trade and, 167
Nonuniqueness of trading equilibrium, 63–
  64
Norman, Victor, 25

Ohlin, Bertil, 31, 56
Oligopolistic industries, 34
Oligopoly, 85–111
Output creation, 108
Output diversion, 108

Panzar, J. C., 35, 68
Parent country definition, 230

Pattern of trade
  multinational single-product model, 231–
    238
  multinational vertically integrated, 250–255
  summary of model results on, 261–263
Pattern of trade indeterminancy, 22
Pearce, R. D., 238, 247
Plant-specific costs, 229
Porter, M. E., 248
Pretrade commodity prices, 155

Razin, Assaf, 139, 204
R & D. *See* Research and development
Reaction function, 106
  Cournot with segmented markets, 106
Reciprocal dumping, 107
Relative country size dispersion measure, 166
Research and development
  product-specific and multinationals, 227,
    228
Restricted entry, differentiated products
  model, 146–151
Reverse engineering, 37
Ricardian theory, 55
Rybczynski effect, 156

Scale and diversity in equilibrium, 187–190
  nontradables with increasing returns, 202
  large country effect, 203
Scherer, Fredrich, 32
S-D-S. *See* Spence-Dixit-Stiglitz
Segmented market assumptions, 105
Segmented markets and transportation costs,
  197
Seller concentration, 86
  partial equilibrium analysis, 86–88
Share isocurves, 174–178
Single-product multinational firms, 227–245
  determinants of, 234–235
  profits, 238
  structure of employment, 235
  trade pattern, 231–238
  volume of trade, 238–241
Specialization
  economies of scale and, 131
  transport costs, 208
  volume of trade, 166, 171
Specific inputs and integrated firms, 39–
  40
Spence, M. E., 117, 248
Spence-Dixit-Stiglitz preferences
  factor mobility, 204
  income distribution, 191
  intermediate goods, 212
  love of variety, 132–134, 138–139, 144
  transport costs, 205
Stability of trading equilibrium, 64
Stiglitz, Joseph, 117, 118
Stolper-Samuelson theorem, 190, 194

generalized to differentiated products
   model, 195
Sunk costs, 146
Sustainability and contestable equilibrium,
   67, 69–70

Taste for variety preferences, 116
Tauman, Yair, 257
Trade creation, 108
Trade diversion, 108
Trade pattern
   bilateral factor content of, 27
   contestable markets model, 74
   differentiated products model, 131–158
   differentiated products model with entry,
      140–142
   external economies, 55–57
   international economies of scale, 57
   seller concentration model, 88–96
Trade volume, 159–178
   differentiated products model, 161–163
   empirical work on, 159, 173
   generalized differentiated products model,
      165–168
   Heckscher-Ohlin model, 159–161
   within group volume, 167, 173
Transport costs, 86, 196, 262
   Cournot model, 104
Transportation costs and nontraded goods,
   197–209
Travis, W. P., 17
Two-level production function, 212
Two-stage budgeting, 118, 122
Two-way trade in identical products, 106

Unequal factor prices
   contestable markets model, 77–78
   multinational single-product model, 233
   summary of implications, 262
   differentiated products model with entry,
      143–144
   FP model, 24–28
   factor reward and factor composition under,
      27

Vanek, J., 11, 18–19, 57, 74, 93
Vanek's chain, 19, 20, 148
Varian, Hal R., 28, 132
Vertical differentiation, 119
Vertically integrated multinationals, 247–266
   rationale for, 248
   trade pattern, 250–255
   trade volume and factor endowment link,
      258
Volume isocurves, 174–178. Also see Volume
   of trade
   factor proportions model, 23
   multinational single product, 239

multinational vertically integrated firms,
   256
Volume of trade
   definition, 23
   factor proportions model, 22–24
   indeterminancy, 22
   multinational single-product model, 238–
      241
   multinational vertically integrated firms,
      255–259
   summary of model results on, 261–263
Von Neumann-Morgenstern utility function,
   184

Weak separability of preferences, 118
Welfare effects
   FP model, 28
Williamson, Oliver, 39–40, 228, 278
Willig, R. D., 35, 68
Wolter, F., 173